Nonprofit Investment Policies

The NSFRE/Wiley Fund Development Series

Nonprofit Investment Policies: Practical Steps for Growing Charitable Funds by Robert P. Fry, Jr.

Planned Giving Simplified: The Gift, the Giver, and the Gift Planner by Robert Sharpe

The Universal Benefits of Volunteering: A Practical Workbook for Nonprofit Organizations, Volunteers, and Corporations by Walter Pidgeon

Beyond Fund Raising: New Strategies for Nonprofit Innovation and Investment by Kay Sprinkel Grace

Critical Issues in Fund Raising edited by Dwight F. Burlingame

Fund-Raising Cost Effectiveness: A Self-Assessment Workbook by James M. Greenfield

The Nonprofit Handbook: Fund Raising, Second Edition edited by James M. Greenfield

The NSFRE Fund-Raising Dictionary by National Society of Fund Raising Executives

NONPROFIT INVESTMENT POLICIES

Practical Steps for Growing Charitable Funds

Robert P. Fry, Jr.

JOHN WILEY & SONS, INC.

New York • Chichester • Weinheim • Brisbane • Singapore • Toronto

Published simultaneously in Canada.

This publication is designed to provide accurate and authoritative
information in regard to the subject matter covered. It is sold with the
understanding that the publisher is not engaged in rendering legal,
accounting, or other professional services. If legal advice or other
expert assistance is required, the services of a competent professional
person should be sought.

Library of Congress Cataloging-in-Publication Data:

Fry, Robert P.
    Nonprofit investment policies : practical steps for growing
charitable funds / Robert P. Fry, Jr.
        p.   cm. — (The NSFRE/WLR fund development series)
    Includes bibliographical references and index.
    ISBN 0-471-17887-X (cloth : alk. paper)
    1. Nonprofit organizations—United States—Finance—Management.
2. Investments—United States.   3. Asset-liability management—
United States.   4. Nonprofit organizations—Law and legislation—
United States.   I. Title.   II. Series.
HG4027.65.F79   1998
658.15'224—dc21   97-38261
                                                                              CIP

Printed in the United States of America.

10 9 8 7 6 5 4 3 2 1

Dedication

For Susan—And I promise never to do it again.

Acknowledgments

The real question when writing a book is not whether you have enough to say but whether you have enough friends to help you say it. In my case, I am deeply indebted to a number of people for their help and encouragement. Most of the ideas in this book were developed while I was with Van Deventer & Hoch, Investment Counsel. I appreciate the many friends at V&H who contributed to my investment education and I am particularly grateful to Dick Snyders, the President of V&H, for giving me permission to write the book.

Before this was a book, it was an idea embodied in a small guide now published by the National Center for Non-Profit Boards. I appreciate the help of Dale Larson in preparing that guide and of my editor at the National Center, Kathleen Enright, for her help on the guide and as a reviewer of portions of this book. In addition, Ray Lyne, the President of Lifestyle Giving in Newport Beach, California, is the source of the idea that charitable organizations need to be worthy of large gifts, an idea that floats throughout the text.

Many significant contributions to the background research were provided by Amy Schroeder, Andrea Harzstark, Anne Larson, and Katie Callas. In addition, numerous friends and colleagues read and commented on portions of the text, including John Cooke, Sue Francis, Dick Graffis, Duke Haddad, Carlee Harmonson, Paul Nelson, Jim Normandin, Charles Schultz, Dixie Skiles, Celia Vorsanger, Stanley Weithorn, and Jeanne Williams. Jeanne also read my earlier guide while serving on the NSFRE's publishing committee and championed the cause of turning it into this book.

Martha Cooley, my editor at John Wiley & Sons, patiently read, re-read, and corrected the entire manuscript. My brother, Eric Fry, an international securities investment manager, provided many helpful corrections to the technical materials on portfolio theory and also created the majority of the charts and graphs. In every case, the book was improved by their questions, criticisms, and ideas. Since I did not follow their every suggestion, however, the errors that remain are mine.

Finally, I am particularly indebted to my friend and colleague, Gerry Kaskel, without whose editing skills and help in receiving and deciphering the reviewers' comments, this book would never have been finished.

Thank you all.

Bob Fry
Irvine, California
1997

The NSFRE/Wiley Fund Development Series

The NSFRE/Wiley Fund Development Series is intended to provide fund development professionals, volunteers including board members, (and others interested in the not-for-profit sector) with top-quality publications that help advance philanthropy as voluntary action for the public good. Our goal is to provide practical, timely guidance and information on fund raising, charitable giving, and related subjects. NSFRE and Wiley each bring to this innovative collaboration unique and important resources that result in a whole greater than the sum of its parts.

The National Society of Fund Raising Executives

The NSFRE is a professional association of fund-raising executives which advances philanthropy through its more than 18,000 members in 145 chapters throughout the United States, Canada, and Mexico. Through its advocacy, research, education, and certification programs, the Society fosters development and growth of fund-raising professionals, works to advance philanthropy and volunteerism, and promotes high ethical standards in the fund-raising profession.

1997–1998 NSFRE Publishing Advisory Council

The Publishing Council would like to extend special thanks to F. Duke Haddad, Ed.D, CFRE, and John D. Cooke, CFP, for their thoughtful critique of the manuscript.

Contents

Preface   xi

PART I

BACKGROUND AND THEORY

1 **The Case for Investment Policies**   **3**
  The Power of Policy   4
  The Investment Context   6
  The Organizational Context   6
  The Unique Charitable Context   9
  Conclusion   10

2 **The Legal Environment: Law, Tradition, and Investment**
Practices   **11**
  What Laws Apply to Nonprofits?   12
  Fiduciary Duty—The Starting Point of Investment Regulation   13
  Trusts, Trusts Everywhere   13
  The Investment Laws   16
  Changes in the Investment Environment   20
  State and Federal Securities Laws—The Philanthropy Protection
    Act of 1995   31
  Conclusion   33

3 **The Investment Environment: Modern Portfolio Theory**   **34**
  Goals of the Process   34
  The Origins of Modern Portfolio Theory   35
  Market Efficiency   37
  Key Investment Concepts Every Director Needs to Know   41
  The Importance of Asset Allocation   52
  The Importance of Time   69
  Risks Most People Do Not Discuss   73
  Conclusion   79

PART II

OPERATIONS

4 **Critical Internal Organizational Components of Investing**   **83**
  First Things First—Who Is on the Board   84
  Critical Organizational Issues   85
  Creating an Appropriate Structure   86

Organizing Investment Systems   89
Conclusion   90

5 Getting Started   **91**
    Categories of Investable Funds   92
    Conducting an Investment Policy Audit   95
    Who Conducts the Study?   96
    Part I: General Information   97
    Part II: Development (Fund-Raising) Information   98
    Part III: Investment Accounting, Gift Administration, and Reporting   103
    Part IV: Investment Philosophy and Objectives   108
    Part V: Fund Information   117
    Conclusion   121

6 Hiring Help   **122**
    Hiring Help, Part 1—Too Many Choices   122
    Investment Management: A Functional Analysis   124
    Investment Advisors   129
    Consulting—Who Gets to Be in Charge?   136
    Hiring Help, Part 2—Putting the Pieces Together   139
    Finding Help   146
    Conclusion   151

7 Investment Accounting and Performance Reporting   **154**
    The Role of Accounting-Based Financial Statements   155
    Accounting Is Not Enough   157
    Investment Management Performance Reporting   159
    Frequency of Performance Measurement   163
    When Should the Manager Be Fired?   167
    Consultant-Driven Performance Analysis   168
    Conclusion   169

PART III UNIQUE NOT-FOR-PROFIT ISSUES

8 Investment Policy as a Fund-Raising Tool   **173**
    The Yield Curve   175
    The Case for Endowment   183
    Establishing an Endowment   186
    Endowment Investment and Spending Policies   186
    Maximizing the Value of an Endowment   190
    Planned Gifts   193
    Not All Planned Gifts Are Created Equal   199
    Conclusion   204

Special Nonprofit Investment Problems **205**
Cultural Vulnerabilities 206
Socially Responsible Investing 207
Serving as Trustee 210
Avoiding Bad Gifts—The Primary Role of Gift-Acceptance Policies 218
Willingness to Trust 219
Conclusion 224

10 **Putting It All Together** **227**
Closing the Loop 227
Conclusion 235

APPENDIXES

A **Glossary** **239**

B-1 **Uniform Management of Institutional Funds Act** **242**

B-2 **Uniform Prudent Investor Act (1994)** **246**

C **Sample Gift-Acceptance Policies** **250**

D **Internal Self-Guided Investment Management Assessment Form** **257**

E-1 **Sample Monthly Report** **271**

E-2 **Sample Quarterly Report** **275**

F-1 **Sample Endowment Resolution** **280**

F-2 **Sample Endowment Trust Agreement** **282**

G-1 **Sample Investment Policies—General** **287**

G-2 **Sample Investment Policies for Operating Reserves** **290**

Bibliography **293**

Index **299**

Preface

There are few things more satisfying than being in the right place and knowing it. Our calling in life, according to one theologian, is to find the place *where our great joy and the world's great needs meet.*[1] The charitable world is one in which great joys and great needs uniquely meet. As a result, nonprofit organizations form a robust, exciting, and increasingly important part of American life.

The world's great needs tend to be obvious. Whether the nonprofit is a social service agency, an art museum, a hospital, a school, or a religious institution, the particular need the organization addresses is usually clearly reflected in its mission and purpose. Only among stagnant charitable organizations will this not be the case. In every case, the existence of the charitable organization represents an effort to address human frailties and improve human conditions. It is from this central purpose that joy is derived.

There is joy in service. It is deeply gratifying to be allowed to give of oneself for the sake of others, even in small ways. A second joy, that of fellowship, sometimes derives from the first. Cambridge professor and author C.S. Lewis once wrote that friends are those who share a common vision.[2] Not infrequently, we find ourselves developing deep and lasting friendships among the staff, directors, and volunteers with whom we work in the charitable world.

Finally, there is the joy of significance. How difficult it is for so many people to find significance in their daily work. From this perspective, those who are employed in the charitable sector are, among all people, most richly blessed. The mission and objectives of the organization infuse even the most menial tasks with an importance those tasks otherwise would not have.

The joys of serving in the charitable world are often more subtle than the needs. This is particularly true for those full-time staff members immersed in the work of the organization. Frequently, it seems as if the organization's needs will overwhelm not just the joys but all the available resources. And it is difficult to be joyful when you're broke! The great challenge of the

---

[1] The exact quote is a definition of vocation from Frederick Buechner's book *Wishful Thinking, A Seeker's ABC:* "The place God calls you to is the place where your deep gladness and the world's deep hunger meet." Robert Frost expresses the same sentiment in a poem entitled, "Two Tramps in Mud Time." He writes:
  But yield who will to their separation,
  My object in living is to unite
  My avocation and my vocation
  As my two eyes make one in sight.
  Only where love and need are one,
  And the work is play for mortal stakes,
  Is the deed ever really done
  For Heaven and the future's sakes.

[2] *The Four Loves* by C.S. Lewis.

charitable world, and one purpose for which this book is written, is to keep those needs from overwhelming the joys.

The point of beginning our work on *charitable* investment policies with a brief reflection on the significance of the work that we are privileged to do and the joy that it brings us is to put investment policies in their proper perspective. Our goal is to strengthen and enhance the effectiveness of charitable organizations and thereby enable them to be good stewards of their resources. It is helpful to remember that sound investing is merely a means to an end. Investment policies are only tools. The true and ultimate goal is to serve our chosen communities joyfully and well.

Few Things Are More Helpful Than a Good Decision

In the world of investments good decisions are ultimately more important than the occasional wizardry of an outstanding portfolio manager. For unlike such wizardry, good decisions can be replicated in good times and bad by anyone who is committed to doing so. Consequently, the world does not need another book on investing. If you walk blindfolded into any bookstore in the United States and purchase the first two books you touch, you are likely to head home with one book on investing and another on having firmer thighs. Both books will promise a richer and more complete life in just five minutes a day.

This is not, therefore, a book about investing. Rather, it is a book about making good decisions and about the process of continuing to make good decisions in an institutional setting over an extended period of time. The particular *good decisions* are those that involve investing any money that the nonprofit organization is holding. The particular nonprofits we hope to help are those that think of themselves as charities, ministries, or other philanthropic enterprises. The intended result is the creation and implementation of a set of policies to guide the investing of those surplus funds.

A Book for Those Who Supervise

This is a book for supervisors—officers and directors—of the investment process. The book's principal goal is to provide the chief financial officer, chief development officer, and members of the investment committee of the board with a sufficient understanding of the overall investment environment so that they can comfortably implement investment policies. To do that, the book functions as an extended analysis of and a guide to the sample investment policies in Appendix G-1. The actual policies are quite brief—a mere four or five pages—and so leave much unsaid. The purpose of the commentary is to identify the work that needs to be done within the parameters that the policies establish.[3] An important presupposition is that the organization will be hiring investment professionals to actually manage the money. Consequently, this book is not intended to equip the reader to pick stocks or bonds but rather to supervise those who do. Obviously, any investment sophistication the reader brings to the table will be helpful. But it is not essential.

Every day we make business and personal decisions that are intended to take advantage of the expertise of others. We select carpenters and auto mechanics, hire computer programmers, use lawyers to draft agreements, and even decide whether or not to have surgery—all without the ability to perform those services ourselves. We do not think less of our ultimate authority nor look to our service providers to decide for us simply because we choose not to write our own computer code or remove our own gall bladder. Making the decisions and supervising those performing the tasks is job enough. So it is with investment management. Selecting the service providers, establishing the parameters within which they work, and supervising their performance is job enough. Let the investment managers decide whether to buy AT&T or MCI. And let the managers read all those other books on how to pick stocks!

Assumed Knowledge

This book does assume that the reader understands the basics of the financial markets. Therefore, it will not cover details of stock and bond investing other than at those unique points where particular aspects of the financial markets are affected by or have an impact on nonprofit investment policies. The book also assumes a certain familiarity with the basics of accounting and of U.S. laws.

In every area, the primary focus is on the policies organizations need and not on the details of how the underlying work is performed. From that perspective, popular investing notions such as how to beat the stock market or how to invest for retirement are not particularly important. Even when we discuss current institutional stock selection techniques, the goal is to provide enough recognition of asset categories, strategies, and techniques that your organization—your board members and your officers—can effectively create and implement policies that supervise those who actually perform the work.

Among the many benefits of this approach is a freedom largely to ignore

---

[3] We also have a summary of the book, which is separately available for those directors who cannot take the time to read an entire book. The summary is an easy-to-read 24-page guide, published by the National Center for Nonprofit Boards, which can be a helpful first step in moving the entire board toward a greater understanding of this area.

the details of very advanced areas such as quantitative portfolio analysis. For those with a mathematical bent, I highly recommend Harry Markowitz's book on portfolio selection, which really launched the modern world of investing. It is a quant's[4] dream come true, filled with mathematical formulas, charts, tables, and theorems.

Welcome to the American Charitable Organization

This book will refer periodically to the American Charitable Organization, or ACO, as if it were a real entity. It is not. And if there is an ACO somewhere, I am unaware of it and am not referring to it. Rather, it is an entirely fictitious organization used for the purpose of illustration. Not only is it fictitious, but its make-believe board is also far less competent than any real board that I have ever seen. This convention permits the illustration of real-life nonprofit problems and mistakes without embarassing anyone and without all the pesky disclosures, disclaimers, and apologies that would otherwise be needed. So enjoy the humor of the ACO's incompetence!

Book Organization

The book is arranged in three parts plus the appendixes. Part I presents the background environmental issues within which investment policies operate. These include the underlying assumptions, the legal environment, and modern notions of portfolio theory.

Part II deals with operational issues. Such issues include appropriate internal structures, how to find and hire outside advisors, and the essentials of investment accounting and performance reporting.

Part III examines some of the special issues and problems faced by nonprofits. The discussion begins with a chapter on endowments and planned gifts, then considers peculiar problem areas for nonprofits, including scam artists and the question of serving as trustee, and concludes with a chapter called "Putting It All Together." This last chapter addresses the first investment problem most nonprofits face: "How in the heck do we get started?"

---

[4] "Quant" is a slang expression in the investment community for those who love the mathematical and largely computer-driven forms of research and portfolio selection.

PART I

Background and Theory

1 The Case for Investment Policies / 3

2 The Legal Environment: Law, Tradition, and Investment Practices / 11

3 The Investment Environment: Modern Portfolio Theory / 34

▼ 1 The Case for Investment Policies

The case for adopting investment policies is simple: The adoption of policies invariably leads to an increase in return on investment and a decrease in fiduciary liabilities. Some results are immediate and effectively result from the mere act of adopting policies. Others take significant time, effort, and commitment. All are worth it.

Most nonprofits operate today under varying degrees of financial pressure. Consistent and disciplined investing provides a wonderful opportunity to increase revenues and decrease pressure on fund raising. Even a modest increase in return on investment can, over many years, make an enormous difference in the financial health of an organization.

To obtain such benefits an organization must integrate investment policies into all aspects of organizational and financial life. That can include everything from cash management to fund raising. After briefly considering the inherent power of investment policies, this chapter introduces the steps and actions that are necessary to put the policies into action. Investment policies, however, are not likely to be put into action at the American Charitable Organization ("ACO").

At the ACO . . .

"JUST ASK US WHEN THE TIME COMES"

It had already been a long board meeting, even by ACO standards, so the chief financial officer probably goofed in bringing up the question in the first place. But it was too late now so he plunged in.

"I really think we ought to adopt a set of investment policies," the CFO said.

"What for?" asked a board member. "We trust you."

"I know you trust me, but I don't know exactly what you want me to do when it comes to investing our funds."

"That's simple," added another director. "We want you to make investments that generate a decent income. Keep it safe, of course. Don't put more than a hundred thousand dollars at any one bank, because then it wouldn't be insured."

"But I'm not even sure it all ought to be in fixed income," protested the CFO. "Some of our long-term money probably ought to be in equities. That's part of the reason I want an investment policy; I want some guidance on how the money should be invested."

"Well, I still don't see why we need a set of policies," said the first director. "Just ask us when the time comes. That way we don't have to deal with a bunch of hypothetical questions."

The CFO sighed.

The Power of Policy

Investing includes virtually any use of capital to earn a return in the form of either *income,* meaning the receipt of dividends or interest, or *capital gains,* meaning an increase in the value of the asset. Therefore, almost any time a surplus exists, those funds are being "invested." Thus, transferring funds from a checking account into a higher-yielding money market deposit account is an example of an investment. Consequently, most organizations already have an investment policy, even if it is as casual as that maintained by the ACO.

But even if the board is populated with investment experts and the treasurer or chief financial officer is capable of making sound short-term cash management decisions, the organization is not well served by the failure to adopt formal policies. The benefits of increased return and decreased liabilities flow from the discipline and order that formal policies represent. The larger the sums and the longer the periods during which they can be invested, the more crucial the policy decisions.

Policies represent big, broad, sweeping decisions that by their very nature simplify our lives. Think for a moment about parents trying to prevent their children from watching violent or sexually explicit movies. One option is to evaluate every movie the children wish to see. If the children are typical, this system will eventually fail; the children will simply wear the parents out. By the hundredth time they ask to see an R-rated film, explain that all their friends have seen it, and declare that their teacher will let them write a report on it, most parents will cave in and let them see the movie. The burden of decision making becomes overwhelming.

If, however, parents drive a stake in the ground and say, "No R-rated movies," then all they need to ask is, "What's the rating?" If parents stick to their guns, after a couple of inquiries they won't even have to have the discussion. The children will simply know there is a *policy* that prohibits those particular films. So it is with investment policies. They represent sweeping decisions that help reduce daily and long-term financial problems to more manageable proportions. This, ultimately, is the reason for adopting investment policies.

THE POWER TO INCREASE RETURNS

In the world of investing, it is impossible to overstate the importance of the basics. Merely adopting and implementing investment policies, for example, frequently *increases* the return on investable resources. This phenomenon occurs whenever *the majority of the return produced by financial investments is attributable merely to the fact of being invested* as opposed to the specific manner in which funds are invested. Not only does "being invested" frequently produce most of the return, but, being invested consistently over time is also fundamental to any ability to earn extraordinary returns through better management.

Despite that fact, the tendency in the world of investing (particularly in the world of institutional investing, of which nonprofits are a part) is to spend enormous time, effort, and energy on either selecting investments or selecting investment managers. But a look at the five-year performance of the 2,267 U.S. stock mutual funds followed by the Morningstar Service shows that the average return was 13.69 percent per year for the period ending December 31, 1996. During that period, the U.S. stock market, as measured by the Standard & Poor's 500 Stock Index, generated a return of 15.20 percent per year. While there were many funds that outperformed the market, it was still the stock market itself that did most of the heavy lifting. When it comes to generating investment returns, it is the ultimate "basic" of getting our funds invested in the first instance that matters most.

THE POWER TO REDUCE LIABILITIES

When it comes to protecting the organization, the basics are equally important. By adopting investment policies, charitable organizations discharge their fiduciary responsibilities in a way that protects the organization and its officers and directors from investment liabilities. Legal developments increasingly are giving board members a choice: discharge or delegate. If they delegate in a prudent manner, they can escape liability for the actions of those to whom they delegate or for any investment losses. Conversely, if they fail to delegate or do so carelessly, they retain full responsibility and liability.

Even the simplest of investment standards will usually also protect us—and our organizations—against ourselves. Almost everyone associated with nonprofit organizations, being aware of the continual need for fund raising, adopts an open and inviting manner in dealing with the public. Consequently, part of the culture of the nonprofit world is gentleness. Where Voltaire would say, "The beginning of wisdom is doubt," a nonprofit officer would say, "Thank you for letting us participate in such a terrific investment opportunity." With such gentleness often comes a certain vulnerability to hustlers and poor decision making.

From the dependency on fund raising also comes a tendency for nonprofit organizations to be more trusting than they should. Many charities have a "Blanche DuBois attitude," having grown accustomed to the kindness of strangers. Nonprofits not only benefit from but also incur potential liabilities to strangers. Consider the following example.

The Philanthropy Protection Act of 1995 (also discussed in Chapter 2) was passed by Congress in response to a massive lawsuit brought in Texas by heirs of a maiden aunt against agencies of her church. The most important observation here is not that several people were willing to bring a lawsuit against their aunt's church for the sake of whatever money they might make but rather that *the plaintiffs were people with whom the defending charities had no previous relationship.* Every nonprofit organization actively involved in receiving planned gifts arguably has a large potential off-balance-sheet liability in the form of future claims by disgruntled heirs.

If nonprofits are to preserve an open and trusting character without giving away the store to unhappy heirs and slick promoters, they will need the protection that investment policies afford. Adopting policies and creating structures by which investment policies are implemented actually lowers the potential liabilities of the board. Sticking to the basics thereafter also greatly reduces vulnerability to fraudulent schemes, inappropriate investments, and inadequate supervision.

The Investment Context

The investment context includes the broad cultural and societal items just mentioned as well as the current state of investment law and investment theory. To equip organizations to understand policy decisions, this book begins with an examination of those broad contextual issues. Chapter 2 discusses the tremendous liberalization of the investment laws as evidenced by the move from the Prudent Man Rule to the new Prudent Investor Rule. While this change started more than twenty years ago, the most recent expression of the new rules, the Uniform Prudent Investor Act, which applies to trusts, was first promulgated in 1994 and so far has been adopted by ten states. Things are changing, therefore, as this is being written.

The change in law is directly related to and in some ways results from changes in investment theory. The field of so-called modern portfolio theory began in 1959 and has evolved rapidly since. All of Chapter 3 is devoted to an explanation of portfolio theory. As intimidating as that may sound, understanding the basics of this theory is fundamental to the work that investment policies are intended to govern.

The Organizational Context

The primary role of investment policies is to provide a stable foundation and a context within which to take *measured* risks. That context includes both the organizational structure as well as the specifics of goals and objectives, available resources, investment time frames, and the limitations, if any, on permitted investment. There is also an important philosophical concept which is the notion of participating in the investment process. Investment policies are intended to facilitate the participation of officers and directors in the investment process, not exclude them from it. As seen in later chapters, investing is not something that can be wound up and pointed down the road to be thereafter ignored.

In pursuing the goal of participation, organizational structure matters. It is not enough to have competent directors, although clearly that is essential. It is not enough to have capable officers and outside advisors, although they can be helpful. The relationships between the directors and their committees and the organization's officers and outside advisors need to be established and maintained in a manner that helps everyone do their work. Chapter 4 examines the appropriate stylization of internal decision-making structures and its relationship to the investment policy process.

KNOWING WHAT WE HAVE TO INVEST

Chapter 5 presents a specific process for identifying investment assets. The chapter is an extended commentary on an internal self-guided investment assessment form or questionnaire. While the specific information this process identifies is important, the process also represents a continuing commitment to participation. The questionnaire is intended to be completed in parts by the executive director, the senior development officer, the chief financial officer, and other key board members. The results should be shared even more broadly within the organization. At every step implementing policy means involving the organization's key people in the process.

Surveying the investment world also means attempting to identify the key characteristics that bear on investment decisions. Consequently, the survey probes for information and attitudes concerning goals and objectives, resources, time frames, tolerance for risk, and specific, known limitations. Just the process of completing this survey will make the typical organization far more "manageable" from a professional investor's perspective. In a sense, therefore, knowing the organization well is also one of the basics.

Goals and Objectives
What are the goals for which the organization is investing? What are the purposes for which a particular fund exists? What planned-gift instruments does the organization accept and administer? These questions, and many more, represent critical components of the organizational context.

Resources
Resources refer not only to the money the organization has to manage but also to the existing structures and relationships in place for managing funds. Which staff members are available and capable of participating in this process? Who are the outside service providers? Which of the outside service providers is doing a good job?

Time Frames
What are the time frames involved? It makes a great deal of difference to the application of a particular policy to know the period for which the funds

will be invested. Obviously, if the money is needed in thirty days, the appropriate choices are considerably narrower than if the money is not needed for thirty years. As will be seen, an important requirement for effective investing is to impose on the charitable organization, at every opportunity, the longest possible time frame the organization can tolerate.

Risk Tolerance
One of the key processes that investment advisors now use is known as asset allocation. It is basically a technique for controlling the amount of risk in a portfolio by combining different types of assets. For the process to be effective, however, the board has to be able to tell whoever is guiding the process just how much risk they are willing to take. Nothing is more "basic" than answering the question, "How much money are we willing to lose?" That, it turns out, is no easy task, but involves asking a series of questions and listening carefully to the answers. A selection of key risk identification questions is included in the Chapter 5 questionnaire.

Limitations
Finally, what are the other limitations under which the organization is operating? Any effective implementation of investment policies must necessarily deal with the limitations within which the organization operates. One example of possible limitations is social or moral restrictions. A number of nonprofits attempt to avoid investing in companies whose activities are antithetical to their goals and objectives. Chapter 9, on special nonprofit investment issues, examines such restrictions.

Nonprofit organizations are also saddled with a host of more mundane limitations on their investment activities. Virtually all forms of planned-gift assets are subject to either tax-related or legally imposed investment restrictions. Gift-annuity reserves, for example, are regulated by the insurance commissioners of several states. Charitable remainder trusts must be invested with an eye toward the tax effects on the distributions to the income beneficiaries. And certain instruments, such as net income charitable remainder trusts, effectively restrict the possible investments by creating a demand for dividend and interest income. All of Chapter 8 focuses on the subject of investing planned-gift assets.

HIRING HELP

An essential component of order demanded by effective investment policies is execution. At the end of the day, someone actually has to do the work. Most nonprofits are hiring investment help now even if they do not recognize it as such. Investing in mutual funds, for example, is a form of hiring investment help. There is little fundamental difference between mutual fund investment management and the management that comes from hiring an investment advisor directly. The differences are matters of fees and expenses, minimum investment amounts, and control over the contents of the portfolio. The "work" that the investment advisor does is largely the same, either way.

All of Chapter 6 concerns the issue of hiring appropriate help. The principal effort of that chapter is to identify the choices that are available and the relationships that exist between the potential service providers—banks, trust companies, brokers, and investment advisors—and the work that needs to be performed—custody, asset allocation, investment selection, securities brokerage, and performance reporting. As will be seen, it is increasingly difficult to discuss service providers in terms of their traditional roles since most providers now offer a wide range of financial services. Still and all, understanding the traditional roles as they relate to the essential tasks, can help bring order to this area as well.

MEASURING PERFORMANCE

An organization can adopt policies, reorganize its board, identify manageable assets, and hire help, but if the organization lacks a system for keeping track of the results, it is likely to be disappointed, or worse. Measuring performance is a continuous process of asking ourselves and our agents (those who are implementing our policies) if we are doing what we have committed to do. While there are highly structured ways to conduct that review, a number of which are discussed in Chapter 7, the crucial point is to ask regularly, "How are we doing?" Chapter 7 examines investment performance reporting and its relationship to normal financial accounting. The first new concept for many officers and directors is that even the best and most thorough financial accounting is not enough if the goal is to do a good job managing investments. Some of the key issues concerning portfolio risks are simply not measured at all by financial accounting. Organizations need to adopt new standards and implement performance reports if they are to do a good job in this area.

Fortunately, the work that will have already been done when creating appropriate investment portfolios lends itself naturally to performance reporting. Any model created for a portfolio can also be used to measure against readily available benchmarks. Thus, completing the process by effectively measuring performance is a logical and easily accomplished step.

The Unique Charitable Context

The final three chapters of the book deal with issues that are largely unique to charitable organizations, meaning those nonprofits that are publicly supported for eleemosynary purposes. Usually such organizations are qualified as tax-exempt entities that may receive tax-deductible donations under section 501(c)3 of the Internal Revenue Code. Their dependency on fund raising and on the services of volunteers is a paramount and fundamental issue.

Chapter 8, as already noted, discusses the investment of planned-gift assets. Chapter 9 examines a number of special nonprofit investment problems including socially responsible investing, the pressure to serve as trustee, and vulnerability to outright scams. In considering these issues the chapter examines the New Era scandal.

Chapter 10 addresses the final nonprofit investment problem, which is the challenge of getting started. An abiding characteristic of all organizations, and of nonprofits especially, is that board members sometimes have a glorious time discussing policy issues without ever coming to an executable decision. The policy-making process, while important, is not the goal. Rather, it is a means to an end. To benefit from having policies, action must be taken to implement them. The last chapter of the book presents a step-by-step approach intended to help even the most hesitant board get off the dime!

Conclusion

The final reason to adopt investment policies is that investment policies do not stand alone. Rather, investment policies affect every other area of the organization, including budgets and fund raising. When dealing with charitable remainder trusts, for example, investing for growth maximizes the value of the gift. Generating too little income, however, can lead to an unhappy donor. But trying to make the donor happy by investing exclusively for income can cause the organization to lose money on every trust it brings in the door. And so it goes. For nonprofits in the fund-raising business, investment policies are critical to the ultimate success of the fund-raising program.

The good news, here as elsewhere, is that sticking to the basics substantially protects organizations. Whether it is a desire to use the latest and greatest investment technique—or a driving fear of missing out on the greatest bull market in history—sticking to the basics helps organizations resist momentary passions. No matter how strong the feeling of being underinvested when the market is hot or how strong the urge to cut and run when the market drops, when we walk into the board meeting to advocate a new position we run into those pesky policies established in calmer times. If we are to pursue our passions of the moment we must first change our policies.

Clearly written investment policies are therefore a critical tool for charitable organizations. Investing is a human endeavor and as such is no less subject to momentary passions or other human weaknesses than anything else we do. Fortunately, we can prepare ourselves and our organizations to use the best of our humanity and to temper our weaknesses. That, ultimately, is the case for having investment policies.

2 ▼ The Legal Environment: Law, Tradition, and Investment Practices

The manner in which charitable organizations are permitted to invest their funds is, largely, a matter of law. As will be seen, those laws are considerably more liberal today than they were just a few short years ago. We are, in fact, in the midst of a tremendous liberalization of the laws of investing as applied to nonprofit organizations. Nonetheless, even the modern, liberal provisions still circumscribe the world of permitted investments.

At the ACO . . .

THE BOARD'S VIEW OF THE LAW

The American Charitable Organization ("ACO") is a twenty-year-old social service agency with religious leanings but with no denominational ties. It runs a series of small residential facilities for recovering alcoholics in the downtown area of a major eastern city. The organization's founder is now in his late 50s and continues to serve as director. He is well respected in the community and has good ties to the other agencies in town, both public and private.

The ACO has a twelve-member board that oversees a $3 million annual budget. Of that amount, roughly 55 percent is derived from rents, fees, and public subsidies paid for up to 72 residents in a total of six homes. The balance of approximately $1.4 million is raised annually, largely through direct donations, a golf tournament, silent auction, and an occasional bequest.

Throughout its 50-year history, the organization has largely been a hand-to-mouth operation, having to raise the portion of the operating budget that they do not earn each year. Nonetheless, despite themselves, they have had some longer-term funds imposed upon them. Two donors left them substantial bequests on the condition that they retain the funds in trust and "use only the income" for operational purposes. With those funds in mind, consider the ACO board.

Two of the twelve ACO board members are bankers, one retired. Both have advised the board repeatedly that the state banking regulations require banks and trust companies to maintain lists of "trust qualified" investments. In addition, they have expressed the opinion that if the law does not permit banks to take risks with trust money, then the ACO ought to be even more cautious. "Whatever the rules are for charities," said one, "they sure can't be any more aggressive than what the state lets our bank get away with." Therefore, the current, dominant understanding of the board is that there are legal lists of "safe" investments for banks, charities, and other similar organizations.

Let's see if the bankers are right.

What Laws Apply to Nonprofits?

There has never been a single "investment law" in the United States that defines and regulates permitted investments by individuals, businesses, or nonprofit organizations. The premise of the federal securities laws, for example, is not to control what may be offered and sold but rather to assure that there is full and fair disclosure of the known information. Consequently, such regulation of investments as has existed has been random and scattered.

Historically, pieces of investment regulation have been found in the trust laws and banking regulations. Beginning in the 1930s, regulation of the securities industry and of the insurance industry and their products was added. More recently, through tax and labor laws, pension, profit sharing, and other retirement plans have been regulated. In virtually all of these areas, however, the rules regulating permitted investments exist to serve some underlying industry need or purpose.

In the last 25 years, however, the situation has changed for both charities and fiduciaries—those individuals or non-bank-regulated organizations who serve as trustees—because there are now in fact specific statutes dealing with investments. These new laws, which are discussed in the following section, were not painted on an empty canvas. So the understanding and application of those laws has been determined by the pieces that formerly existed as well as by the centuries-old common-law notions that have controlled fiduciary investing in the absence of specific, controlling statutes.

To appreciate the investment freedom that we now have—and to be aware of those remaining areas where that freedom is compromised—one needs to first understand the common-law tradition known as the Prudent Man Rule. With that as background one can better understand the enormous change in philosophy and approach that the new Prudent Investor Rule represents. It is the Prudent Investor Rule that is embodied in the investment-specific statutes that now apply to charities and to trustees. The ability to implement the precepts of the Prudent Investor Rule is, at times, limited by other, usually older, laws, including the rules of the various state insurance commissioners and, to a lesser extent, the state and federal securities law statutes. Rather than encumber the present discussion with problems, however, such issues will be examined in Chapter 9. The present focus is on the major investment laws with which a nonprofit organization's policies must comply and the freedoms within those laws around which policies are constructed.

Fiduciary Duty—The Starting Point of Investment Regulation

The first piece of the puzzle—the legal concept that plays the most important role in both the current and the historic development of our investment laws—is the notion of fiduciary duty. A fiduciary is a person or an entity who holds a trust relationship to another. Anyone who controls assets or exercises power or authority for the benefit of someone else is said to be a fiduciary, and such a person's responsibilities are referred to as fiduciary duties. It is a broad concept with deep roots in Anglo-American law.

The terms *trustee* and *fiduciary* are frequently used synonymously, largely because the first and most common fiduciaries were trustees. A trustee is, literally, the person who exercises control over property, in the manner of an owner, for the benefit of someone else. The ability to allow one person to exercise such control over assets for the benefit of another person has proven so helpful over the centuries that there is a tremendous body of long-established law dealing with trusts and with the rights and obligations of those with interests in a trust. It is from this body of trust law that many of the concepts of prudent investing originated. To see how this has occurred, and to better understand the continuing role of trust law concepts in prudent investing, a brief examination of the nature of the trust relationship is in order.

Trusts, Trusts Everywhere

Whenever a trust relationship exists, it has four elements:

1. The beneficiary(ies) are those for whom the trust relationship exists;
2. The trustee is the person or entity who exercises control over whatever property, rights, or other assets are being held "in trust";
3. The trust corpus is the property or other assets being held in trust; and,
4. The trust purposes are the collection of terms and conditions under which the trustee (item 2) holds and administers the assets (item 3) for the beneficiaries (item 1).

Obviously, the trustee is in a tremendously powerful position. The trustee has, for most purposes, the same degree of control over the property in the trust as would an absolute owner. The difference is that the trustee is charged with exercising that power *solely* in the best interests of the beneficiaries of the trust.

Human nature being what it is, the law has been forced over the years to articulate and prescribe a number of specific duties with which a trustee is charged. Those duties include:

- A duty of loyalty to trust beneficiaries
- A duty to keep records
- A duty to furnish information
- A duty to exercise reasonable care
- A duty to take and keep control of trust property
- A duty to protect property of the trust
- A duty to enforce claims of the trust
- A duty to defend the trust against claims
- A duty to pay income beneficiaries
- A duty to deal impartially with beneficiaries

And there are others. The point is that all of these "duties" are obligations that come to rest upon an individual or an organization that serves as a trustee. A trustee is, primarily, a position of responsibility.

EXPRESS AND IMPLIED TRUSTS

Trust relationships can be express or implied. A charitable remainder trust is an example of an express trust. It comes into existence when the donor executes the trust document and then funds the trust by making a contribution to it.

Trusts can also exist on an implied basis. If I give you $100, for example, so that you can purchase concert tickets for me, we have created an implied trust. At the time I hand you the cash, you have the same control over those funds as would any legal owner, simply by virtue of possession. It is within your power to do whatever you wish with that money. If instead of buying concert tickets for me, you visit a wine merchant and purchase a bottle of expensive Bordeaux, the wine merchant will not look at the $100 bill and say, "Oh my gosh, that's Bob Fry's money." Rather, he will simply take the money and make change. So far as he is concerned, it is your money.

Now if you are a good trustee, you will honor our understanding that you are to buy concert tickets with the corpus of the trust—my $100—and not buy yourself wine. You hold the money, in other words, for my benefit; you are the *trustee*, and I am the *beneficiary* of our implied trust. And just as with an express trust, your fiduciary duty continues until you have satisfied the terms of the trust—in this case by delivering to me the tickets, along with my change.

While this example is a bit silly, it does serve to illustrate how easy it is to create an implied trust relationship. From this idea of an implied trust, a further concept has emerged that completes the transition to a broader notion of fiduciary duty. That is the idea of a public trust.

PUBLIC TRUSTS

The theory of a public trust is that someone is the holder of a general responsibility of which the public is the ultimate beneficiary. A great deal of recent environmental legislation and regulatory activity is based on "public trust" concepts. In the environmental arena, the underlying presumption is that natural resources are (or should be) held for the benefit of all people, regardless of who happens to be the owner of the land on which those resources reside. In a very real sense, the "owner" of the property becomes a "trustee" of the resources and is charged with preserving and protecting them for the public good.

CONSTITUENCY TRUSTS

Such "public" trust concepts can also exist for the benefit of a smaller group or subset of the general public. The constituents of a charitable organization can be a group for whose benefit the organization holds its assets. The organization—through its officers and directors—acts as a "trustee" of an implied or public trust of which the constituents' and the organization's charitable purposes are the beneficiaries.

TRUST CONCEPTS FOR CHARITABLE ORGANIZATIONS

We have now come full circle in applying trust concepts to the management of charitable organizations' funds. The notion of fiduciary duty expresses itself in the understanding that none of the assets under the control of a charitable organization actually belong to the nonprofit. Rather, all such assets are held by it "in trust" for some purpose, even when those assets are not, on the face of things, so restricted.

In many states, this notion is an express part of laws that declare that all assets of charitable organizations are deemed to be held in trust for the benefit of the constituencies and purposes for which the organization exists. This is a trust concept, written into state statutes, that creates regulatory oversight of the nonprofit world. Under California law, for example, the attorney general is authorized in extreme cases to go to court to enforce that trust by preventing the misapplication of charitable funds.

Development of an investment policy rests on the fundamental understanding that every asset of a charitable organization is held in trust. It is impossible to overstate the importance of this concept. It flows through our laws and informs our organizations' relationships with constituents, regulators, board members, employees, outside advisors, and the general public.

If those serving in the nonprofit world think of themselves as trustees, they will be well on their way to an understanding of the specific investment laws that govern the nonprofit world.

The Investment Laws

For many years, the operative rule governing investments by fiduciaries was the Prudent Man Rule. Not surprisingly, the Prudent Man Rule emerged from the law of trusts, where it initially governed the actions of trustees under so-called express trusts. Subsequently, by both judicial and statutory action, the concepts in the Prudent Man Rule came to be applied to virtually all funds held in a fiduciary capacity, whether by trustees, banks, or charities. Though currently being replaced by the Prudent Investor Rule, both the substantive provisions of the Prudent Man Rule and the manner in which it was developed and applied remain important to a complete understanding of the *current law* of investing by charities.

HISTORY AND APPLICATION OF THE PRUDENT MAN RULE

The Prudent Man Rule traces its roots to the 1830 case of *Harvard College v. Amory* in the Supreme Judicial Court of Massachusetts. In that case, the judge wrote that when investing, a trustee "is to observe how men of prudence, discretion and intelligence manage their own affairs, not in regard to speculation, but in regard to the permanent disposition of their funds, considering the probable income, as well as the probable safety of the capital to be invested."

As written, the Prudent Man Rule was reasonable and accommodating. In some jurisdictions, such as Massachusetts, subsequent decisions followed a reasonable and reasoned approach in determining the investment standard of care. However, in a great many jurisdictions the actual, practical standard under which trustees and directors acted on a day-to-day basis was considerably narrower and more restrictive. It is important to understand how the lessening of investment freedom occurred in the wake of a patently reasonable rule because the forces at work that led to the decline of freedom continue to inhabit our legal system. The notion of the common law, in particular, and the role that this odd bit of our legal history *continues* to play in the formation and interpretation of our laws today is important.

THE COMMON LAW

The idea of the common law arises from the English practice of establishing laws through a body of judicial decisions over a long period of time rather than through the legislative enactment of statutes. The practice, dating back to medieval England, was followed in colonial America and continued by the states after the Revolutionary War. Thus, for many years, laws dealing with crimes, contracts, wills, trusts, and real estate were all primarily governed by centuries of judicial decisions as opposed to specific, legislatively created statutes.

In the United States in the late nineteenth and early twentieth centuries, there was a strong movement toward codifying the common law. The result has been that much of what was common law is now reflected in state statutes, which supersede the common law when enacted. The legacy of common law is that the state and federal courts still interpret how specific laws are to be understood and applied. Thus, for most purposes, the statute on a particular subject is the beginning point when we want to know "the law." Having found the statute, we then look to subsequent judicial decisions to round out the understanding of exactly how that law will be applied.

Constriction

Investment law took one of three turns from its common law roots. The first was the natural consequence of ongoing judicial development and interpretation of the Prudent Man Rule as established in each state by either case law or by statute. One might think of that as a process of "constriction."

For example, a bank agrees to serve as trustee on a trust. During its tenure, the bank invests a small portion of the fund in a relatively young company with good growth prospects. Since most of the fund is invested in either older, established companies or government bonds, the bank reasons that it is reasonable (i.e., prudent) to try to earn a greater return on a small portion of the fund. Unfortunately, this small, young growth company goes broke, and the entire investment is lost. The income beneficiary sues the bank.

The judge in the case is an older lawyer who just happens to invest his own money exclusively in government bonds. His natural inclination, therefore, is to think that the bank was gambling with the trust's money. In support of his position are, literally, thousands of cases on a trustee's duty to preserve and protect the assets in the trust. Since the asset is gone, he reasons, isn't it obvious that the bank breached its duty? He rules for the plaintiff.

At this point we still have not created any new law as trial court decisions in the United States are not, for the most part, recorded and reported for subsequent citation. But the bank in this example is the trustee on hundreds of trusts and has purchased shares of the same growth company in a number of them. Consequently, the bank does not want the word to get out that it paid for losses in one of those trusts. So it appeals the judgment.

The bank then loses on appeal and now new law has been created. When the appellate court issues its opinion, that opinion is recorded and may be cited by lawyers and judges in the future. In our appellate court opinion, the judge writes, "It was imprudent for the bank, as trustee, to invest trust funds in the shares of an *unseasoned company*. Rather, the bank should have confined its equity investments to shares of established companies with a long history of regular dividend payments. In the case at hand, this start-up company, in fact, paid no dividend, thus lending further weight to the reckless nature of this investment." While this quote is a hypothetical example, hundreds just like it exist in cases decided throughout the fifty states.

Here is what happens next. In subsequent lawsuits, attorneys for the plaintiffs argue that investments in "unseasoned companies" are imprudent as a matter of law. In other words, it is always imprudent for a trustee to invest trust funds in such companies. By the time that there are three or four appellate court cases that come to that same conclusion, or only one at the state supreme court level, the proposition—that investments in *unseasoned companies* are imprudent for trustees—is now, in fact, the law of the land. And it will remain so until changed by an act of the legislature.

This brief example demonstrates the entire development of common law in a microcosm. First, there is a dispute between parties that, *wholly apart from the development of new laws,* needs to be resolved. The issue of the day is not what is the best law for all concerned but, rather, has a wrong occurred on these particular facts. Developing a new rule of law is, at best, a secondary concern.

Secondly, there is a natural tendency in this situation to focus on the problem. The question before the court is whether this particular investment was prudent. It takes extremely broad-minded people, when faced with such a narrow question, to step back and look at the bigger picture.

Within the investment environment the tendency of the common law to develop one problem at a time led directly to one of the truly damaging and insidious aspects of the Prudent Man Rule. Investments tended to be judged for prudence on an investment-by-investment basis, wholly apart from overall portfolio performance, let alone portfolio theory. As anyone who has ever invested in the stock market is aware, having losing positions in a portfolio is a virtual certainty, given enough positions and enough time. Faced with an investment-by-investment standard, most trustees concluded that the prudent course (for them at least) was to invest primarily if not exclusively in U.S. government bonds.

Legal List Statutes
The second response to or variation from the Prudent Man Rule was legislative. Some states migrated from the original broad-based approach of the Prudent Man Rule by statute as opposed to judicial decision. Unfortunately, these initial legislative approaches were frequently even more restrictive than judicial decisions interpreting the Prudent Man Rule. In a number of states, the legislature actually prescribed lists of acceptable investments. Such laws became known as legal list statutes.

The legal list statutes generally restricted fiduciaries to investments in U.S. government securities and high-grade corporate bonds. Common stocks were often prohibited. So the effect of these laws was more or less the same, in terms of limiting investment options, as the narrowest judicial developments discussed above.

Nondelegable Duties

The final significant trust legacy in the growth of investment management rules was a general prohibition on delegating investment responsibilities. This restriction, which is to modern investors counterintuitive (as we now hire help for everything), made a great deal of sense from the perspective of someone naming an *individual* as the trustee of his trust. For example, if I have asked Al Gore to act as the trustee on my family's trust, and he has agreed to do so, I probably do not want him to turn around and delegate responsibility for the trust to Newt Gingrich. Wholly apart from your views of the relative abilities of these two well-known politicians, it is clear that their views on many things are different; it makes sense that if I choose one, I might not want the other.

What developed in trust law, therefore, was a general rule that the duties and obligations of a trustee were nondelegable. This meant in the context of managing trust assets that it was much more difficult and less rewarding to hire professional investment management assistance. Why was that the case?

Hiring help was not a rewarding exercise because it in no way diminished one's responsibility and liability as trustee. If the trustee's manager made a poor investment and the trustee was sued for the losses, the fact that the trustee relied upon expert advice was not a defense. It might, in fact, *increase one's liability;* if a judge determined that the trustee had delegated a nondelegable responsibility, that alone could be a basis of liability.

Faced with that hurdle, help would have to be hired, if at all, on an advisory as opposed to discretionary basis. When an individual invests in a mutual fund, the individual hires discretionary investment management. The mutual fund managers have discretion to buy and sell stocks with the mutual fund's assets *without having to get the individual investor's permission in advance.* The individual has given them blanket permission by investing in the fund. And that is the manner in which the overwhelming majority of directly managed funds are handled. The manager is given discretion, usually through a limited trading authorization, to buy and sell securities in the account without having to ask the client's permission each and every time. It should be obvious that without such discretion it would be extremely difficult for managers to handle very many accounts. They would constantly be on the phone. In addition, they would need to document (as they are in fact still required to do in nondiscretionary accounts) that they were given permission to take a particular action. Nondiscretionary accounts are an administrative headache.

Add it all up and trustees had a difficult time retaining investment help.

They could not be relieved of the daily burdens, and they still "participated" in the manager's mistakes. It was a lose-lose situation.

THE PRACTICAL LEGACY OF THE PRUDENT MAN RULE

The result of the foregoing evolution is that the Prudent Man Rule in practice could be summarized as follows:

1. Never lose money—as each investment is judged on its own.
2. Income matters most—as non-income-producing investments are inherently suspect.
3. Do not attempt to delegate responsibility—as it is probably a breach of duty to do so.

Taken together, these three characteristics of judicial interpretation made it almost impossible to invest in common stocks, even when such investments were not actually prohibited by either statute or case law. As will be seen, one of the great ironies of the Prudent Man Rule was that it was actually less restrictive of investment freedom than everyone believed. But the "beliefs" prevailed, so that the profile of a "prudent man" was one who invested in U.S. government bonds.

The attitudes created during the 150-year primacy of the Prudent Man Rule still linger in the nonprofit community. Many organizations continue to invest endowment and other long-term funds exclusively in certificates of deposit and U.S. government bonds; however, such an approach no longer complies with the law of prudent investing.

Changes in the Investment Environment

Two broad changes in the 1960s and 1970s heralded the need for revised standards for fiduciary investments. The first was a dramatic increase in the rate of inflation. With inflation reaching an unprecedented 13.3 percent, holders of fixed-income portfolios found themselves consistently losing money. As a practical matter, they were lending dollars and being repaid in dimes. Second, much of the academic work on portfolio theory (discussed below) was published and available for practical application.

THE FORD FOUNDATION STUDIES

These two trends—high levels of inflation and the development of modern portfolio theory—merged most notably in two Ford Foundation studies published in 1969 and 1974. The first, entitled *The Law and the Lore of Endowment Funds,* was prompted by a general recognition that the nation's universities needed to be doing a better job managing their endowments. Those

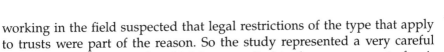

working in the field suspected that legal restrictions of the type that apply to trusts were part of the reason. So the study represented a very careful examination of just exactly which laws applied to the management of university endowment funds.

The results were surprising. The authors focused primarily on the question of what constitutes "income," and, specifically, whether income could include realized and unrealized capital gains. They also briefly examined what they called the "other legal problems affecting endowment funds." Within this category they considered the law of permissible investments, the fear of directors' liability, and the delegation of investment authority. Their overall conclusion was that the law was not the principal source of the problem.

> If the managers of educational endowment funds are being hampered in their efforts to develop sound investment policies, the fault cannot fairly be said to lie in the law. Legal impediments which have been thought to deprive managers of their freedom of action appear on analysis to be more legendary than real.
>
> If the managers of endowment funds wish to seek long-term appreciation in their investments, the need of their institutions for current yield should not dissuade them. We find no authoritative support in the law for the widely held view that the realized gains of endowment funds can never be spent. Prudence would call for the retention of sufficient gains to maintain purchasing power in the face of inflation and to guard against potential losses, but subject to standards which prudence dictates, the expenditure of gains should lie with the discretion of the institution's directors.
>
> The law allows the managers of endowment funds wide latitude in their choice of investments, and no conscientious director need fear liability for an honest mistake of judgment. The administration of the fund can be handled within the corporate structure by the persons best suited to the task, and it would seem that outside investment counsel can be given wide responsibility for investment decisions, provided that the institution's directors do not abdicate their power of supervision. (*The Law and Lore*, p. 66)

The irony of the initial Ford Foundation study is their principal conclusion that there are no legal reasons why endowment fund managers could not invade principal for distributions and thereby manage funds on a total return basis. The actual restriction of investment freedom under the Prudent Man Rule was driven more by the fear of liability than by actual liability in either specific court cases or statutory restrictions. The fact that such a study was necessary shows the power that the fear of liability had on trustees and other fiduciaries under the old rule.

As helpful as the conclusion was, what may have been an even more important part of the study was the observation that there was not very much law that applied directly to investing, at least for college endowment funds: "The law relating to charitable corporations in general, and particularly to the administration of endowment funds, remains throughout the nation both 'rudimentary and vague.' The great and rapid increase in the number and aggregate wealth of charitable corporations has taken the law by surprise, and the courts and commentators are still groping for a solution" (*The Law and the Lore*, p. 14).

Repeatedly the study traces legal concepts to their roots in the laws of either trusts, corporations, or contracts, only to conclude that *there is nothing in the statute that deals specifically with charitable organizations* or that *the courts have not ruled specifically* on some particular point. In the absence of clear direction, the trust law concepts discussed earlier came to dominate the thinking of charitable boards of directors with the result being a somewhat paralyzing fear.

Out of the first study came a recommendation for a new model act that would deal specifically with fiduciary investing. The recommendation stated that "ideally" such an act would establish standards for:

1. Selecting investments under a prudent man rule but in a way that allowed protecting capital against inflation
2. Utilizing gains as part of income as needed
3. Permitting delegation of investment authority.[1]

Such an act was in fact adapted and embraced a new standard that became known as the Prudent Investor Rule.

THE NEW PRUDENT INVESTOR RULE

As with many broad legal concepts, the Prudent Investor Rule is not itself a law. Rather, it is an idea embodied in state statutes and eventually reflected in judicial decisions interpreting those statutes. Currently, there are two statutory expressions of the Prudent Investor Rule. The first, promulgated in 1972 following publication of *The Law and the Lore*, is the Uniform Management of Institutional Funds Act (UMIFA). A copy of the UMIFA, which has been enacted in 40 states and the District of Columbia, is found in Appendix B-1.

The UMIFA applies broadly to any "incorporated or unincorporated organization organized and operated exclusively for educational, religious, charitable, or other eleemosynary purposes" (§1). Its express purpose is to

---

[1] The latter point—delegation—was so important (and dealt with only cursorily in this first study) that the authors revisited that subject five years later. In their report, *The Developing Law of Endowment Funds: The Law and the Lore Revisited*, the authors again conclude that the law is not the problem and that directors by all rights ought to delegate investment authority.

"establish guidelines for the management and use of investments held by eleemosynary institutions and funds."

More recently, the National Conference of Commissioners on Uniform State Laws promulgated the Uniform Prudent Investor Act (UPIA), which applies these same investment concepts to trusts. The UPIA has been enacted in 19 states, including New York, Florida, and California, since its promulgation in 1994. A copy of the UPIA is found in Appendix B-2.

The most important point in this context is that the Prudent Investor Rule is rapidly becoming the law of the land. Both statutes—the UMIFA and the UPIA—vary in certain details but at their core reflect the same investment standards. Consequently, it is important for all nonprofit boards to review their investment policies for compliance with these legal expressions of the Prudent Investor Rule.

The following discussion focuses primarily on the Uniform Management of Institutional Funds Act for two reasons. First, it is the older and more widely adopted law. Consequently, its provisions apply to most charitable organizations in the country. Secondly, the UMIFA applies, by its terms, to institutional funds as opposed to those that are literally held in trust. Consequently, a portion of the discussion of the UPIA and its focus on trusts is reserved for that part of Chapter 9 that deals with the special problems charities experience when they serve as trustees.

For immediate purposes, two areas of the Prudent Investor Rule as reflected in both statutes matter most. The first is the investment standard of care. What, exactly, is the standard under which the boards of our charitable organizations now operate? From what we have already read, we can guess that there will be some movement toward portfolio theory. But where, exactly, does that take us?

Secondly, what are the current rules with regard to hiring help? Are investors allowed to delegate investment responsibility? If so, what are the rules that must be followed? These questions go to the heart of the legal side of our investment world.

THE STANDARD OF CARE

Under both acts, the measure of prudence focuses on investment processes as opposed to classifying an investment or course of action as prudent or imprudent per se. The initial language is familiar: "In the administration of the powers to appropriate appreciation, to make and retain investments, and to delegate investment management of institutional funds, members or a governing board shall *exercise ordinary business care and prudence*" (emphasis added) (UMIFA § 6). The beginning point is the same as it has always been.

Permitted Investments
While not part of the paragraph in the UMIFA labeled standard of care, the scope of permitted investments is nonetheless an important component of

the overall standard. Under the UMIFA, the range of permitted investments is incredibly broad. The language of section 4 begins by stating that this authority is "in addition to an investment otherwise authorized by law or by the applicable gift instrument, and without restriction to investments a fiduciary may make." The board, in other words, is *not* subject to the restrictions that other laws may impose on trustees. Rather, the governing board may:

> (1) invest and reinvest an institutional fund in any real or personal property deemed advisable by the governing board, whether or not it produces a current return, including mortgages, stocks, bonds, debentures, and other securities of profit or nonprofit corporations, shares in or obligations of associations, partnerships, or individuals, and obligations of any government or subdivision or instrumentality thereof;
>
> (2) retain property contributed by a donor to an institutional fund for as long as the governing board deems advisable;
>
> (3) include all or any part of an institutional fund in any pooled or common fund maintained by the institution; and
>
> (4) invest all or any part of an institutional fund in any other pooled or common fund available for investment, including shares or interests in regulated investment companies, mutual funds, common trust funds, investment partnerships, real estate investment trusts, or similar organizations in which funds are commingled and investment determinations are made by persons other than the governing board.

This rather lengthy quotation governing permitted investments provides the easiest way to get a "feel" for the liberality of the Prudent Investor Rule. What possible investment instrument might be precluded from the items listed in the preceding paragraphs? While there is no express mention of derivatives, private placements, or venture capital funds, for example, most of those investments occur in forms such as partnerships, which are mentioned. Hence, they are permitted. Here, ironically, the UPIA is more concise:

> (e) A trustee may invest in any kind of property or type of investment consistent with the standards of this [Act].

The succinctness of the UPIA language is undoubtedly a response to the incredible flood of new products in the investment world in the last twenty years (see Chapter 3). Things have been changing so quickly that it simply does not make sense to keep lists of any sort.

Clearly, we have moved from a restrictive to a permissive approach. Any investment is appropriate if it is prudent in light of the overall game plan and portfolio strategy.

No Hindsight

The standard of care language from the Uniform Act continues by stating that prudence is measured "under the facts and circumstances prevailing at the time of the action or decision" (UMIFA § 6). In other words, hindsight is no longer a component of the investment standard. Section 8 of the UPIA states this explicitly: "Compliance with the prudent investor rule is determined in light of the facts and circumstances existing at the time of a trustee's decision or action and not by hindsight" (§ 8). This is most important as a piece of the movement away from an investment-by-investment standard. If an investment made sense *at the time* as part of the investment strategy, the law is not going to second-guess a bad result.

Total Return

In addition, the board is to consider "expected total return on its investments" (UMIFA § 6). This is very important. The ability to manage a fund for total return (in other words, dividends and interest *and* capital gains) is an essential component of modern portfolio theory (see Chapter 3). Thus, this language represents another step in that direction. The use of the plural, *investments*, in the short phrase above, is also intended to convey a portfolio approach.

When a fund is managed on a total return basis, it may or may not produce a level of current return or yield that is sufficient for intended distributions. If the emphasis on total return results in a higher percentage of the fund being invested in equities (stocks) and a corresponding decrease in bonds and other fixed-income investments, then whatever else happens the current income portion of the return will be less than it would be otherwise. So a law that permits investing on a total return basis but still requires that distributions be made only from dividends and interest would be self-defeating.

Therefore, in order to permit a total return approach, the board has to be able to make distributions out of both realized and unrealized capital gains. Consequently, Sections 2 and 3 of the UMIFA enable that access. Section 2, Appropriation of Appreciation, specifically provides that "the governing board may appropriate . . . so much of the net appreciation, realized and unrealized, . . . as is prudent under the standard established by Section 6."

Section 3, Rule of Construction, then attempts to anticipate the real world problem of interpreting the language of gifts and bequests. It begins by stating that a donor may in fact express an intention that "net appreciation shall not be expended." In that case, the permission granted by section 2 would not apply. But, that may not be the case. Rather, the rule of construction (our rule for interpreting language of gifts) will be that neither a "gift to an endowment" nor a general instruction to spend only the "income" may be used to imply "a restriction upon the expenditure of net appreciation." In other words, if a donor wants to restrict such expenditures, he or she will have to be explicit.

Taken together, these provisions allow the board to manage on a total return basis. If the income is insufficient for whatever level of distribution the board determines is necessary from the fund, then the board may invade principal. As will be seen in Chapter 8 in the discussion of ways to use investment policy to facilitate fund raising, an endowment spending policy that is crafted to take advantage of this legal right to invade principal can do wonderful things for the health and growth of endowment funds. It is one of the linchpins of successful long-term investing.

Diversification

Inherent in a portfolio approach is a diversification requirement, which is implied in the UMIFA and again made explicit in the UPIA: "A trustee shall diversify the investments of the trust unless the trustee reasonably determines that, because of special circumstances, the purposes of the trust are better served without diversifying" (§ 3).[2] This is really not new as trustees have long been held to have a duty to diversify. Its primary significance from an investment management perspective is that diversification is also a fundamental component of portfolio theory.

Inflation

The last piece of the puzzle is the explicit permission in both acts for fiduciaries to consider the effects of inflation. The second half of section 6, Standard of Conduct, of the UMIFA authorizes the board to "consider long and short term needs of the institution in carrying out its educational, religious, charitable, or other eleemosynary purposes, its present and anticipated financial requirements, expected total return on its investments, *price level trends*, and general economic conditions" (emphasis added).[3] The reference to "price level trends" means "inflation." The UPIA states in section 2 that:

> (c) Among circumstances that a trustee shall consider in investing and managing trust assets are such of the following as are relevant to the trust or its beneficiaries:
> (1) general economic conditions;
> (2) the possible effect of inflation or deflation.

---

[2] I speculate that because the UPIA was written a little more than 20 years after the UMIFA, the commissioners took the opportunity to make explicit a number of concepts that the UMIFA clearly intends but does not state directly. That, at least, is a detectable pattern between the two statutes and would also be consistent with the intervening rewriting of the Restatement Third of Trusts discussed below.

[3] As a quick aside, notice also that the board is entitled to take into consideration the organization's *"educational, religious, charitable, or other eleemosynary purposes."* This is good news for organizations with strong political or religious beliefs. If such organizations wish to eschew investments that are philosophically incompatible with their purposes, they may do so. The way in which social and moral concerns can be factored into policies, and the cost on performance that such policies can impose, are discussed in Chapter 9.

In both instances, inflation and its devastating impact on largely fixed-income portfolios at the nation's universities was one of the principal causes of the effort to update our investment laws. Many of the new rules and standards already considered here have their genesis in the attempt to deal with inflation: "The portfolios of many endowment funds have been far too heavily laden with fixed income securities to resist the relentless erosion of inflation. In a decade when the average price of common stocks has risen seven times as fast as the cost of living, and dividends on common stocks have risen three and a half times as fast, many endowments have been exceedingly hard pressed even to keep abreast" (*The Law and Lore*, p. 5). We want to be able to invest in common stocks, in other words, as a means of dealing with inflation. But by doing so there may not be enough dividend and interest income to spend. So the investor has to be able to invade principal for distribution purposes, but after doing so he or she has to manage on a total return basis, counting both realized and unrealized capital gains, or the investor will never know where the portfolio stands. And so it goes. The need to deal with inflation has driven large portions of the rewriting of the investment laws.

Final Thoughts on the Standard of Care

It seems clear from the standard of care language that *all* the essential requirements of a portfolio approach to investing are now mandated or allowed:

1. Permitted investments include any imaginable financial instrument on either a direct or a pooled basis.
2. Investments will be judged as part of an overall portfolio, not position by position.
3. Prudence is judged at the time the portfolio is created, not on the basis of hindsight.
4. Capital gains are treated the same as dividends and interest in order to allow a total return standard.
5. Managers may take account of inflation in order to preserve the long-term value of investment assets.

Collectively, these provisions allow the nonprofit community to pursue superior investment management as aggressively as individuals or businesses. Truly, the legal barriers that once existed to optimal investing, either at law or in the minds of fiduciaries, are gone. The ultimate standard now is a commitment to excellence. To pursue that, however, may require more specialized expertise than many nonprofit officers and directors possess. Fortunately, the new laws also permit delegation.

Delegation of Investment Authority

Both the UMIFA and the UPIA expressly authorize the delegation of investment authority. The UMIFA, written earlier, contains a direct grant of authority to (1) delegate internally to boards and committees, (2) hire outside service providers, and (3) "authorize the payment of compensation for investment advisory or management services" (§5). The actual language of part 1 of this paragraph provides that the board may "delegate to its committees, officers or employees of the institution or the fund, or agents, including investment counsel, the authority to act in place of the board in investment and reinvestment of institutional funds" (§5). The permission to delegate "the authority to act in the place of the board" is tremendously important. As discussed earlier, organizations have always been allowed to hire investment help. The question has been, how tight a hold on the reins does the board need to retain? And even more to the point, if a board delegates and losses occur, is that delegation in and of itself grounds for the board's liability? Clearly under this language a board would not be liable for investment losses solely on the basis of its delegation of authority to internal or external service providers. Arguably there remains some question as to the liability of a board for the errors and omissions of those to whom the investment authority is delegated. The question turns on a fairly fine point of law: are those you hire working *for you*, as your agent, or are they working *in your place*? If they are mere "agents," you remain liable for their actions, whereas if they are allowed to work in your place and to assume your responsibilities directly, you do not.[4] It would seem that the UMIFA was attempting to authorize a true delegation of responsibility.

Once again, the UPIA, with its additional 20-year perspective, deals directly with this issue.

§ 9. Delegation of Investment and Management Functions.

(a) A trustee may delegate investment and management functions that a prudent trustee of comparable skills could properly delegate under the circumstances. The trustee shall exercise reasonable care, skill, and caution in:

(1) selecting an agent;

(2) establishing the scope and terms of the delegation, consistent with the purposes and terms of the trust; and

(3) periodically reviewing the agent's actions in order to monitor the agent's performance and compliance with the terms of delegation.

---

[4] Here and elsewhere discussions of the "law" are oversimplified and are intended for a general audience.

When you are ready to implement your new investment policies, have them carefully reviewed by your attorney. And ask for an opinion on the issues that concern you, such as the amount of liability that you, as a board, now have when you act under your policies. Given that even adoptions of the UMIFA and UPIA vary (significantly at times) from state to state, there is no other safe way to proceed. If you in fact get advice of counsel, then my generalizations will be far more helpful than harmful.

(b) In performing a delegated function, an agent owes a duty to the trust to exercise reasonable care to comply with the terms of the delegation.

(c) A trustee who complies with the requirements of subsection (a) is not liable to the beneficiaries or to the trust for the decisions or actions of the agent to whom the function was delegated.

(d) By accepting the delegation of a trust function from the trustee of a trust that is subject to the law of this State, an agent submits to the jurisdiction of the courts of this State.

I think this is one of the most helpful new additions from the UPIA. The idea of establishing a standard and, to some extent a methodology, for delegation is the best kind of law; it does not just establish a rule but helps the organization comply with the rule in a relatively certain manner.

Subparagraph (a), above, establishes three requirements for effective (that is, liability limiting) delegation of investment responsibility. The board must use reasonable care in selecting an agent, must establish the scope and terms of the agent's authority, and must periodically review the agent's performance. These are all things that an organization that adopts and implements investment policies in the manner recommended by this book will in fact be doing. Chapter 7, which deals with hiring investment help, outlines such a process. Any reasonable effort at hiring competent investment counsel that includes a measured and disciplined search for such help is likely to satisfy the first requirement above. Certainly, virtually any consultant-driven search for managers of the type that has become standard among larger funds would satisfy this requirement.

Interestingly, the adoption of investment policies and the application of those policies to specific funds ought to satisfy the second requirement. The purpose of the policies is to provide guidance and direction to those who are actually managing funds on a daily basis. So point two is a lay down.[5]

Similarly, the policies mandate periodic performance reporting and review. Insisting upon such reports and conducting such reviews ought to satisfy the third point. Thus, without extraordinary effort, it is possible to satisfy the delegation requirements of the UPIA.

This leads naturally to the promised land. Paragraph (c) of §9 provides that "a trustee who complies with the requirements of subsection (a) is not liable to the beneficiaries or to the trust for the decisions or actions of the agent to whom the function was delegated." In other words, simple diligence in the delegation process leads to clear relief of liability for actions of the investment managers.

---

[5] A "lay down" is a hand in a card game such as bridge in which it is certain and obvious that the player will win all the remaining tricks, so he simply lays his cards down on the table and forgoes the rest of the play.

This provision of the UPIA is very important. First, in those states in which the UPIA has been adopted and for those trusts to which it applies, the UPIA becomes an additional, compelling reason to delegate investment responsibility for charitable trusts. Secondly, when interpreting a law such as the UMIFA that, in the area of delegation, is not precise, judges typically look to similar laws for guidance. Thus, one may expect that the new delegation standard of the UPIA will, in the course of time, be read back into the UMIFA when disputes under that act are resolved in courts. Therefore, it makes sense to delegate investment authority in a stylized manner that complies with the UPIA provisions in all circumstances and not just those in which the UPIA technically applies.

Finally, the ultimate importance of the delegation provisions is not that the organization escapes liability if there are investment losses or that the potential relief from liability is a compelling reason to delegate. Rather, the new provisions represent genuine freedom to delegate, as opposed to grudging permission. The language permitting the delegation of investment authority is sufficiently enthusiastic that boards may rely on it with a clear conscience and without the risk of second-guessing and recriminations that existed before. It is a subtle difference on the one hand, but it is all the difference in the world on the other.

The Role of the Restatement of the Law of Trusts

The Restatement of the Common Law is a series of treatises published and maintained by the American Law Institute. It is a topical guide to the provisions of the common law, arranged by subject matter, for attorneys, judges, and others. Because of its thoroughness and the quality of the associated scholastic commentary, it also tends to influence and not just report law.

In May 1990, the American Law Institute adopted a partial Restatement Third of the Law of Trusts, which completely revised the sections dealing with investments by adopting the Prudent Investor Rule. In a certain sense, therefore, not only the UMIFA and the UPIA but also the Restatement Third of Trusts may be consulted as sources of the Prudent Investor Rule. The Restatement's version of the Prudent Investor Rule is functionally identical to that which we have seen in the uniform acts. Given that, and the extensive and growing adoption of the uniform acts, why does the Restatement matter?

Before a uniform act is adopted by a state legislature as law, the legislature frequently makes changes. At times, those changes include exemptions for certain categories of charitable organizations. Therefore, in some states, churches and other religious organizations might ultimately be exempted from all or a portion of either of the uniform acts. In addition, there are still states that have not adopted one or the other or both of the uniform acts. So what happens when a dispute arises in a state that has not adopted the uniform act or that involves organizations that have been exempted from the acts' provisions?

The short answer is that the judge in any case will apply some law. Enter the role of the Restatement. In the absence of a specific statutory provision, the judge will look to the "common law," to which the Restatement is a guide. Hence, even if a religious organization is exempt from a particular state's statute, the judge may well apply exactly the same prudent investor standard as set forth in the Restatement of Trusts, Third. Thus, the existence of the Restatement's provisions tends to nullify specific statutory exemptions. Given the clear trend toward adopting the Prudent Investor Rule and the position of the restatement, prudent behavior for virtually all charitable organizations will be to act as if these rules apply to them, particularly when serving as a trustee. Ultimately, this will be the safest course.

State and Federal Securities Laws—The Philanthropy Protection Act of 1995

State and federal securities laws tend to be complementary and regulate to the same overall effect. In those areas where federal securities laws exist, they either preempt state statute or allow the states to add particular additional requirements. As a practical matter, there is little substantive difference between the effect and content of state laws and the effect and content of federal laws in this area. Therefore, while it is technically incorrect to refer to "securities laws" as if they were a single body of law, it is helpful for the purpose of discussion.

WHAT IS A SECURITY?

The most important concept is that of a security. A security is any agreement under which more than one person hopes to profit solely from the efforts of others. A number of entities not normally thought of as securities are included in this definition. Thus, bank accounts, pooled-income funds, and limited partnerships are securities. Securities laws regulate both the offer and the sale of securities by requiring specific and highly stylized disclosures about the securities being offered.

The laws have become more manageable by the creation of two broad categories of exemptions from their requirements. There are exemptions by category of issuer (the organization that creates and offers the security), and there are transactional exemptions that apply to the particular security being offered. Among the more important issuer exemptions is the exemption of all bank and trust companies. Described here are the requirements and application of the Securities Act of 1933 and related state statutes.

SECURITIES LAW EXEMPTIONS

The nonprofit community has for years operated under the assumption that the funds it manages for its benefit are exempt from state and federal securities laws. In some cases, there has been support for this position in specific statutory provisions. The California Securities Statute, for example, exempts both securities issued by any charitable organization, meaning a 501(c)3 organization, along with pooled-income funds issued by such organizations. In the absence of case law on the subject, the general thinking has been that the exemption for securities issued by a charitable organization extended to pools formed out of assets irrevocably dedicated to such charities including things such as gift annuity reserves.

THE PHILANTHROPY PROTECTION ACT OF 1995

Most of the uncertainty that existed in this area was eliminated by the passage of the Philanthropy Protection Act of 1995 (PPA). The PPA, passed in response to the Texas gift-annuity litigation, specifically exempts pools of charitable assets from the application of the major securities laws. In addition, the statute specifically preempts the application of state law for a period of three years. Therefore, in the absence of subsequent state legislation, pools of charitable assets are exempt from both state and federal securities laws for the foreseeable future.

For a general understanding of which laws apply to charitable organizations, it is now sufficient to know that all pools of charitable assets should be exempt from those laws with one exception. That is the pooling of revocable trust assets where the revocation provision is not restricted to either a revocation due to a change in the financial circumstances of the donor or a change of the designated charitable remaindermen. Regarding revocable trusts that are not so limited, there is an interim provision that allows charities under certain restricted circumstances to continue pooling such funds for a period of 36 months, following which they must either divest themselves of such funds, manage them separately so they are no longer pooled, or segregate those assets and qualify them under the applicable securities laws. The latter option is practically unthinkable for most charities, since it would mean converting pools of revocable trust assets into a fully licensed mutual fund with all the audits, SEC filings, and other requirements associated with such funds. Because it requires between $50 million and $100 million for a mutual fund to be cost-effective, it is highly unlikely that any charitable organization will choose to pursue that option.

The last observation on the applicability of the securities laws is that separately managed trusts or interests (those not pooled with the assets of other donors) are also generally thought to be exempt from state and federal securities laws. We are now on somewhat shakier ground because the exemptions created by the PPA specifically apply to pools and say nothing about nonpooled interests. But the long-standing rationale for the belief that these nonpooled or individually managed interests are not subject to the securities laws is that they do not constitute a security. The basis for this position is that the essential element of multiple participants is missing. Regardless of whether that rationale would stand up to aggressive scrutiny, it is clear that the securities laws were not intended to apply to such instruments, and there is no apparent constituency among state or federal regulators for changing that state of affairs.

Conclusion

As we now know, our ACO bankers were incorrect in believing that rigid investment rules still apply to charities. With the widespread adoption of the Uniform Management of Institutional Funds Act and the fairly rapid adoption in a number of large states of the Uniform Prudent Investor Act, the clear trend in the legal environment is toward the dominance of the Prudent Investor Rule. Under that rule, charities are allowed to manage each fund: (1) on a portfolio basis, (2) in light of the goals and character of the organization, (3) based on the knowledge available to the decision makers at the time, and (4) with clear permission to delegate investment management responsibility. If the ACO is to do the best it can with the funds under its control, the first step is to breathe the air of investment freedom that the law now permits.

All in all, this is a great time to be investing for the benefit of charitable organizations, as the legal environment has never been more favorable to the success of charitable fund management. That same sense of open-ended possibilities and the unrestricted ability to pursue excellence exists in the investment environment as well. That environment, which includes the basics of modern portfolio theory, is the subject of the next chapter.

3 The Investment Environment: Modern Portfolio Theory

An understanding of modern portfolio theory is a prerequisite to the effective use of investment policies. Being an antiquarian at heart and one who believes that civilization peaked around 1910, I am somewhat suspicious of any use of the word "modern" as an endorsement. However, so-called modern portfolio theory and its progeny serve to enhance our understanding of the operations of markets and to improve our ability to invest wisely. Ironically, a fair amount of the academic work represents the ability to describe more precisely what common sense has told investors for centuries. The detailed analysis of the ways diversification reduces portfolio risk is a prime example. The general proposition is as old as the first person who dropped the single basket of eggs on the way back from the chicken coop. Nonetheless, recent advances also include legitimate discoveries that are not intuitive; for example, the fact that not all risks carry a commensurate reward.

Goals of the Process

Before plunging into the most technical discussion in the book, it may be helpful to recall that the objective is to achieve the basics which lead to the lion's share of investment returns and help organizations avoid mistakes that erode capital. Toward that end, the overarching goal is to help officers and directors of nonprofit organizations establish parameters within which good investment decisions may be made. To do that, certain investment concepts need to be made accessible to those who do not have significant investment experience. Those who already understand investment theory may comfortably skip the next section and go directly to the discussion at the end of the chapter concerning risks that are normally ignored.

The balance of this chapter is divided into three sections. The first is an overview of the history and development of modern portfolio theory. Following that is an examination of six key concepts every nonprofit officer and director needs to know. The chapter concludes with a brief examination of the risks most people do not discuss. Before proceeding, however, let's see what is happening at the ACO.

At the ACO . . .

STOCKS ARE TOO RISKY

"I don't care what the law allows," roared one of the banker board members, "there's no way we ought to be taking chances with our money. Since stocks are a lot riskier than government bonds, I don't think stock market investments are appropriate."

"That's not true," replies another. "Bonds can drop in value just like stocks."

"Has the government ever defaulted on a bond?"

"No."

"Well lots of companies—including a lot of big, formerly successful companies have gone broke. Remember Penn Central? How about Chrysler? If the government hadn't stepped in and bailed them out, we'd only have two automakers today. So clearly stocks are a lot riskier than bonds, and I don't think we ought to put our money at risk. After all, it's not really our money."

The foregoing expresses the sentiment not just of the banker board member but of thousands of board members across the country. Even though many, perhaps most, of such board members are stock market investors personally, they judge themselves more able to bear the risk of loss than the charity on whose board they are serving. To our board member's credit, he or she wants to be more cautious, not less cautious, with other people's money.

And to make matters worse—or at least more difficult to understand—the board member is right, to a point. Stocks are riskier than bonds one-on-one, short-term, and without considering the impact of inflation. But put those same stocks into portfolios, judge the results over 20 years (not just one or two) and measure results net of inflation—and the whole story changes.

The heart of the matter is this—how much risk are we really taking when we invest in stocks and bonds? And which of those risks can we reduce, control, or eliminate? That effort, controlling the risks that we take, is at the heart of modern portfolio theory. And the result, to which both academics and investment pros have contributed, is surprising, to say the least.

The Origins of Modern Portfolio Theory

While countless academic papers, books, and textbooks have been written on various aspects of modern portfolio theory, three broad areas of development are most significant. They are (1) the efficiencies of markets, (2) the behavior and characteristics of stocks or bonds in a portfolio, and (3) the application of portfolio theory to broader categories of assets, such as U.S. stocks or real estate investments, which will be discussed under the rubric of asset allocation.

The field of modern portfolio theory traces its roots to the work of Harry Markowitz, who in 1952 published a paper entitled "Portfolio Selection."

That paper, which became the basis for his Ph.D. dissertation and then a book in 1959, earned Markowitz a share of the 1990 Nobel Prize in economics. Markowitz discovered that securities can be combined in a portfolio in such a way that the combination has less overall risk, as measured by the standard deviation of returns, than any one security individually. He discovered, in other words, a way to measure and explain the effectiveness of diversifying a portfolio.

Subsequently, William Sharpe and others focused on exactly what risks were being eliminated by the use of the Markowitz theory of portfolio construction. This work led to the development of the capital asset pricing model (CAPM), for which Sharpe also earned a portion of the 1990 Nobel Prize in economics. This model continues to influence investment management.

The work of Markowitz and Sharpe focused on creating optimal portfolios of securities. Markowitz looked for the best risk and reward relationship by comparing all of the securities with one another. This took a lot of time. Sharpe's approach was simpler and more useable in that he compared each security with the market as a whole. In both cases the goal was to identify the mix of securities that had the best risk-reward relationships. The graphical picture of these relationships became known as an "efficient frontier" (see Exhibit 3.1).

While still used at the portfolio level, the notion of combining assets in such a way that one takes the least amount of risk for any given level of return, has found its most widespread and enthusiastic acceptance in the area of "asset allocation." The asset-allocation process applies the Markowitz optimization concept to classes of investments as opposed to individual securities. Thus, instead of trying to "optimize" a portfolio of common stocks, an investor optimizes the mix of common stocks, bonds, foreign stocks, and other "classes" of assets. The result is again an efficient frontier but on a grander scale.

Finally, Eugene Fama and other academicians have contributed over the last 30 years to the development of the so-called random walk theory of market efficiency. The theory draws its name from a mathematical concept. When there is no particular relationship between a series of numbers, they are said to be random. It does not mean that the numbers are irrational, it just means that one cannot tell what the next number will be by looking at its predecessors.

Flipping coins is the classic example. No matter how many heads or tails are flipped in a row, the chances of flipping either the next time *is exactly the same*—50:50. There is no relationship between the previous flips and the likelihood of a particular result the next time. Each occurrence is random.

When applied to securities prices, the theory argues that there is no particular relationship between yesterday's price and tomorrow's price. One cannot, in other words, predict future prices based on past price trends. Random walkers advance the concept of market efficiency as the reason for the randomness of stock price movements. The most widely embraced ver-

EXHIBIT 3.1. Efficient Frontier

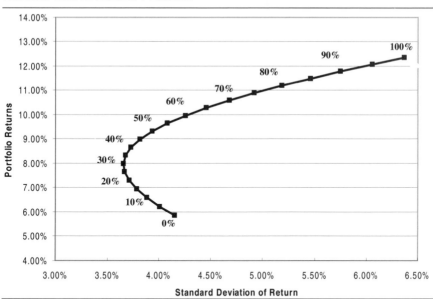

Produced by Capital Markets Research

sion of this theory argues that markets so efficiently price securities and so thoroughly reflect all that is known about the true value of securities that no one can produce above-market returns for any given level of risk by selecting stocks. Obviously, that is a bold assertion which calls into question much of the work of investment professionals. Therefore we must now examine that theory.

Market Efficiency

It is the belief in the efficiency of the securities markets that supports the proponents of the random walk theory. It has also led to the increasingly widespread use of passively managed investment vehicles such as index funds. Consequently, effective creators and supervisors of investment policy must have a solid understanding of what people mean when they declare that the stock markets are efficient.

An efficient market is one that accurately prices the commodity being sold. In a perfectly efficient market, price and "value" are the same at all times. For economists, perfect markets exist when there are a large number of buyers and sellers, a free flow of information between all the parties, and low or nonexistent transaction costs. In such an environment, prices change rapidly to reflect new information as it becomes available.

The U.S. securities markets are clearly very efficient, as all of these elements exist. Hundreds of thousands of people are doing their best every day to put a proper value on assets, and there is a tremendous flow of information from companies to investors and between investors. In addition, transaction costs are low, so all the ingredients of the economists' perfect market exist: multiple, fully informed buyers and sellers, free-flowing information, and low transaction costs.

The random walk theory is built on the notion of efficient markets. The heart of the theory is that there is no significant relationship between the past price movements of a stock and the future price movement of the stock. The fact that a stock has gone up daily for 8 trading days or 800 trading days tells us nothing about what will happen tomorrow. The day-to-day movement of prices is therefore "random" in the sense that it is independent of any relationship to prior price movements.

The random walk theory and a belief in efficient securities markets are not the same thing, but they are related. Proponents of efficient markets believe that all publicly available knowledge is so rapidly reflected in stock prices that there is no exploitable inefficiency in the pricing of securities. The market price is itself, moment by moment, the best indicator of true value. The assertion of the random walk theory that day-to-day pricing is random is a conclusion that grows out of a belief in efficient markets.

When dealing with both concepts it is important to understand what is *not* being said. Neither concept asserts that stock prices are irrational. There is, for example, a clear long-term upward trend in stock prices, which is consistent with the underlying growth of earnings and dividends from the companies being priced. Similarly, the shares of strong, profitable, and growing companies will, over time, increase in price while the shares of weak or failing companies will decrease in price. The claim that the market is efficient does not mean that reasonable and to some extent foreseeable changes in price to reflect true value do not occur.

The only thing being said by all proponents of the random walk theory is that there is no useful data in the pattern of past price movements. Even this form of the random walk theory discards virtually all charting and technical analysis from the battery of available investment management tools.

Some random walk theorists go further and argue that the market is so efficient that virtually everything that is knowable about the stock is reflected in its price and that no amount of study or effort, including so-called fundamental analysis, will create an advantage for the investor. The evidence for this strongest position of market efficiency is simply the relative performance of the market compared to most mutual funds and most portfolios managed by independent investor managers. Over long periods of time the market has done a reasonably good job of clobbering both mutual funds and investment managers.[1]

The ultimate irony is that the markets are as efficient as they are at pricing assets largely because so many skilled and diligent people are working ev-

---

[1] See "On Studies of Mutual Fund Performance, 1962–1991," *Financial Analysts Journal*, Jan.–Feb. 1993, pp. 42–50.

ery day to determine appropriate prices for those assets and to take advantage of perceived mispricing. Charles Ellis in a very good little book entitled *Investment Policy* makes the point that professional investment managers cannot outperform the market *because they are the market*. It is as if the snake is trying to swallow its own tail.

So where does this leave us in terms of market efficiency? Are the markets as efficient as academicians claim? If so, should we simply use index funds and abandon the use of investment professionals altogether?[2] I can only give my own somewhat biased answer.

First, I instinctively distrust the effort to have an "answer." It seems to me that members of the academic community, from which efficient market and random walk theories derive, are seeking systematic or technical solutions to the problem of selecting investments in a manner similar to that which they criticize in the investment community. Their ideal appears to be a mathematically certain approach that relieves investing of any need for reason, experience, or judgment. The movement toward hands-off management calls to mind the unsinkable Titanic or the U.S. Navy's infallible Aegis radar system. The former sank and the latter shot down a 747 full of passengers over the Persian Gulf.

Second, the markets are clearly not as efficient as the strongest proponents of the random walk theory assert. The 500-point drop in the Dow on a single day in October 1987 is an example of inefficiency. While there may well have been good reasons for stocks to drop such that the move was not "irrational," that kind of radical repricing of assets in one day is clearly not efficient.

There are also academic studies showing that some market segments, such as very small company stocks and value stocks, actually outperform the market over time. Because our measures of risk are so anemic, it is not clear if the better performance of these areas represents inefficiency or merely the assumption of greater risks. But one suspects, at least, that there is in fact some inefficiency in the pricing of financial assets.[3]

There are also abundant examples in the current manic stock market of companies that are priced many times higher than they were just 24 months ago. While one possible outcome of an analysis is that hundreds of American businesses are now worth two or three times what they were just two years ago, it seems more reasonable to believe that the market was wrong on the low side then or is wrong on the high side now. Either way, it may be efficient but it is imperfect.

---

[2] An index fund is a mutual fund that consciously mimics a broad stock market index, such as the S&P 500, by buying and holding shares in exactly the same percentages as are included in the index. The managers of the fund do not exercise any judgment as to which shares to purchase based on perceptions of value. They simply maintain a portfolio that tracks the index.

[3] For a very good discussion of efficient markets and their limitations, see Richard Roll's article "What Every CFO Should Know about Scientific Progress in Financial Economics: What is Known and What Remains to Be Resolved," in *Financial Management*, 1994, 23(2), 69–75.

The markets are in fact very efficient at establishing a fair value for assets—over time. As prices fluctuate month in and month out, reflecting the confluence of opinions, opportunities, demands for capital, hopes and fears, price and value circle each other in closer or further approximation of reality. This seems to be a picture of an efficient market. It is one that prices assets well but that is incapable of always pricing assets perfectly simply because of the magnitude of the task.

In applying this thinking, keep in mind that some markets—and some segments of a given market—are more efficient than others. The New York Stock Exchange probably represents one of the more perfect markets in the world, as every company whose shares are traded on this exchange is actively followed by multiple analysts, traded by many brokers, reported on by numerous financial services, and owned, at a minimum, by thousands of investors.

If one purchases shares instead on the Colombo stock exchange in Sri Lanka, one may find a radically different situation. Many markets are not nearly so active, well-researched, reliable, and inexpensive as those we tend to think of as "the market" in the United States. Even in North America, on smaller exchanges like Vancouver and Alberta, it is not unusual for a single trade to change the valuation of an entire company: the stock last changed hands at 5 cents and someone bid 10 cents. Do not expect to be able to index accurately in such funds or in certain asset classes, such as emerging markets, as the necessary efficiencies are not there.

My personal expectation is that index funds and actively managed funds will eventually reach a natural equilibrium. Remember, the market is as efficient as it is because so many bright people work hard at accurately pricing securities. Indexing, on the other hand, represents blind buying and selling of shares in order to remain synchronized to a particular index. While I have no idea how large a number would be required for this to happen, at some point the indexing of a sizeable enough percentage of the total market would actually distort valuations of the underlying shares. For that to happen, were the unthinking buying and selling of all shares in an index to become a dominant factor in determining stock prices, exploitable opportunities for actively managed funds would be created. The irony is that the belief in an efficient market followed to its logical conclusion would ultimately reintroduce a level of *in*efficiency in the market.

POLICY IMPLICATIONS OF EFFICIENT MARKETS

The primary policy implication of efficient markets is to increase the importance of the asset allocation decision and decrease the relative importance of selecting the vehicle by which the charitable organization participates in the market for each particular class of asset. If one believes that markets are efficient and that there are few exploitable opportunities for the better manager to deliver superior performance, one can use index funds, other mutual funds, or active portfolio managers interchangeably, with the selection based on incremental service, price, and reliability. Even if one believes, as I do, that although the market is efficient, it is still traumatized by crowd psychology and unable to deliver a perfect valuation for any particular asset, the process still begins with asset allocation decisions. Either way, the efficiency of the securities market is an important concept.

MODERN PORTFOLIO THEORY IN A NUTSHELL

The essence of modern portfolio theory is the belief that assets—either individual securities or classes of investments such as "stock" and "bonds"—can be combined in optimal ways. These optimal combinations are intended to produce the lowest amount of risk for any given level of anticipated return (or conversely the highest return for any given level of risk). The technique of optimizing investments is now most commonly practiced under the name of asset allocation, which focuses on combining classes of assets.

With the increasing emphasis on asset allocation, the investment community is tacitly admitting that the securities markets are in fact very efficient. From this perspective, establishing asset allocation parameters—that is, deciding what percentages of our funds may be invested in each class or category of investment asset—becomes more important than "picking stocks," which is selecting the particular investments within each class. That alone is a pretty radical change of perspective from the "let's find someone who picks winners" mind-set of the relatively recent past.

When Burton Malkiel surveys the world of modern portfolio theory under the broad heading of "the new investment technology," he makes the following statement: "None of these titles [of various portfolio theories] conveys the heart of the matter, which is that when all is said and done, risk is the only variable worth a damn in the market."[4]

Everything to be discussed under the rubric of modern portfolio theory in the following section has as its ultimate goal the management of investment risk. Investment policies are created to achieve this purpose. To do that some basic concepts need to be understood.

Key Investment Concepts Every Director Needs to Know

The handful of investment concepts that every board member should understand include the following:

1. The meaning of total return
2. The relationship of risk to return

---

[4] *Random Walk Down Wall Street* (1995), p. 227.

3. The use of diversification, Markowitz style, as a portfolio technique
4. The critical role of asset allocation
5. The importance of time

In addition, performance reporting could justifiably be considered the sixth investment management tool. The process of inspecting the results in and of itself improves the results, particularly when it is done in a disciplined and stylized manner. The role of reporting is so important that all of Chapter 7 is dedicated to the subject. Keep in mind throughout this section, therefore, that expectations in all the areas that follow will need to be inspected.

TOTAL RETURN

Total return is the full amount an investment earns, as opposed to the current income it produces. In other words, total return is the sum of dividends and interest plus capital gains less any capital losses, realized or not, and expenses. Frequently, an investment's total return is different from its current yield. This is an extremely important concept, an understanding of which distinguishes the knowledgeable investor from the novice.

If, for example, you buy a 6 percent bond for $1,000 and hold it for one year, you will receive $60 in interest. But if at the end of the year you sell the bond for $950, your true gain would be only $10; $60 in interest payments reduced by a $50 capital loss. Consequently, the total return on your 6 percent bond would be 1 percent.

Measuring an investment on the basis of its total return is the only way to actually know how well or how poorly it is performing. Why? The principal reason is that the "yield" or current income portion of an investment is only part of the total return. We understand this intuitively in the stock market. Almost no one buys common stocks expecting to receive only the dividends. Most investors also hope that the price of the stock will "go up." They invest in the hope, therefore, of capital gains. Their total return is then the sum of their dividends received and any capital gains less any expenses they incurred in making the investment and less any capital losses.

This same rationale applies to fixed income investments (bonds and other interest-bearing debt obligations), although it is less intuitive. With a fixed-income investment, the interest payments tend to be a much greater percentage of the total return than the common-stock dividends are of their return. So as a practical matter yield is often closer to total return on fixed-income investments than it is on equities. But fixed-income yields and fixed-income total returns are not the same, and the fact that they are different and the reasons for the differences are very important.

When we purchased our $1,000 bond at 6 percent, we received an agreed-upon income stream—$60 per year—and repayment of the $1,000 at maturity. Let's assume that the 6 percent payment represents fair compensation at the time we purchased our bond. But now, some time later, the general level of interest rates has changed, and identical bonds due at the same time are now paying 7 percent or $70 per year. What rational investor is going to buy our bond for $1,000 when for the same $1,000 she can receive $10 more per year in interest? No one. If we then try to sell our bond in the market, it will probably be worth something less than its $1,000 face amount, particularly if the due date is far away.

The risks associated with shifts in interest rates will be discussed in much greater detail in the section of Chapter 8 entitled "The Sin of Reaching for Yield." For now the important point is that yield and total return are frequently different, even with fixed-income investments (see Exhibit 3.2). Unless investment performance is judged on the basis of total return, one misses the capital gain or loss characteristics of the investment and, quite simply, one has no real idea how the investment is performing. Measuring investment performance on a total-return basis is fundamental to all other investment management work.

Within the investment community, total return is usually measured annually. To compute annual total return, the amount of capital gain or loss is calculated by assuming that the investment was purchased on the first day of the year and sold on the last. To the amount of capital gain or loss so determined, the analysis adds the total of all dividend or interest payments made during the year.

A common objection to this approach is that it treats unrealized gains or losses the same as realized gains or losses. Doubters ask why it matters that a bond has decreased in value if the investor intends to hold it to maturity. The truth is that it matters a great deal; the loss is real whether one is forced to realize it or not. At that moment, the organization has fewer assets on its books and less money available for its charitable purposes, no matter how certain the future appreciation may seem.

Exhibit 3.3 shows the price in the secondary market of a 20-year treasury bond, paying 6.75 percent issued in 1973. By 1982 that $1,000 bond could be sold for only $650. What if you had a $1,000,000 portfolio of such $1,000 bonds and for whatever reason had to sell? Your then unrealized loss of $350,000 comes home to roost.

Even if one never has to sell, unrealized losses represent an opportunity cost in every current investment. Continuing to hold a security is essentially the same as deciding to buy it instead of another. This is particularly true in highly liquid markets with low transaction costs. Clearly, if the organization wished to switch to another investment, it could do so only with the reduced amount.

The final irony of the importance of total return is that it is in the fixed-income area—in which the traditional focus has been on yield—where switching to a total-return perspective can produce the greatest results. The most sophisticated fixed-income operations in the country manage their assets on a total-return basis. The further step that professional fixed-income managers take is to evaluate the universe of possible fixed-income investments based upon the *anticipated* total return of each.

EXHIBIT 3.2. Intermediate Term Government Bonds—Interest Rate vs. Total Return

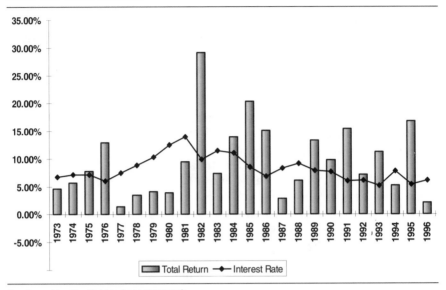

Produced by Capital Markets Research

Essentially, the manager considers the current yield, yield to maturity, duration (meaning a tool that measures a bond's risk based on maturity), interest rate, and yield[5], and the likelihood of being able to earn a greater or lesser amount when reinvesting interest income, all on a discounted-to-present-value basis. If foreign bonds are involved, then possible currency fluctuations enter the picture as well. The result is the ability to compare apples and oranges—for example, a 6 percent bond due in five years to a 6.5 percent bond due in seven years—and make a judgment as to which is the better buy at a particular point in time. Expenses such as commissions incurred on buying and selling bonds can be factored in as well when deciding whether it is advantageous to swap from one bond position to another. Clearly, this entire effort at maximizing returns from fixed-income investments is dependent on a total-return perspective.

Ultimately, there is no rationale for not managing investments on a total-return basis, no matter how long one has been focusing on yield. Even in those situations that require current income—and thus to some extent must be managed to produce a certain level of yield—one would still want to track total return as well in order to know how much the pursuit of yield was costing.

---

[5] See Chapter 6 for a formal definition of duration.

EXHIBIT 3.3. Yield vs. Total Return—Market Value of 20-Year Treasury Bonds—Issued February 15, 1973, with a 6.75% Coupon

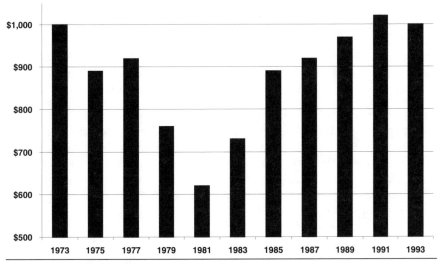

Produced by Capital Markets Research

THE RELATIONSHIP OF RISK TO REWARD

Risk is the possibility of a bad investment result. More technically, it is the measurable possibility of losing value. There are numerous types of risks, the more important of which include

1. Specific risk—the risk associated with any one individual stock or bond
2. Market risk—the risk that all stocks and/or bonds will decline in value
3. Liquidity risk—the possibility that market conditions will preclude selling an asset
4. Inflation risk—the possibility of a decline in the purchasing power of the currency in which the investment is denominated.

Each of the foregoing risks is usually present in varying degrees in every investment. Obviously, some investments are encumbered with greater risks of one sort or another than are others. Real estate, for example, has far greater liquidity risk than do shares of stock traded on a major exchange. Conversely, real estate investments tend to have less inflation risk than do some fixed-income investments, such as long-term government bonds.

In recent years, an enormous amount of literature from the professional and academic investment communities has focused on risk. As a result, the understanding of the risk-reward relationship is slowly improving. It has long been known that there is a correlation between the amount of risk an investor assumes and the anticipated reward. Fifty years ago, investment professionals would have said, "The greater the risk, the greater the reward."

As a result of modern studies, we now know that investors are rewarded with greater returns for taking some risks but not others. The risks for which there is a corresponding reward are generally those that cannot be avoided. Today's investment professional declares, "The greater the *unavoidable* risk, the greater the reward." Let's look at what that means. Before doing so, however, we first have to understand how risk is measured.

The Measurement of Investment Risk

The most widely used measure of risk is the variance or the standard deviation of return.[6] As explained in the footnote, the greater the standard deviation, the greater the risk. The rationale for using this measure of risk is twofold. First, it is a calculable statistic. For any group of numbers one can determine the dispersion around an average. So there is an easily determined benchmark.

Now it is not immediately apparent that the variability of returns is a good measure of risk. We do not care, after all, if we get unexpectedly good results. Standard deviation measures the dispersion of numbers both above and below the average. It includes the good with the bad.

As it happens, however, most groups of numbers tend to be distributed symmetrically around the mean as shown in Exhibit 3.4. If that is in fact the case, if returns as a group for any particular asset or group of assets are roughly symmetrical such that the number of above-average returns roughly equals the number of below-average returns, then the variance from the average is a reasonably accurate way to measure the *likelihood* of a disappointing return. The wider the range, the greater the variance or standard deviation and therefore the greater the risk.

Virtually all reporting of financial risk, including charts, graphs, and tables that purport to show either risk-adjusted returns or risk and return relationships, are based on standard deviation of returns. It has become one of the fundamental concepts of modern portfolio management. So for our purposes, the first important thing to know is that most of the time when you read about risk, what is being measured is the standard deviation of returns of that asset or asset class.

Three other statistical concepts related to risk have come into widespread use in recent years. Both covariance and the correlation coefficient are mea-

---

[6] Standard deviation is a statistical measure of the degree to which one value in a distribution of returns tends to vary from the average (mean) of those numbers. The higher the standard deviation, the greater the dispersion of returns. Thus two sets of numbers, 1, 2, and 3 as set one and −8, 2, and 12 both have the same average: 2. But the range for the first set is much narrower than for the second set. The first set will have a lower standard deviation. If the numbers in the two sets represented annual percentage returns from a portfolio, we would say that the first set has less risk because the range is narrower—the standard deviation of returns is lower.

EXHIBIT 3.4. Normal Distribution

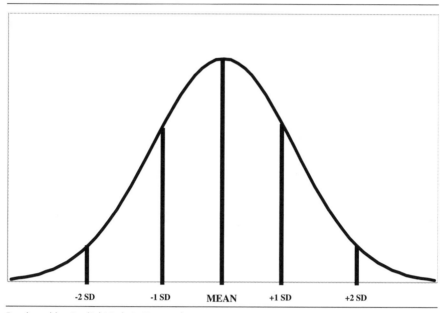

| -2 SD | -1 SD | **MEAN** | +1 SD | +2 SD |

Produced by Capital Markets Research

sures of the degree of relationship between two series of numbers. Covariance is the statistical measure that underlies most of the Markowitz portfolio theory. The usefulness of the correlation coefficient (often referred to simply as "correlation") is that the result of the calculation is always a number that falls somewhere between minus one and one. Thus, the closer the correlation is to positive one, the more perfectly the two series move together.

Conversely, as the correlation between the two portfolios approaches negative one, the more the two series move in opposition to one another. A correlation coefficient of zero means that the numbers are uncorrelated. Thus "correlation" provides a measure that is both readily understandable and somewhat intuitive of the degree to which two series of numbers tend to move up or down together.

Finally, the most common use of the covariance and correlation concepts is in calculating the so-called beta of a stock or portfolio. Beta is a measure of the correlation between a stock or portfolio and an index intended to represent the market as a whole. When calculating beta, the S&P 500 (or other market index representing the market) is assigned a beta of one. A stock with the same volatility as the market also has a beta of one. A stock twice as volatile as the market has a beta of two.

One can quickly see the appeal of such a statistic. If the standard deviation of returns is a proper measure of risk, then beta is merely an extension of that concept. Beta uses the average return of the market itself as the baseline against which the variability of the returns of a particular stock or portfolio of stocks is being measured. Beta becomes a proxy for measuring the risk of a stock in comparison to the market. A low beta stock is presumed to have less risk than a high beta stock. Similarly, a portfolio with a higher beta than the market would be thought to be more risky than the market or than a portfolio of lower beta stocks.

Limitations of Risk Measurement Tools

Standard deviation of returns and its progeny are, at best, imperfect measures of risk. Both the usefulness and inadequacy of the measures are obvious if we simply ask what is being measured. Beta, for example, measures the historical relative volatility of a security or portfolio in comparison to the S&P 500. All we really know about high beta stocks is that they have tended to be more volatile than the market over whatever trailing period of time is being used to determine beta. We don't know why. Clearly, there is some extent to which greater volatility in securities prices in fact represents greater risk. But just as clearly the historic volatility of returns is not measuring all of the risks in any investment. So the most important limitation to keep in mind for all discussions of risk management and of risk-adjusted returns is this: such efforts use standard deviation of return or related statistical concepts because they are readily known, not because anyone believes such measures to be complete or to accurately measure all risks.

DIVERSIFICATION—PORTFOLIO TECHNIQUES CAN REDUCE RISKS

Modern portfolio theory focuses on controlling risks. By combining assets in a portfolio an investor can to some extent reduce the amount of risk taken for a given level of anticipated reward. The risk of illiquidity, for example, can be virtually eliminated by confining the portfolio's investments to major markets. Beyond that, the most important portfolio risk reduction techniques are diversification and asset allocation.

When Markowitz began his work on portfolio selection, he proposed calculating the correlation or the covariance relationships between all the potential securities in a portfolio as the method of optimizing the portfolio. Optimization means the process of finding that combination of assets that produces each anticipated level of return at the lowest level of risk. When portrayed graphically, these relationships are referred to as an efficient frontier, as seen earlier.

If there are a thousand potential stocks in an investment universe and for each stock one must calculate the covariance relationship with each of the others, an enormous amount of data-processing muscle is required. The ability to do a million or more such calculations in the mid-1950s when this concept was first proposed was such a daunting task that it greatly hindered its application.

When Sharpe, along with John Lintner and Fisher Black, extended Markowitz's theory to develop what became known as the capital asset pricing model, he made the assumption that the stock market itself is in the aggregate the most efficient portfolio. Therefore, if one knows how a stock behaves relative to the market, that is a sufficient proxy for how it behaves relative to all other stocks. If the variability of return is an appropriate measure of risk, then beta—which measures the relative volatility of a stock or a portfolio to the market—becomes the ideal substitute for market risk. With the capital asset pricing model, therefore, one can "optimize" a portfolio based on the beta of each stock—a much, much simpler proposition than calculating millions of covariance relationships.

The capital asset pricing model came to be reflected in what is known as the capital market's line as shown in Exhibit 3.5. This is a line that intersects the risk-free rate of return (typically the rate on 30-day treasury bills) and the market rate of return as measured by the S&P 500 or some even broader market index. In theory, one can determine whether a particular portfolio, and by extension the managers who constructed it, is performing as well as, better than, or worse than the market by plotting performance on the same graph as the capital markets line. Performance above the line indicates superior stock selection or market timing on the part of the managers, and performance below the line indicates inferior performance.

The chart in Exhibit 3.5 portrays the distribution of returns for a group of growth managers headquartered in California, all of whom manage at least

EXHIBIT 3.5. Return vs. Risk Analysis—Third Quarter 1991 to Second Quarter 1996

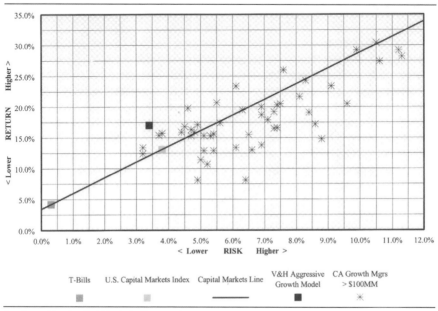

$100 million. Each manager's performance number is representative of a portfolio of stocks and the capital markets line reflects the risk-reward relationship of the market itself. In other words, when moving up the line, one gets an increase in return that is exactly commensurate with the increase in market risk. Consequently, if a portfolio performs above or below the line, then someone is doing something to either under-perform or out-perform the market on a risk-adjusted basis. That something could be stock selection, market timing (i.e., being invested or not invested in the market), or any one of a number of techniques for changing the composition of the portfolio.

Whether the capital asset pricing model (CAPM) works as well as is claimed is the subject of significant debate among both academics and practitioners. Without digging into the details of that debate, suffice it to say that very few investment professionals believe that CAPM is the last word on market theory. Sometimes, however, even a blind sow finds an occasional acorn. In this case, the acorn is the helpful explanation that there is a difference between market risk and specific risk.

The risk of any investment may be thought of as the sum of a group of risks. Under the CAPM approach, there are only two categories of risk. The first is the specific risks associated with a particular investment, and the second is the risk inherent in the market. When one constructs a well-diversified portfolio, that diversification eliminates specific risk. This is illustrated by Exhibit 3.6. The amount of specific risk in the portfolio is reduced

EXHIBIT 3.6. Portfolio Theory Reduces Risk—Diversification— Elimination of Specific Risk

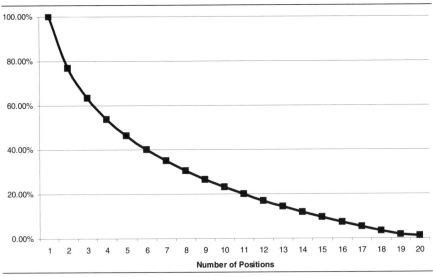

Produced by Fry Capital Advisors

to near negligible proportions as the number of securities in the portfolio approaches 20. The risk that is left is market risk. Absent some other factor, the performance of a well-diversified portfolio should be on the capital markets line.

The most important implication for investment policies is that each portfolio be adequately diversified. We could quibble all day with academicians and practitioners on exactly which risks are being eliminated and which are not, but diversification is clearly reducing some risks and leaving us with portfolio returns that are more directly related to the market as a whole than to any one issue. Thus, the sample policies in Appendix G-1 *require* diversification by providing that no investment in any one security be more than five percent of the portfolio on a cost basis. This is one of the few places where the sample policies mandate a component of portfolio construction.

The reason, quite simply, is attributable directly to the capital asset pricing model: there is no reward for taking avoidable risks. If it is possible to eliminate (or greatly reduce) specific risk, why would the market compensate someone for not doing so? And how could the market compensate anyone for not doing so? That would require 20 investors, each of whom holds a portfolio composed of *only* one stock (e.g., IBM, MicroSoft, Intel, etc.), to earn a greater return than the investor who holds five percent positions in the same 20 stocks. Clearly, such a result is impossible.

The CAPM view, however, that there is only specific risk, individual stock risk, and market risk is not quite right. Both experience and logic dictate that for diversification to be effective, one must also eliminate the risks associated with various industries or sectors of the economy. For example, it is intuitively clear that a portfolio of 20 airline stocks is not representative of the market, and therefore is not adequately diversified. Hypothetically, while there is some amount of risk associated with owning American Airlines as opposed to United, Delta, or any other carrier, there are nonetheless overriding factors that affect the industry as a whole and that can cause an increase or a decrease in the level of their stock prices as a whole. Large increases in fuel prices, for example, would have a negative impact on profits of the entire industry and ultimately on future earnings, thereby lowering stock prices of all the carriers.

The sample policies therefore also require sector diversification. Sectors are groupings of companies within the economy that tend to share common characteristics. Exhibit 3.7 shows the approximate sector allocations within the S&P 500. The sectors used are basic industry, consumer cyclical, consumer noncyclical, energy, financial services, industrials, other services, technology, and utilities. Even the sector allocations shown in Exhibit 3.7 probably underrepresent some areas of the economy, such as technology. Many large technology companies are traded on the NASDAQ (National Association of Securities Dealers Automated Quotations system) as opposed to the New York Stock Exchange. Nonetheless, the S&P 500 sectors

EXHIBIT 3.7. Representative Sector Allocations

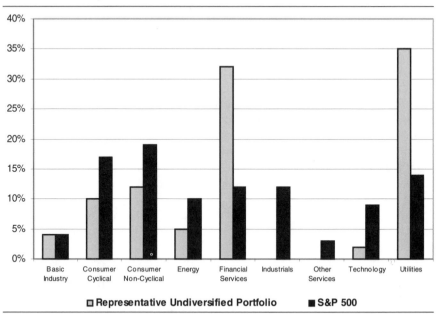

Produced by Capital Markets Research

are a widely followed and convenient proxy for broad and therefore complete diversification.

When a portfolio is completely diversified, as occurs when buying the market through the mechanism of an index fund, we are still left with an enormous amount of risk—the risk inherent in the market as a whole. Pure capital market theorists suggest controlling those risks either by borrowing funds at the risk-free rate and leveraging the portfolio or by loaning money. While some approximation of these techniques is now available to most investors, there is a better way to reduce market risks in a portfolio. It is to that technique, known as asset allocation, to which we now turn our attention.

The Importance of Asset Allocation

Asset allocation is the process of choosing the classes of assets in which one wants to invest. The broadest classifications are stocks (equities), bonds (fixed-income investments), and cash. Stocks represent an ownership interest in businesses, while fixed-income investments generally represent debt instruments of either businesses or governmental entities. The investment community defines cash as money invested for very short periods of time in highly liquid fixed-income investments, such as short-term treasury bills, certificates of deposit, or money market funds.

The statement frequently made today is that anywhere from 87 percent or more of the total return on a portfolio is determined by asset allocation. This claim traces its roots at least as far back as a study of investment performance prepared by a national investment consulting firm.[7] The graph in Exhibit 3.8 is a visual presentation of the now-standard claim.

The first thing to remember is that the consultants who prepared the study were in the asset allocation business. In other words, as investment consultants their clients hired them to decide what the mix of investment assets should be, in turn to hire investment managers who specialize in each of those areas, and finally, to supervise their performance. This is a common model of consulting work in the world of institutional investments. Did self-interest in the conclusion that asset allocation is responsible for 87 percent of the total return compromise the results? Probably not. But to understand the full story, we have to first understand the choices, which is to say the different classes of investment assets and, in particular, the nature of cash.

BEEF AND BEEF BY-PRODUCTS

When normal people think about cash, they picture money in their wallet or, if they are at all like me, they picture twenty-dollar bills emerging miraculously from an ATM machine. If you asked a normal person what kind of a return do you earn on your cash, the answer would be I don't earn any kind of return, I spend it every day on a low-fat latte and a blueberry scone, and the answer would be technically correct. Unless we are in a period of deflation, in which case the purchasing power and therefore the value of the actual dollars that we are holding is increasing, or unless we are comparing values on a global basis, and the value of a dollar is increasing relative to most major currencies, then we are not "earning" any return on the money in our pocket. Similarly, we are not earning any money on non-interest-bearing accounts, such as the typical checking account. When the investment community, on the other hand, talks about cash, they almost always mean "cash or cash-equivalent." What on earth is a cash-equivalent? The term reminds me of the phrase "beef and beef by-products" that you read on the labels of pet food cans or, worse, packages of hot dogs.

Essentially, a cash-equivalent is any short-term, highly secure investment that, by its nature, is so liquid that it can be immediately converted to cash. For individuals, a pass book account at a federally insured bank or savings and loan would be a cash-equivalent. The money is on deposit and earning interest, but can be withdrawn (i.e., converted to real cash as opposed to "equivalent cash") at any time without cost or penalty. In the institutional world, cash-equivalents include such things as banker's acceptances, commercial paper, repurchase agreements, 30-day treasury bills, and money-

---

[7] For a discussion of asset allocation studies see Barton M. Biggs, "Asset Allocation Is Crucial," *Morgan Stanley Perspectives*, April 9, 1985.

EXHIBIT 3.8. Investment Performance Factors

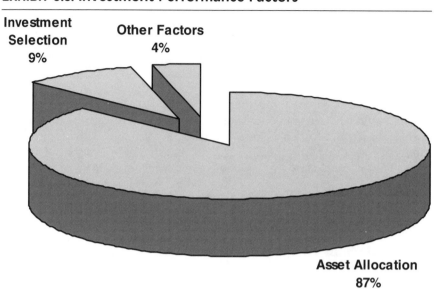

Produced by Fry Capital Advisors

market mutual funds. The 30-day treasury bill makes the list even though it is technically a 30-day obligation, because the secondary market for treasury bills (the market in which investors buy and sell bills that the government has previously issued) is extremely liquid. On any given day hundreds of millions of dollars of treasury bills change hands in the markets, meaning that one can always sell them, quickly and at very little cost. Selling a bill means converting a cash-equivalent into cash.

Today the most common form of a cash-equivalent is a money-market mutual fund, which is commonly referred to as a money market account. These are issued by banks, major brokerage houses, and mutual fund companies. The liquidity is achieved in two ways. First, the mutual funds themselves are invested exclusively in fairly short-term instruments, usually a combination of treasury bills and commercial paper.[8] The second way is the normal redemption obligation of all open-ended mutual funds.

Open-end funds pledge to redeem shares on demand by the shareholder for the amount of the net asset value represented by each share. In the case of the money-market mutual funds, they make every effort to maintain net asset value at $1.00, which helps maintain the image, if you will, that these are truly a cash-equivalent even though the typical money-market mu-

---

[8] Because these instruments are actual mutual funds and are not direct obligations of the U.S. government even if they invest predominantly in such instruments, you have to be careful about the quality of the money market fund that you use. (See further discussion in Chapter 8.)

tual fund has a weighted average maturity of anywhere from 45 to 90 days.[9] Consequently, "cash," when it actually means cash-equivalents, does in fact earn a return.

So now let's return to the question of asset allocation and whether asset allocation is in fact responsible for 87 percent of the total return that one earns in investment portfolios. If the assumption is that the return, apart from asset allocation decision, is zero, then certainly asset allocation accounts for a very substantial portion of the total portfolio return. Another way to say this is that if one assumes that the comparison is to cash, in its pure nonearning form, as opposed to cash and cash-equivalents, then asset allocation certainly contributes a very substantial portion of the total return. But as we have already seen, there is no such thing as an organization (nor, really, even an individual) who takes their funds, their endowment, or other long-term money and fills a suitcase with hundred-dollar bills and buries it in the backyard. So when we declare that asset allocation determines 87 percent of the total return that is earned on a portfolio, we are crediting the asset allocation decision with the decision to dig the money up out of the ground and do anything with it at all. We are including in the general asset allocation decision-making process, the decision to move buried cash out of the backyard and into "cash" in a money-market mutual fund.

The problem is that when investment advisors, stockbrokers, or consultants talk about asset allocation, they are usually talking about the technique of establishing a mix of investments. Invariably they are speaking to people or organizations who have already made a decision to invest and, typically, who are already invested in something. That something might range from money market funds and government and corporate bonds to portfolios of U.S. equities and fixed-income instruments. In other words, 99.9 percent of the time when investment professionals are talking about asset allocation, the starting point for their audience *is not* money in the ground.

So if we then claim that asset allocation is responsible for 87 percent of the return that a portfolio earns we might be tempted to believe (and here's where the vested interest of the consultant enters in) that the particular techniques currently being promoted for determining the mix of assets in a portfolio are responsible for all of the return, including the movement from zero to the 5 percent that one currently earns in a money market account. Clearly, that part of the 87 percent statement is incorrect.

ASSET ALLOCATION IN ACTION

Although asset allocation is not the *only* important investment issue, as its proponents sometimes claim, it is nonetheless tremendously important. To

---

[9] The $1.00 net asset value for money-market mutual funds is so important to their success that the larger issuers of these funds will go to great lengths to protect that figure. Several years ago, a fund maintained by Bank of America, currently the nation's third largest bank, incurred substantial losses, which if reflected in the value of the fund, would have driven its NAV below

understand why, consider the construction of a model portfolio using asset allocation techniques involving two asset classes. The asset classes are stocks, as represented by the S&P 500, and bonds, as represented by a five-year U.S. Treasury bond.

Exhibit 3.9 shows the basic return relationships over a 50-year period from 1945 to 1995. As we move from left to right on the graph, each dot represents an additional 5 percent equities. So the first dot, on the far left, is the average annual return of five-year treasury bonds, calculated on a rolling five-year average for the last 50 years. In other words, we start in January 1945 and look forward five years. During that period, the bonds averaged 1.66 percent. We then move forward one quarter to April 1, 1945, look forward another five years and come up with another average annual return, 1.47 percent. We do that for all of the five-year periods (20 quarters) between January 1, 1945, and December 31, 1995.

We then calculate the average of all of the rolling five-year periods. That average is represented by the first dot on the curve. As one can see, on a rolling five-year basis the average annual return of five-year treasury bonds for the fifty years ending December 31, 1995, was just under 6 percent (5.85 percent).

We then repeat this process for the stock market as represented by the S&P 500. The average for the S&P 500 for that same period of time was just over 12 percent (12.34 percent). That figure is represented by the last dot on the curve on the far right side of the graph.

The dots in-between represent portfolios composed of both stocks and bonds. As you move from left to right across the graph, each dot represents 5 percent more stock and 5 percent fewer bonds. Thus, the second dot from the left is the average annual return on a rolling five-year basis of a portfolio that is 5 percent stocks (the number shown on the horizontal axis) and 95 percent bonds. The next dot is 10 percent stocks and 90 percent bonds. And so it continues until you get to the all-stock number on the far right.[10]

The first observation is that stocks here produced higher returns than bonds over the last 50 years. Thus, adding stocks to a portfolio increases returns. Stocks, in fact, have historically produced nearly twice the return of bonds. This is the reason why the initial reaction of every financial consultant, investment advisor, or stock broker to an organization's all-bond portfolio is usually, "Oh my gosh, why don't you have any equities?"

Exhibit 3.10 shows the same average return figures as the middle line flanked by an upper and lower line. The average, as we now know, represents all the rolling five-year periods from 1945 to 1995. That works out to 180 annual return figures averaged into each dot on the middle line. If we

---

$1.00. Rather than have that occur, Bank of America chose to voluntarily contribute several million of its own dollars to the fund in order to preserve its $1.00 net asset value.

[10] Using rolling five-year averages produces numbers that are more likely to be experienced by investors than are one-year numbers. The averages are very similar, but the range (which we will look at next) will be much different.

EXHIBIT 3.9. Asset Allocation (1)—Five-Year Rolling Averages: 1945–1995—S&P 500 and Mid-Term Government Bonds

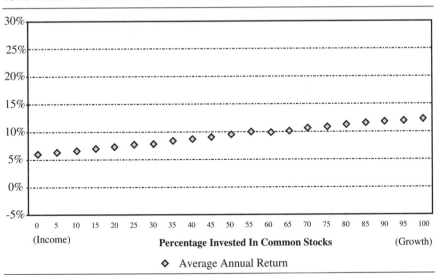

(Income)   **Percentage Invested In Common Stocks**   (Growth)

◇ Average Annual Return

Produced by Capital Markets Research

were to show every five-year period as a dot, there would be a range of dots above and below the line.

The upper and lower lines represent one standard deviation of return from the average. In other words, two-thirds of the 180 rolling year periods fall between the upper and lower lines. So in an all-bond portfolio (the far left-hand dot) the average return is 6 percent, and the range of returns within one standard deviation is from a low of 2 percent to a high of 10 percent.

This means that while the average return over 50 years was 6 percent, two-thirds of the time the actual number ranged somewhere from 2 percent to 10 percent. The standard deviation is ±4 percent. Notice now the far right-hand dot, which measures the average all-stock return. There the average is 12 percent, but the range is from 6 percent to 18 percent. The standard deviation in other words is ±6 percent. Consequently, the all-stock portfolio experiences a wider range of returns; it is more volatile than an all-bond portfolio. This observation agrees with our instinct and common experience that stock prices fluctuate more wildly than do bond prices.

So now we know the averages, and we have some idea of the range of likely returns. But the range of likely returns does not give me, a truly conservative and anxious board member, all the comfort that I might want in making a decision. The upper and lower lines only tell me the range of what is likely, the range of what happens two-thirds of the time. What about the other third of the time and, more to the point, what is the worst that can happen? How bad can it get?

EXHIBIT 3.10. Asset Allocation (2)—Five-Year Rolling Averages: 1945–1995—S&P 500 and Mid-Term Government Bonds

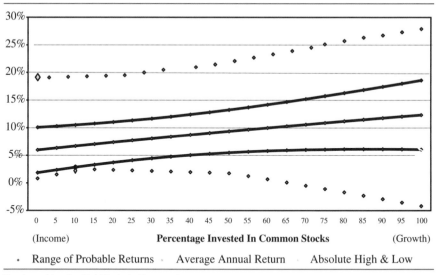

(Income) **Percentage Invested In Common Stocks** (Growth)

• Range of Probable Returns · Average Annual Return · Absolute High & Low

Produced by Capital Markets Research

Exhibit 3.11 adds two more lines to the chart: the top line shows the best averages for a five-year period and the bottom line shows the worst averages for a five-year period (the lower line). On the far right side, the all-stock portfolio, we can see that the top five-year numbers knocked the lights out with returns of nearly 30 percent. But in the worst five-year period, the all-stock portfolio actually lost money with an annualized return of negative 5 percent. This again agrees with common experience—it is possible to lose money in the stock market.

But notice as we move from left to right across the graph we get all the way to a 65 percent allocation to equities before we have a losing portfolio on a five-year average basis. In other words, there is no five-year period from 1945 to 1995 in which a portfolio invested 60 percent in the S&P 500 and 40 percent in five-year treasury bonds lost money. That is significant.

We have now seen faintly, almost as if cloaked in shadows, that some power exists in the combination of assets. Stocks generate greater returns than bonds, on average, but at times actually lose money. In addition, stocks appear to fluctuate more in value. Add it all up and the "typical" charitable board would ideally like the returns of stocks but the stability of bonds. Can we write that into our policies? Not exactly, but we can come closer than you might think. Let's take a look at these same numbers but from a slightly different perspective.

Exhibit 3.12 shows our now-familiar line of rolling five-year averages but with a curved line of dots added as well. This line, measured against the right-hand vertical axis, is the standard deviation of returns for our average

EXHIBIT 3.11. Asset Allocation (3)—Five-Year Rolling Averages: 1945–1995—S&P 500 and Mid-Term Government Bonds

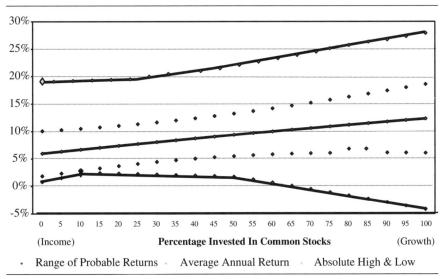

Produced by Capital Markets Research

EXHIBIT 3.12. Lowest Risk Investing (1)—Five-Year Rolling Averages: 1945–1995—S&P 500 and Mid-Term Government Bonds

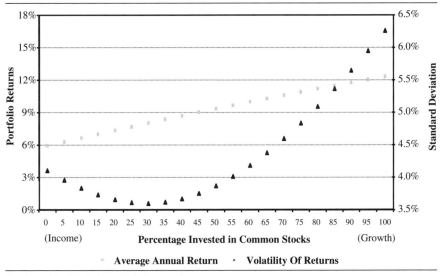

Produced by Capital Markets Research

returns. Here one can see more clearly than before that the standard deviation for the all-bond portfolio at just over 4 percent is a good deal lower than the standard deviation for the all-stock portfolio at nearly 6.5 percent. The stocks are riskier.

But now notice in Exhibit 3.13 that the lowest risk allocation is *not* all bonds. Rather, the lowest risk allocation is 30 percent stocks. At that point, the standard deviation is only 3.5 percent. In other words, a portfolio of 30 percent stocks and 70 percent bonds will produce lower volatility and will fluctuate less in value than an all-bond portfolio. In a very real sense, *we lower our risks by adding stocks to our portfolio.*

Notice also in Exhibit 3.14 that a 60 percent allocation to equities has approximately the same standard deviation of return as an all-bond portfolio. Yet, over the last 50 years, the average annual return for a 60 percent stock portfolio was nearly 10 percent versus 6 percent for the all-bond portfolio. The return on our 30 percent stock portfolio was over 8 percent. So when we move from all bonds to 30 percent stocks, we increase our annual returns while *decreasing volatility.* This would seem a rather compelling move to make.

More importantly, it demonstrates the benefit of combining assets, in this case stocks and bonds, which respond differently to the same outside economic events. Because stocks and bonds do not always move up and down together, combinations of such assets in portfolios tend to smooth out the ups and downs. The countervailing movements tend to offset one another

EXHIBIT 3.13. Lowest Risk Investing (2)—Five-Year Rolling Averages: 1945–1995—S&P 500 and Mid-Term Government Bonds

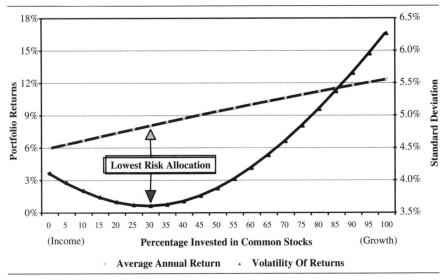

EXHIBIT 3.14. Lowest Risk Investing (3)—Five-Year Rolling Averages: 1945–1995—S&P 500 and Mid-Term Government Bonds

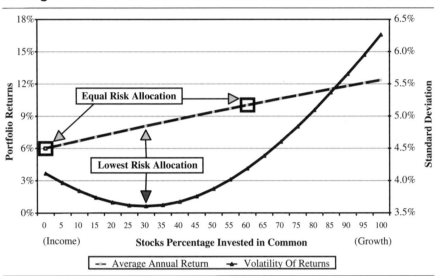

Produced by Capital Markets Research

and result in a more stable portfolio. That offsetting effect is at the heart of asset allocation.

Exhibit 3.15 (which you saw earlier as 3.1) is simply a combination of both the risk line and the return line from the preceeding charts into a single line. Portfolio return is measured on the vertical axis and portfolio risk (our old friend standard deviation) is portrayed on the horizontal axis. As you move up, you increase returns. As you move right, you increase risk. It is even easier to see in this view that the 30 percent portfolio is the lowest risk point and the 60 percent allocation has exactly the same risk as the all-bond portfolio.

The foregoing series of charts highlight the first significance of asset allocation. It is a technique that identifies the portfolio with the lowest risk for any given level of anticipated return. This represents the first and perhaps most important use of asset allocation modeling.

The technique also allows us to construct portfolios that have risk characteristics with which we are comfortable. The benefits of managing to an acceptable level of risk are legion. The direct advantage is that of limiting losses in times of bad market performance. The collateral benefit is the absence of worry. To the extent that we can eliminate a category of organizational worries, everyone is better off.

From the chief financial officer's perspective, managing portfolios within the comfort zone means being able to devote energy to issues other than explaining losses in the investment portfolio at the quarterly investment policy meeting or at the annual board meeting. In addition, managing within

EXHIBIT 3.15. Efficient Frontier

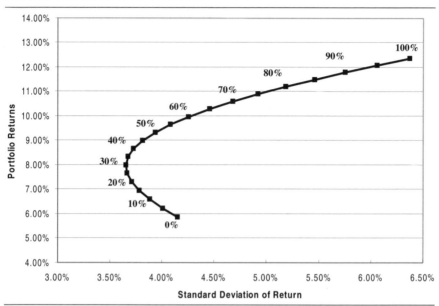

Produced by Capital Markets Research

the comfort zone allows an organization to stay the course, which inherently improves investment performance.

Imagine that ACO's board has, in a fit of ignorant enthusiasm, authorized the CFO to invest 100 percent of the long-term reserves in equities. That is actually twice the board's true level of comfort, but they did not know it. Now the market drops significantly. What happens? The board panics and in the absence of a plan instructs the CFO to sell the investments and go to cash.

At that point, the ACO has incurred round-trip commissions, first by establishing all the positions in the portfolio and then by liquidating them. Incurred frequently enough, such costs will adversely affect performance. In addition, whatever investment strategy was being pursued is now in the dumpster, along with last year's annual report. Finally, and ironically, the heretofore unrealized losses from which the portfolio may have ultimately recovered, are now realized and therefore locked in. All in all, such panic decisions in response to being invested beyond the comfort zone usually range from poor to disastrous.

WHAT RISKS DOES ASSET ALLOCATION STRATEGY ADDRESS?

The broadest categories of risk are specific risk—those associated with any one stock or bond—and market risk—those associated with a broader market. Diversifying a portfolio by including multiple securities greatly reduces specific risk. Asset allocation reduces market risk. To some extent, in the very simple two-asset-class model we have been using, we are reducing market risk simply by reducing our exposure to the market. To the extent that stocks are riskier than bonds, reducing a portfolio's exposure to stocks reduces market risk. But that is not the whole story. If it were, the risk line in Exhibits 3.12 to 3.14 would be as straight as the return line instead of curved. Something else is going on that may best be understood with an illustration.

ASSET ALLOCATION AT WORK

To illustrate why asset allocation reduces market risk, we will look back at the stock market of 1973–1974. This two-year period was the last time the market was so bad that brokers were thankful their high-rise office windows would not open. In 1973, the stock market as measured by the S&P 500 was down 25 percent. In 1974, the market was down another 15 percent. Thus, for every dollar invested on January 1, 1973, only 60 cents remained by December 31, 1974 (ignoring compounding effects). The investment committee that confidently plunged 100 percent of its funds into the stock market late in 1972 had, after costs and fees, reduced the organization's endowment by nearly one half.

Exhibit 3.16 portrays the annual percentage return for the S&P 500 and intermediate-term government bonds for the 10 years from 1970 to 1980. The solid bar is the S&P 500. Notice the bloodbath of 1973 and 1974. At the

EXHIBIT 3.16. Annual Performance by Asset Class—Bear Market: 1973 & 1974

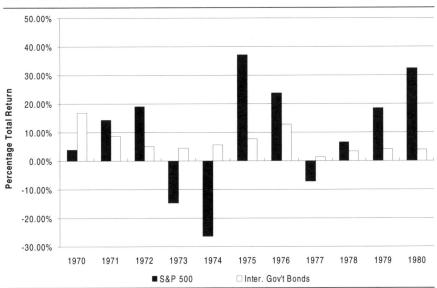

Produced by Fry Capital Advisors

same time, the government bonds (the clear bars) continued to generate modest, if unspectacular, returns. In the bounce-back year of 1975, the S&P 500 returned more than 35 percent, while the bonds continued their modest course.

We have seen earlier that on a five-year basis our 30 percent equity/70 percent bond portfolio was our lowest risk portfolio. Let's now compare such a portfolio to the S&P 500 for this same 10-year period. Exhibit 3.17 compares the compound growth of $100 in our lowest risk portfolio to the compound growth of $100 in the S&P 500. Notice first that the lowest risk portfolio does not drop nearly so much in the terrible 1973–1974 market, although it does decline slightly.

Notice further that it does not rebound as quickly during the strong market of 1975–1977; the leveling effect cuts both ways. But for risk-adverse boards, the fact that the low risk portfolio tremendously muted the sharpest stock market decline since the Great Depression is probably worth more in terms of peace of mind and staying power than whatever was lost on the upside. During this particular example, it is not until 1980 that the pure stock market portfolio overtakes the lowest risk portfolio. There are fully seven years in which the lowest risk portfolio outperforms the 100 percent equity portfolio.

To complete the picture, Exhibit 3.18 extends compound growth comparison of the two portfolios out to 1996. We can see that, given a tremendously strong stock market, the pure stock portfolio eventually outperforms our

EXHIBIT 3.17. Compound Growth of $100 by Asset Class—Through Bear Market: 1973 & 1974

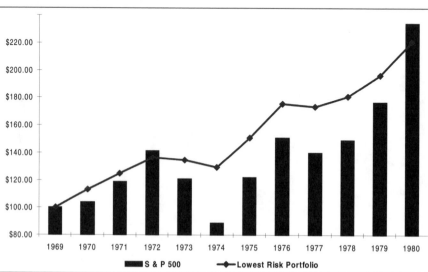

Produced by Fry Capital Advisors

EXHIBIT 3.18. Compound Growth of $100 by Asset Class

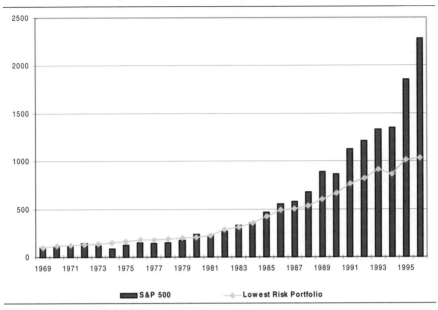

Produced by Fry Capital Advisors

lowest risk portfolio by a significant amount. Taking the safer course reduces returns in a strong market.

But it is even more interesting to note the extent to which the lowest risk portfolio outperforms the six-month treasury bill, which might be thought of as money in the bank. We have taken risk out of the portfolio and yet maintained exposure to the equity markets. The result is a growth rate that the board can live with.

ASSET CLASSES

A list of asset classes is included as Exhibit 3.19. It is actually a list of asset class specific investment funds taken from the Common Fund's 1996 Annual Report. As there is no single standard set of asset classes, names, order, and emphasis vary with the consultants or institutions involved. Allowing for such variations, the list in Exhibit 3.19 is fairly representative of the classes that are commonly used among larger endowments and for larger pools of money.

The interesting thing about this list is its historical orientation. Notice that when the Common Fund began its operation, it offered an equity fund. Shortly thereafter it offered a short-term fund and a bond fund. The three initial asset classes, in other words, were U.S. equities, managed cash, and bonds. The list then shows rather dramatically a "typical" progression in

EXHIBIT 3.19. Common Fund Annual Report—Assets

The Common Fund 1996 Annual Report

Landmarks
1971 – 1996

"On behalf of all the Members of

The Common Fund, the Board of

Trustees wishes to express its

appreciation to the Ford Foundation

for the substantial grant which has

made this undertaking possible.

McGeorge Bundy, President of the

Ford Foundation, stirred consider-

able discussion when, in the

Foundation's 1966 annual report, he

was critical of existing attitudes and

practices in the management of

educational endowments. The

study, *Managing Educational*

Endowments, published by the

Foundation in 1969, made a strong

case for professional investment

management, and for a change from

the traditional emphasis on income,

to a recognition of the greater

importance of long-term total return

from both yield and appreciation."

– John F. Meck
Founding President, Board of Trustees
Writing in the first Common Fund
Annual Report (For the Fiscal Year
July 1, 1971 – June 30, 1972)

1971	The Common Fund organized with 72 Members and $63 million in assets
	Equity Fund
1974	Short Term Fund
1976	Bond Fund
	$500 million in assets
1983	International Equity Fund
	$1 billion in assets
1984	Equity-Income Fund
1985	Global Bond Fund
1986	South Africa Free Equity Fund
	Intermediate Cash Fund
	Tactical Asset Allocation Program
1987	South Africa Free Bond Fund
	Endowment Planning Model I
	$5 billion in assets
1988	Endowment Advisers, Inc.
	Endowment Realty Investors I
	Endowment Partners Fund I
1989	Endowment Energy Partners I
1990	Endowment Venture Partners I
	South Africa Free International Equity Fund
	Endowment Planning Model II
	$10 billion in assets
1991	Absolute Return Funds
1992	Growth Equity Fund
	Core Equity Fund
	High Quality Bond Fund
	Endowment Energy Partners II
	Global Equity Fund
	Emerging Markets Fund
1993	International Bond Fund
	Endowment Venture Partners II
	More and Less Currency Hedged Alternatives of Global and International Funds
	Endowment Institute
	Three Books on Management and Growth of Endowments
	$15 billion in assets
1994	Endowment Realty Investors II
	Small Cap Growth Fund
	Small Cap Value Fund
	Hedge Fund
	Endowment Private Equity Partners II
	Distribution Management Service
1995	Domestic Equity Fund
1996	25th Anniversary of The Common Fund
	Endowment Energy Partners III
	Publication of *A Common Vision: Working in Partnership for the Benefit of All*
	Colloquium on *The Financial Challenges Facing Education Today*
	$17 billion in assets

The Common Fund is itself a nonprofit organization founded by the Ford Foundation to provide investment services to the nation's colleges and universities. Its outstanding success is a credit to the vision of the Ford Foundation.

the increase in number and variety of asset classes as the size and sophistication of the organization increases. By the time of this report, the asset classes have grown to include style specific funds (growth, value, and small capitalization), a wide range of international alternatives, multiple fixed-income funds, and various specialty funds, including hedge funds, funds with social or more investment restrictions, and real estate investments (See also Exhibit 7.2 for a companion Common Fund list.)

Even today, organizations with smaller funds, or who are new to investing, often invest only in U.S. stocks, bonds, and cash while organizations with larger pools of money usually add additional asset classes. Three things control the movement from three-class models to multiclass models. The first issue is expense. There are still economies of scale to be had in managing pools of money. Basically, the larger the amount, the lower the management fees and transaction costs on a percentage basis. There is an understandable hesitancy, therefore, to break up pools of money into smaller pieces, since doing so invariably increases costs and fees. Thus, it is still quite common for funds of less than $5 million to have allocations only to U.S. stocks, bonds, and cash. Conversely, by the time an organization has several hundred million dollars under management, allocations to seven or more asset classes does not significantly increase expenses.

A second factor is administration. Each allocation to a new asset class represents at least one more fund or one more manager to track and to factor into a matrix. The consulting services available to large charitable organizations are, for the most part, not available for funds of under $10 million. (See Chapter 6 for a further discussion of this point.) Therefore, most smaller charitable organizations must rely on either a broker-consultant or a single investment manager to provide some of the horsepower necessary to establish the models, monitor performance, and continuously rebalance the allocations. For organizations with less than $5 million in a single manageable fund, reaching for an elaborate multiple-asset-class model may not be worth the effort.

Finally, the law of diminishing returns is at work. The degree of low correlation between equities and short-term fixed income investments, in particular, is much greater, historically, than the non-correlation between different types of equities, such as value and growth stocks. Consequently, in terms of reducing risks for a given level of return, easily the most important decision is the one establishing the mix of equities, fixed-income investments, and cash.

ASSET ALLOCATION CONCLUSIONS

Asset allocation works to reduce risk when the asset classes chosen have a low correlation to one another. That low correlation ultimately means that the assets respond differently to the same external economic events. In our particular example of low correlation in practice, the Arab oil crisis that sent the stock market reeling in the early seventies did not have that same impact on the short-term bond market. Consequently, the lowest risk portfolio enjoyed a much smoother ride through those turbulent times.

Asset allocation is a viable technique for controlling the level of market risk in any portfolio. Its principal risk management virtue is that it allows the investor to establish positions that can be maintained with a clear conscience and untroubled sleep, even during periods of profound market declines. That experience then allows an organization to stay the course and greatly increases the chances that it will achieve the purposes for which it is investing.

Moreover, while it was not the primary purpose of this discussion, notice the wonderful effect that even a 30 percent exposure to the equity markets has on the portfolio's overall value, compared with the all-bond or all-cash portfolio. Even that modest equity exposure greatly increases returns over the time frames that govern most charitable mandates.

Asset Allocation as an Investment Policy Tool

Selecting appropriate asset allocations and settling on a model for each portfolio is also a powerful policy setting tool. By establishing an asset allocation model appropriate for each portfolio or fund, the organization's investment committee is able to establish a range of anticipated returns and a range of likely risk, both of which can be fine-tuned by taking into account the time frames for which each fund is permitted to invest. Most importantly, the organization has not just handed the funds over to one or more managers and told them to go forth and manage. Rather, it has created a reasonable framework within which managers can work. As we will see in later chapters, this also provides a foundation upon which to measure the overall performance of both the investment portfolios and the manager or managers who are doing the investing.

Rebalancing

Rebalancing the portfolio is the process of moving money between asset classes to maintain the previously established allocations. The need for this final step in the asset allocation process arises naturally because some investment classes perform better than others. The following example will suffice to illustrate the benefits of this approach.

Let us assume that in January 1973, an organization had a $1 million portfolio invested 60 percent in equities, 35 percent in intermediate-term government bonds, and 5 percent in cash. By the end of the year, after a 25 percent drop in the equity market, it would only have $450,000 left in the equity fund, representing 53 percent of the diminished portfolio. The loss in the equity portion of the fund was $150,000.

What do we do? I submit that if the treasurer or CFO walks into the board meeting at that point and says, "Since we lost so much in the stock market this past year, I would like to purchase an additional $60,000 of equities in order to get us back to a 60 percent allocation," there is exactly a 0 percent chance of the board taking that step *unless they have committed to maintaining an asset allocation strategy ahead of time.*

Think about it. Would your natural inclination after a $150,000 loss be to buy more of whatever produced that loss? I doubt it. It is a counterintuitive response.

And it would be really gut-wrenching in this particular example as the equities are going to lose another 15 percent or an additional $76,000, in 1974. At that point the equity pool of $433,000 now represents only 56 percent of the total $775,000 fund. To maintain the targeted 60 percent allocation, the organization must again purchase $35,000 of additional equities.

Now comes payday. In 1975, with the S&P 500 up nearly 32 percent, the organization enjoys a 32 percent return on its $468,000 equity position, resulting in a $150,000 gain. This is nearly $40,000 more than the gain would have been had it not rebalanced the portfolio. The rebalancing strategy forced the organization to buy low in the teeth of a declining market.

The effect of rebalancing in down markets is to maintain the desired equity allocation and thereby increase returns when the market turns positive. The effect of rebalancing in up markets is to sell as asset classes are performing well and thereby maintain the originally targeted risk exposure. In both cases, it represents a conscious effort to control the investment process and not be inadvertently controlled by the markets themselves.

The Importance of Time

In the world of investing, time frequently cures a multitude of sins. Over very long periods, investors have found that equity investments eventually turn profitable. What is even more important, however, is that longer periods of time actually reduce investment risk. In addition, the "mere" act of matching the investment time horizons to the period of time for which the funds are in fact available for investment can greatly increase returns without any commensurate increase in risks. This is one of the few places where an investor really can get something for nothing. Let's see why that is the case.

FIXED-INCOME INVESTMENT TIME FRAMES

Investors' time frames are invariably too short. Interestingly, this is a problem that is as common in fixed-income investing as it is in the equity markets. On the fixed-income side, the assets being managed are usually considered some sort of reserve. In approaching the management of such funds, the most common thought is that since we do not know exactly when we'll need the money, we had better keep it accessible in the money market account. Frequently, the result is that balances far in excess of 90-day cash flow requirements are maintained in an asset with a weighted average maturity of something less than 90 days. This can be an expensive mistake, as we shall see when fixed-income investing is discussed in more detail in Chapter 8.

TIME AND THE EQUITY MARKETS

In the equity markets, investors also tend to be too short-term in their focus. Although a number of the funds typically maintained by charitable organizations are effectively perpetual in their existence, most organizations do not manage their money from that perspective. Those that retain outside advisors, for example, usually pay a great deal of attention to quarterly numbers and occasionally terminate managers for poor performance over as few as two quarters. While such micro inspection of manager performance does not necessarily mean that the overall investment time frame is short-term, it certainly implies thinking in that direction.

Lengthening investment time horizons produces a number of positive results. The most important of these are:

1. Reducing the risks of equity investments
2. Increasing the allocations to higher total return asset classes
3. Requiring fewer cost-generating changes in portfolios.

Let us examine each factor.

Recall, if you will, that standard deviation of returns is the fundamental measure of risk. One standard deviation can be thought of as the range of likely returns, as two-thirds of the observations will fall within one standard deviation of the average. Thus, an investment with an average return of 5 percent and a standard deviation of 10 percent is an extremely risky investment in that two-thirds of the time the range of likely returns is going to be anywhere from −5 percent to +15 percent. And since the one standard deviation measure only includes two-thirds of the incidents, then one-third of the time the return will be outside that range. So fully one-sixth of the time the actual return will be worse than −5 percent. Conversely, if the average is 5 percent but the standard deviation is only 1 percent, the investment is much safer, as the range of likely returns is only going to move from 4 percent to 6 percent.

As we extend investment time horizons to longer and longer periods, the range of likely returns around the mean narrows considerably. Exhibit 3.20 shows the range of stock market returns as measured by the S&P 500 on a 1-, 3-, 5-, 10-, and 20-year basis. Notice first that the *average* return for each of the rolling periods changes very modestly, hovering within half of 1 percent of 13 percent. But notice, further, the range of probable returns. On a

EXHIBIT 3.20. Portfolio ROR

Portfolio ROR

	1 Year	3 Years	5 Years	10 Years	20 Years
■ Max ROR	30.92	22.71	19.91	19.32	18.83
□ Min ROR	-5.99%	3.49%	5.86%	6.07%	7.13%
□ Mean ROR	12.46	13.10	12.89	13.00	12.98

Produced by Capital Markets Research

one-year basis, the standard deviation of average returns is over 18 percent. This produces a range of probable returns from −5.99 percent to 30.92 percent. By the time the investment time horizon is 20 years, the standard deviation of these returns is less than 6 percent. With that drop in volatility the likelihood of a losing period (based on historic numbers) also drops significantly. To the extent that the variability of return is an accurate measure of at least a portion of our investment risk, *the long-term equity investor is clearly taking significantly less risk than the short-term equity investor.*

Exhibit 3.21 illustrates this truth with three versions of the efficient frontier for the two-asset-class model used throughout the asset allocation discussion. The curves are based on 5-, 10-, and 20-year rolling averages, respectively. What do we see? First, extending the time horizons shifts the entire curve to the left. The overall level of risk diminishes as the time hori-

EXHIBIT 3.21. Efficient Frontier—Rolling Averages: 1945–1995

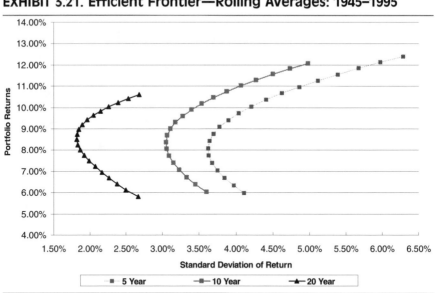

Produced by Capital Markets Research

zons are extended. Second, the lowest risk point also changes from 30 percent equities on a rolling five-year basis to 50 percent equities on a rolling twenty-year basis. Consequently, even the most risk-averse board can still optimize its portfolios at higher overall equity levels *if* it can determine that a fund is perpetual and therefore bring itself to invest on the basis of twenty-year time horizons or longer.

Finally, consider Exhibit 3.22, which brings these ideas together. Here one sees the average return for an all-bond portfolio and an equity portfolio over periods ranging from 1 to 20 years. Those average lines are then surrounded by the standard deviation lines with a result that looks like two trumpets. In both cases the range of likely returns narrows considerably over time.

When time horizons are long enough, the volatility risk in both equity and fixed-income investments is diminished. If one adopts a time frame of 20 years or longer, there is no need to address intermediate-term volatility by optimizing asset allocation models around five-year numbers. Doing so invites shorter term thinking that will produce sub-optimal returns over the intended 20-year time frame.

POLICY IMPLICATIONS OF INVESTMENT TIME HORIZONS

There is almost nothing that a board or finance committee can do to enhance returns that is as direct, simple, and relatively riskless as establishing appropriate investment time horizons for each fund that the organization main-

EXHIBIT 3.22. Compression of Volatility

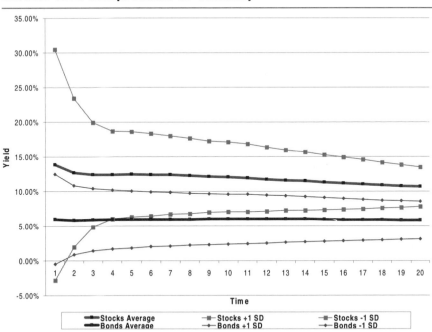

Produced by Fry Capital Advisors

tains. The exact allocation will vary with the recommendations of the organization's advisors and the asset classes the organization is using, but the process is the same. As time horizons lengthen, allocations may be shifted more aggressively toward equities, including more volatile but higher yielding asset classes such as small capitalization stocks or emerging markets in more sophisticated models. Understanding the effect of long time horizons on the standard deviation of returns allows a more aggressive posture. For both novice and sophisticated investment committees, identifying the time horizons of each fund is a basic decision that leads to incremental return likely to far exceed the income and returns to be had by picking the most successful investment managers or mutual funds for each asset class.

Risks Most People Do Not Discuss

There is a great scene in Neil Simon's *Brighton Beach Memoirs* in which the main character describes how his family never discussed *"death"* or *"cancer"*—each time with his voice dropping to a stage whisper. Similarly, there are a number of concepts and risks essential to all that we do in managing

funds but that are rarely if ever discussed. Chief among these is our dependence on historical data.

Lurking in the background as well are at least four other risks worth
mentioning. Those include

1. The risk of the complex
2. Innovation risks
3. The risk of quantifiability
4. The risk of isolation

Let us examine the importance of history for investment management and
then briefly discuss these other concerns.

OUR EYES ARE GLUED TO THE REARVIEW MIRROR

With the recent increase in the national speed limit from 55 to 65 miles
per hour, the need for keeping one eye glued to the rearview mirror has
diminished. Nonetheless, anyone who drives on the interstate checks the
rearview mirror every minute or so to spot a highway patrol car before the
officer has time to establish that he or she is doing 80 miles per hour.
The role of historic data in investment management is at least as pervasive
as the fear of being ticketed when driving over the speed limit. Because of
that, it is worth understanding the weakness and the limitation our dependence on history represents.

Every investment management technique, portfolio theory, stock selection strategy, economic forecast, and financial projection associated with the
management of funds rests on a foundation of historic financial data. A few
examples will suffice. All the work on portfolio theory ultimately rests on
covariance relationships between different assets or classes of assets. Those
relationships, in turn, are derived from the past price behavior of the assets
or asset classes under consideration. This means there are one, two, three,
or more factors or relationships that intervene between what we would like
to understand and what we are actually able to measure.

A low beta stock, for example, means a stock that is less volatile than the
broad market. From that we infer that it is a less risky investment because
we have previously agreed that we would accept the variability of returns
as one measure of risk. Thus we conclude that low beta stocks are less risky.

But our conclusion is really a radical leap from what we actually know.
All we really know is that in the past, the price of this particular stock fluctuated less than the market as a whole. What we do not know is *why*. Certainly, on an issue-by-issue basis, one can speculate about why some stocks
are less volatile than others, and in some cases the reasons are more apparent than in others. Nonetheless, the entire effort is dependent on an analysis
of historic patterns in the belief that such patterns provide some guide for
the future.

One example, developing at the time this was written, illustrates the weakness of our dependency on historic data. The stocks of electric utilities have for many years been very low beta stocks. In the language of the brokerage community, utility stocks are appropriate for widows and orphans. Underlying this low beta, low volatility, and therefore presumed low risk investment are two solid reasons readily apparent to any analyst. First, electric utilities have long been regulated industries, shielded from competition and guaranteed a reasonable return on their investment assets. Second, utility stocks have traditionally paid significantly higher dividends than any other segment of the stock market, meaning that the current income stream represents a larger percentage of the anticipated total return than does future appreciation in the price of the stock. Combine those two factors, and it is reasonable to conclude that these low beta stocks are less volatile because they are less risky.

There are a number of flies in this historic ointment. First, because these shares pay substantial dividends, they have some tendency to trade on yield. They are, for many investors, a bond substitute. So, over many years in this century during which there were relatively modest changes in the level of interest rates, those modest interest rate changes masked the exposure of these investments to substantial changes in interest rates. Consequently, when interest rates did rise sharply at times in recent years, utility stocks as a group dropped sharply in price.

Second, there is currently a widespread and probably irreversible national movement under way to deregulate the electric energy generation and transmission industry. In a number of states, large industrial consumers are already permitted to purchase directly from multiple competing utilities, and legislative changes are under way to compel utilities to share their transmission lines with competitors to facilitate similar choices for residential customers. As a result, there are going to be winners and losers in the electric utility industry similar to any other competitive environment but completely dissimilar to the historic environment that produced the low beta numbers.

Add it all up and what do we have? Beta as a measure of historic volatility relationships tells us nothing about the exposure of electric utility shares to radical changes in interest rates. In addition, the historic beta numbers of a formerly regulated industry are obviously no guide to the future when that industry will be deregulated. *The academic quest for the ability to reduce investment relationships to mathematical certainty founders on the limitations inherent in the historic record.*

The dependency on history that exists when calculating covariance relationships or beta is as profound in virtually every other area of investing. Growth managers compare projected growth rates to historic norms, value managers compare current price-to-earnings ratios to historic norms. Economists compare the current level of interest rates to historic norms. And so it goes. When it comes to predicting what will happen in the markets tomorrow or a year from now, we hope and believe it will be similar to what has happened before, but the truth is that we do not know. History is an imperfect guide. By reminding ourselves that we do not know we are less likely to make egregious errors or be led astray by those who claim that they do.

COMPLEXITY RISKS

I believe it is a mistake to invest in anything I do not understand. Admittedly, that rules out many possibilities. But I am not alone in this thinking. Peter Lynch in *Beating the Street* declares, "Never invest in any idea you can't illustrate with a crayon."[11] While this position may seem obvious, a couple of examples show that it is not.

In the early 1980s, when tax shelters were quite the rage, I spent five years as an attorney preparing offering memoranda for oil and gas limited partnerships. In retrospect, and despite my best efforts at clarity, I am convinced that most of the investors had no idea what they were buying. And in hindsight, virtually all of them would have been better off if they had passed on the investment, simply because they did not understand what they were buying.

More recently, huge, sophisticated companies have lost hundreds of millions of dollars investing in derivatives. There is nothing inherently wrong with derivatives. But they are complicated, and their complexity makes them prone to producing unintended results.

Contrast these new investment instruments with the fact that investors have been trading stocks and bonds on public exchanges, first in England and then in the United States, for more than 300 years. Hence, the behavior and characteristics of these traditional instruments are well known. Absent compelling evidence to the contrary and until sufficient understanding of the complexities of each new instrument exists, I believe in sticking to the basics. I think this is also sound advice for most charitable organizations.

INNOVATION RISKS

Closely related to complexity risk is the risk of investing in new financial devices. I am convinced that the overwhelming majority of investors do not appreciate the impact of the unprecedented wave of new investment techniques and instruments in just the last 20 years.

Take a look at the list in Exhibit 3.23. Notice that every one of these instruments, many of which now represent billions or even trillions of dollars of investments, came into being since the last sustained bear market in 1973–1974. The true mettle of an investment strategy or instrument is a bit like the true character of marriage—it is tested and proven over long periods of time.

---

[11] *Beating the Street*, p. 27.

Consider the example of index funds. Clearly there is a place for new instruments such as index funds in the world of charitable investment management, particularly for the most efficient segments of major markets. They can be helpful tools around which one can build larger portfolios. School is still out, however, on the ideal role of such funds primarily because of their relative youth. The Vanguard S&P 500 Index Fund, begun in 1976, is the oldest index fund. *Consequently, there is not a single endowment fund, investment committee, stock broker, or financial advisor in the United States with experience holding positions in an index fund through a sustained bear market.* It seems unlikely that being fully indexed to the market will be as comfortable when the market is going in the tank as it has been attractive in recent years. All the evidence of efficient markets notwithstanding, I am not yet convinced that unmanaged funds will wear well over time.

The second concern is that many of the new *instruments were created for one purpose but are being used or marketed for another.* Most financial futures contracts fall into this category. For the treasurer of a major multinational corporation who is conducting millions of dollars of business in a dozen different currencies, the ability to buy or sell foreign exchange futures contracts and thereby control currency risk is an unalloyed blessing. It is a device that reduces surprise and thereby facilitates commerce.

When you or I, on the other hand, buy a futures contract in yen because we believe it is underpriced relative to the dollar, we are speculating. The legitimate players in the market appreciate our presence because we increase trading volume, narrow spreads, and add liquidity. But in terms of prudent investing, such activities are folly. The reason to tie this into the proliferation of new financial instruments is that the newness itself should be a red flag that causes us to question whether we understand the investment and whether we are investing or speculating.

QUANTIFIABILITY

Closely related to our dependence on history is the belief that "I count therefore I manage." Thanks to the size of the financial markets, the number of people involved, and the widespread use of increasingly powerful computers, we can now measure almost anything.

Among the newer services available to financial managers, for example, is portfolio attribution software. These programs analyze the performance of each stock in a portfolio from numerous vantage points and attempt to help the manager determine whether stock selection, general market movements, timing, or other factors contribute to the relative success or failure of the portfolio. As helpful as such tools may be, it is appropriate to remember that just as our dependency on history reveals our feet of clay, the fact that we can count or measure something does not necessarily mean we can control it.

Even tools as compelling as asset allocation have a natural tendency to

EXHIBIT 3-23. New Investment Vehicles

Year	Investment Vehicle	Comments
1973	Listed Stock Options	Chicago Board of Options Exchange (CBOE) begins trading
1976	Index Funds	Vanguard starts first index fund on S&P 500
1977	Centralized Asset Accounts	Merrill Lynch introduces the Cash Management Account (CMA)
1978	Index Options	CBOE begins trading options on S&P 500 and other indexes
1980s	Adjustable-Rate Mortgages	Banks & S&Ls introduce adjustable rate mortgages in response to high, inflation-driven fixed-mortgage rates
1982	Stock Index Futures	Introduced on the Kansas City Board of Trade
1982	NASDAQ	NASD introduces National Market Automated Quotation System for the over-the-counter market
1985	Financial Futures	NYSE begins trading currency and other financial futures
1989	Program Trading Baskets	Device to purchase shares of an index for program trading
1992	Style Specific Index Funds	Vanguard creates S&P 500 Value and Growth Funds

oversell themselves. When viewing a beautiful series of charts showing risk/return relationships and predicting a 10 percent annualized return from a 60 percent equity portfolio, the natural inclination is to believe that you are actually going to get such a return. Although I can very accurately *calculate past correlations between asset classes* and thereby state what would have happened had you invested five years ago, I cannot control the next five years by virtue of that exercise. It is a very easy thing to forget.

ISOLATION RISK

Finally, there is some risk that comes from being *unaware* of the developments in the financial world. Most commonly, this is characterized by the statement "That is not the way we have always done it." It is possible to pay dearly for such insular thinking.

In the charitable world, the two most common types of insular investment thinking are the maintenance of substantial sums in certificates of deposit and the excessive aversion to equity investing. Most organizations able to purchase multiple $100,000 one-year CDs from the local bank are leaving money on the table in comparison with portfolios of relatively short-term treasuries or high-grade corporate bonds. Similarly, investing long-term funds exclusively in fixed-income instruments is a mistake. In eschewing the risk of the equity markets, the organization virtually guarantees lower returns and, ultimately, losses due to inflation. Even the ACO needs to embrace the enormous advances of the last 50 years that permit the most cautious investors to participate in the securities markets in a reasonable and measured way.

Back at the ACO . . .

INVEST IN STOCKS

"OK, I'm convinced," said our banker. "I'm willing to let the long-term funds have some equity investments. If that consultant's chart is correct, we lower our risk with 30 percent stocks, so I say go to 30 percent. Let's do that for a few years and see what happens."

Victory. It is an enormous step to learn something new, particularly when doing so requires setting aside the beliefs of a lifetime. Many an executive director would gladly give up a month's pay or a week of vacation to have board members who were willing to change their minds when presented with a compelling reason to do so. So as a quick aside, never underestimate the time and effort it will require to raise the level of investment sophistication of your board. It can be a daunting task. But it is also worth it. To the extent that you regularly recruit new board members, you can "cheat" by recruiting one or two with significant investment expertise. That is, in fact, an essential step.

For the next thing our banker board member will say is something like this: "OK, we're going to invest in stocks—who's going to pick them? Are we going to spend our entire meeting in the future picking stocks? I sure hope not because I don't want to be responsible when the market goes in the tank. On the other hand, even if we hire somebody, who's going to watch them? Or are we going to just hand the money over to a stock broker and let him start buying things?"

Once again, however, our banker's right. We have to be able to supervise those who select investments on our behalf. Solving that problem is the focus of Chapter 5.

Conclusion

The investment environment today is innovative, accessible, and overwhelmingly friendly to the success of charitable participants. While there are always risks in any activity, the investment community and the academic community have worked well together to craft tools designed to control those risks. There is no longer any reason for a charitable organization of any size to fail to participate in the securities markets in a measured and disciplined way. Such effort, when consistently pursued, will yield the tremendous benefit of growing charitable funds.

Operations

4 Critical Internal Organizational Components of Investing / 83

5 Getting Started / 91

6 Hiring Help / 122

7 Investment Accounting and Performance Reporting / 154

4 ▼ Critical Internal Organizational Components of Investing

Thus far, this book has examined the external world within which directors or officers must guide nonprofit organizations. In doing so, it has looked at the broad world context along with both the legal and the investment environments. In this section, the focus turns inward, beginning with an examination in this chapter of the organizational structure, which is essential for effective investment management. Chapter 5 then presents an "investment audit" as a tool for determining what the organization has to manage. That leads naturally to hiring help (Chapter 6) and to establishing appropriate investment accounting and reporting requirements (Chapter 7).

At the ACO . . .

ON THE BOARD

The ACO board has always taken a hands-on approach to investment management. In particular, the two bankers are adamant about retaining control over investment of the organization's funds at the board level. So, at every meeting the chief financial officer gives his report, and the board reviews and discusses it, en masse.

They operate without formal investment policies on the theory that, as one board member put it, "Why fiddle with a policy when we are making all the decisions ourselves?" There is, of course, an informal set of policies that one could discern from the long history of past discussions. They have, in essence, a "common law" set of policies, established by past arguments and resulting decisions. Those who care about the investments have a reasonable feel for what will fly with the rest of the board.

There is also a makeshift investment committee. It consists of the two bankers, a stock broker who is not on the board, and the chief financial officer. The organization's ready funds are on deposit in one of the banker's banks, and securities are purchased through the broker who gives them a 40 percent discount from retail on all trades. This group meets periodically, which works out to about every six or seven weeks to review the accounts, decide what else to buy, and whenever the chief financial officer needs funds, select items to sell to generate additional cash.

This group was formed several years back by the CFO as an act of desperation. It is not an official committee of the board, even though it does effectively make all the investment decisions. Prior to forming this group, the board discussion of investment matters took even longer than it does now. Today, it is not uncommon for a board discussion to sound something like this:

> Broker: This past quarter we moved some of our reserves out of six-month CDs and into a one-year treasury because we are able to earn 30 basis points of additional yield.
> Board member #1: What's a basis point?
> Board member #2: What's a treasury?
> Board member #3: What happens if we need that money in less than a year?

The CFO quietly sighs, looks at his watch and wonders how long the following discussion will take. The broker, smiling, sits silently for a moment. The board members assume he is organizing his thoughts before answering their questions. He is actually trying to calculate how large the organization's funds will have to be to justify the time he is spending on the account.

The silence seems to the executive director like a good moment to make a contribution of his own, so he asks, "Anyone want to go to the Dodgers game tonight? One of our donors gave me four tickets!"

First Things First—Who Is on the Board?

Charitable organizations need wisdom, reputation, vision, and fund raising from their board members and other major supporters. Clearly, however, not all supporters of an organization bring all these characteristics to the table. Therefore, to implement the correct investment structures, which ultimately begin with the board, an organization has to have the right people serving as directors.

The reality, however, is that people serve on charitable boards for a number of different reasons. With young, entrepreneurial organizations, for example, it is not uncommon to find boards populated with the founder's friends. In that case, a large part of their role is helping to create the appearance of the substantial organization that they hope someday to become. Even mature organizations tend to fill board positions for reasons other than organizational governance.

A better way to approach the issue of board membership is to recognize expressly the abilities needed and to create a place for those abilities to be used. Most important, some support can be had more effectively *off the board*. People who are essentially lending an organization their name and reputation, for example, do not necessarily need to be directors. They can serve instead on a board of reference. This is a much better arrangement for the community leader who is willing to endorse a particular charity's work but who does not have the time or the desire to be an active supervisor. It also allows the actual board of directors to be smaller and filled only with those people who are willing to be active in supervising the organization's work. The first "structural" decision, then, is to create areas that are not in the chain of command but where important supporters and major donors can be recognized, appreciated, and involved.

This is still not enough. The liabilities are real, the work is real, the time commitment is substantial. Consequently, for those who do serve on the board, an organization needs to be zealous in (1) protecting them with appropriate directors and officers liability insurance, (2) informing them of the decisions to be made, and (3) reimbursing them for the expenses they incur. With regard to information, the model is probably one of quarterly meetings in which the agenda, minutes of past meetings, management reports, and financial information are all provided sufficiently far in advance that genuine review and reflection is possible.

Critical Organizational Issues

There are three essential board functions in the nonprofit world: (1) setting policy, which can include goals and direction, (2) providing support and accountability to the staff and in particular the chief executive officer, and (3) fund raising. Except for fund raising, these are supervisory functions.

There is a lot of confusion in the nonprofit world with regard to the role of a board of directors. While some of the same confusion occurs in the business community, the problem tends to be worse among nonprofits. Largely, this is because the nonprofit board of directors has significant fundraising responsibilities. In an ideal setting, virtually all of the board members are also active fund raisers for the benefit of the corporation. As they discharge that role they frequently find themselves working with (and to some extent for) either the CFO or the senior development officer. From there it is easy to slide into an executive as opposed to a supervisory role with respect to the board functions noted above.

Ironically, some boards subtly resist fund raising by retaining executive responsibilities for investment management. Picking stocks is fun; picking stocks *with someone else's money can be even more fun.* And it is certainly more pleasant and exciting than asking friends for money (fund raising). The relationship between directors' fear of fund raising and the desire to be directly involved in investment management is that doing the latter provides the rationale for not doing the former. *Let someone else ask for money, I'm helping by managing what we already have.*

Therefore, nonprofit executive directors often have boards that willingly discuss policy and actively involve themselves in certain financial matters, yet rarely help raise money to the extent that they should. None of which makes the investment management task any easier. The good news is that this is one of those areas in which the correct structure can make a world of difference.

Creating an Appropriate Structure

Appropriate organizational structures are like any of the basic disciplines of life—going to work every day, getting up at the same time, exercising at the gym—they help keep us on track. There are many days when we do not feel like working or working out, but we're up, we're dressed, we're in the car and before we know it, despite ourselves, we are doing something useful. An appropriate organizational structure provides exactly this same sort of discipline. Board and committee structures create a framework within which investment policy is established, implemented, and supervised. Because that framework actually affects how officers and directors spend their time, it is very important.

Arguably there is an optimum structure, which is illustrated in Exhibit 4.1. The structure consists of three components:

1. The board of directors adopts policy
2. The finance committee supervises the implementation of policy
3. Employees or outside advisors do the actual work.

Consider the intended application of this structure.

FUNCTION 1: ADOPTING POLICY

The essential first step, adopting a policy, begins at the board level. Only the board is authorized to establish policy; it is uniquely their role. Adopting a policy is also what lawyers might call the *sine qua non* of more effective investment management; that is, it is absolutely essential.

First of all, one cannot delegate authority without a policy. So ACO board members are in fact typical of many boards where there is a strong desire to retain control. They resist adopting policy as that defeats delegation.

But what else can be lost? Accountability. Organizations without investment policies can rarely say anything meaningful about their investment performance. Policy leads to delegation, which in turn leads to accountability. Each is dependent on the previous step.

Consider the expense side of Exhibit 4.1 with which we are probably more familiar. Every year the board establishes a spending policy. We do not usually refer to it as such because the process is so familiar; we call it a budget. When adopting the budget, the board authorizes the organization to spend funds within the prescribed limits for the various budgeted purposes.

After that, the board's direct involvement is very nearly at an end. The board does not subsequently discuss which checks to write or when. The board does not deal with the payroll service or even decide whether to book expenses on a cash or accrual basis. All that is left to others.

Investment policies perform the same role for managing assets that a budget does for managing expenses: they provide a vehicle for delegation of authority. In many organizations the board explicitly delegates authority in

EXHIBIT 4.1. Optimum Structure for Nonprofit Organizations

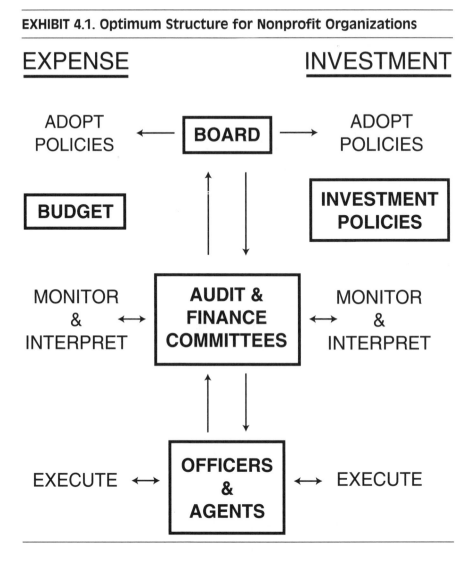

the form of either an audit committee, on the expense side, or a finance (or investment) committee, on the investment side. Forming such committees is the next step.

FUNCTION 2: DEVELOPING ACCEPTABLE COMMITTEE STRUCTURES

There are two types of board-formed committees—those that exercise board authority and those that do not. If a board wishes to delegate some of its actual decision-making authority to a committee, it must do so in accordance with a specific bylaw provision or by formal board resolution. In either event, such a committee must be composed of at least two board members and may not include any nonboard members. In addition, all the actions of such a committee must be in accordance with the same rules that apply to actions of the full board. This includes giving notice of meetings, recording votes, taking formal minutes, and the like.

The board may also form what might be thought of as advisory committees. These may be composed of whomever the board wishes and are not subject to any of the formal requirements which apply to "true" board committees. The important difference is that such advisory committees have no authority to act on behalf of the full board. Rather, the board itself would have to act by resolution or otherwise (e.g., Unanimous Written Consent) to carry out any action recommended by such an advisory committee.

True board committees can be powerful tools. As just noted, a board may delegate actual board authority to such a committee. That allows the committee to take legally binding actions within the scope of their delegated authority in the place of the board. When they do, and assuming they do so properly, board members who are not on that committee are entitled to rely upon the committee's actions. Every state incorporation law allows the creation of board committees to which board authority may be delegated.

Consider again the example of an audit committee. The board has a duty to supervise the budgetary authority of its financial officers and to prudently manage its affairs. But how many board members really know their way around a financial statement? It may in fact be quite a few but it is rarely all. And more to the point, if the board can legally and properly delegate the task of overseeing the budget to only a few of its members, why not do so and save everyone else's time for other things? As the experience of thousands of businesses and charities over the years has shown, using board committees in this manner is a powerful and helpful tool.

FUNCTION 3: THE INVESTMENT OR FINANCE COMMITTEE

The heart of the three-part structure on the investment side of our chart is the investment or finance committee. Why is this so important? First, on many boards there are typically only a few people with significant investment experience. Investing really is a world apart and not necessarily an area in which even very successful business people or professionals (attorneys and CPAs) have significant experience. Even financial officers running operations involving hundreds of millions of dollars do not necessarily consider investment expertise part of their background or training.

For good financial reporting and effective discussion to occur between the supervisors and the practitioners, the greater the expertise of everyone involved the better. In addition, the closer the levels of expertise between the supervisors and those they have hired, the more easily the conversations flow. It is difficult for an investment advisor to report to a group if some members do not understand basic investment concepts, such as the difference between a stock and a bond, while others are wondering why the allocation to emerging markets isn't greater. In such meetings, either the investment-savvy folks talk among themselves (over the heads of the others) or the entire conversation is reduced to the lowest common denominator. Both represent a disservice to the organization. Using an investment committee reduces or eliminates these problems.

It also helps to remember that when a board retains investment authority it also retains investment liability. The worst of all possible worlds is illustrated by the ACO example at the beginning of the chapter. The board's partial delegation creates a group they cannot effectively supervise, and yet leaves the board fully liable for their actions. Even the regular meetings of an investment committee, typically quarterly, are not an activity that lends itself to large groups. Here, more than in any other area of corporate governance, forming a true board committee and thereby allowing delegation to a smaller group of the most qualified board members is an essential step.

THE SUPERVISORY ROLE OF THE FINANCE COMMITTEE

The existence of a finance committee is also important because it enables true supervision over those doing the work. The finance committee itself should not do the actual investing any more than the board should. If that happens, as in the ACO example above, then the organization is back to square one. Either the whole board must supervise the finance committee members, or there is no supervision at all—the latter is the more common result.

The mere fact that any kind of serious oversight might result in criticism of a fellow board member will frequently be enough to dissuade oversight in the first instance. Most people who serve on boards consider their fellow directors to be colleagues, business contacts, and future friends. The last thing they want to do is criticize another board member in front of the group.

Therefore, in establishing the investment or finance committee it is important to make clear that they are intended to be the active supervisors, not the actual implementers, of investment decisions. Such supervision is a big enough job. Recall the provisions on delegating investment responsibility in the UPIA (Chapter 2). This was a three-step process that required diligence in selecting investment advisors, clear communication of goals and objectives, and regular oversight of the outside service providers. That is the substantial job that the investment committee is to perform.

Organizing Investment Systems

The actual supervision of investment policies begins when the policies are adopted by the board and the investment committee is authorized. At that point, the committee begins its work of supervising those actually doing the investing. In virtually all organizations this work will be directed to varying degrees by the chief financial officer. This is a very important position.

The final box on the bottom of the organizational chart in Exhibit 4.1 lists "officers and agents" jointly as those who actually execute investment strategy. They are listed together on purpose as there is really very little functional difference between the two from an investment perspective. Work performed by staff people should be supervised and reviewed in exactly the same way and to the same extent as that performed by outside advisors.

There are at least two reasons for this. First, one cannot, as a practical matter, hire competent investment professionals in-house without spending many times the cost of outside help. As a small operation, even the most expensive outside investment management rarely costs more than 1.5 percent per million dollars, not counting trading costs and custodial expenses, which the organization will incur no matter who is selecting securities. That is only $15,000 per million dollars per year, and the percentage declines as amounts increase. Even when an organization is spending 1 percent on $10,000,000, how much help—with staff support, research services, computers, and the like—can you hire for $100,000? Not much.

By the time the organization has the hundreds of millions of dollars really needed to manage in-house, typically (but not always) the desire for in-house management is gone. By that time the organization has a full-time consultant under contract and is allocating assets across nine different classes, each of which is managed by a firm that specializes in that area. So you could do it yourself, but not as elegantly nor, in all likelihood, as well.

Secondly, even those areas of investment management that an internal staff can run on its own should be supervised in exactly the same manner as one would supervise outside providers. This will include: (1) comparing what the in-house staff can do to what is available in the market; (2) clearly communicating investment responsibilities and expectations; and, (3) reviewing and supervising their work. Everyone does their best when they know people are watching. Your staff is no different. Hold them to the same standards that you would outsiders, and you will likely get equally good results.

Conclusion

The purpose of the structure outlined in Exhibit 4.1 is to provide clear direction, accountability, and freedom to operate for those to whom authority is delegated. This organizational structure provides a firm foundation upon which policies are successfully implemented. While not as integrally important as the policies themselves, such a structure can determine success.

Getting Started

The hardest part of any job is getting started. Organizations that want to do a better job managing their funds frequently stall at the very beginning. They do not adopt, let alone implement, formal investment policies, because the burden of getting started is too great. For many such organizations, there is an understandable hesitancy to begin contacting potential investment advisors or other professionals before they are clear, in their own minds, what they have to manage or are hoping to achieve.

The purpose of this chapter is to help organizations set those fears aside and start down the investment management road. The principal tool in this effort is an investment policy self-assessment form designed to assist organizations in conducting an investment policy "audit" of your organization, as a precursor to the implementation of investment policies.[1] The material here is an introduction to and extended commentary on the self-assessment form presented in Appendix D.

The self-assessment exercise is designed to help an organization answer the seminal questions. Those questions include the following:

1. What assets do we have to manage?
2. What is the status of our organization's fund-raising efforts?
3. What are the current attitudes of our board toward investment risk?
4. How have we been managing our funds up to this point?
5. Who has been helping us in this effort?

The answers to these questions circumscribe our investment world. As such they help identify the task, the context in which it exists, and the resources presently available to the effort. Surprisingly, many organizations start on down the investment management path with only the vaguest notions of these things.

---

[1] The internal study or review that you will be conducting is not, of course, an actual audit. There is no independent auditor, any report you might produce will not be certified, and there is no need for the same level of accuracy or balancing of books that an audit requires. We are trying to get the big picture.

In this context, we need to know what assets we have to manage and the character of those assets, but exact amounts are unnecessary. For investment management purposes, there is no practical difference between an endowment fund with $20 million and endowment fund with $21 million. While the idea of a million dollar discrepancy in audited financial statements would be enough to make most CPAs catatonic, for our purposes it is inconsequential. Policies, procedures, and goals and objectives that we would establish for a $21 million portfolio would be exactly the same as those for a $20 million portfolio.

At the ACO . . .

"I DON'T KNOW"

The ACO both currently and historically maintains its operating reserves in a money market deposit account at the bank. They are allowed to make so many transfers per quarter between their checking account and the money market account, which the treasurer typically does on an ad hoc basis. When the balance in the checking account seems high, the treasurer moves funds to the money market. When it seems low, he moves some back. The treasurer believes that the incremental interest earned on the money market account covers most of the account charges the bank imposes on the checking account.

At a recent meeting, one of the board members asked, "Why don't we invest our reserve funds in treasuries and earn more interest?" The treasurer answered that he did not think that the average balances justified the effort. The board member then asked, "What are the average balances?"

"I don't know."

Categories of Investable Funds

"What assets do we have to manage?" should be the first question any organization considering the adoption of investment policies asks. While there are probably as many fund names as there are organizations, manageable nonprofit assets fall broadly into five categories:

1. Operating reserves
2. Capital reserves
3. Retirement funds
4. Planned gift assets
5. Permanent funds.

Each category of funds has its own sources and characteristics.

OPERATING RESERVES

Operating reserves can be anything from a positive checking account balance to a segregated pot of money. However labeled and wherever invested, operating reserves have two important characteristics. First, they are funds available to pay the organization's day-to-day expenses and as such are usually unrestricted in an accounting sense. If there are restrictions, then even if the treasurer or the board is thinking of using such funds for operating expenses, there is a barrier to doing so that removes the funds from the operating reserves category. Second, because these funds may be needed for short-term expenditures, they should not be invested in equities or in any other investment with a substantial risk of fluctuation in principal value.

CAPITAL RESERVES

One of the most common and yet least optimized forms of reserves at charitable organizations is capital reserves. These are funds the organization holds in anticipation of constructing or renovating a building. A great many nonprofits of every stripe have at least some funds in this category. They are the least optimized because they are frequently not invested well. Let's return to an ACO Board meeting for a minute to see why.

It is two hours into the quarterly meeting, and the board is halfway through old business. All of the nonretired board members are reevaluating their commitment to the board at this point by asking themselves if there is enough good public relations and resume value to justify wasting a day like this.

Of the retired members, one is telling himself that he is only losing one day of golf, and the other is in hog heaven, having nothing else to do. He has been leading the conversations up until now. At this point the senior development officer gives a report on the campaign for a new residential facility: "As you know, we are now in the second year of our $3.5 million dollar campaign, which will enable us to purchase and renovate the apartment house on South Main. The campaign is going very well. We have had the lead gift of $750,000 in-house for nearly a year, which has really given a boost to the entire effort. Since that time we raised an additional $125,000, and we have tentative commitments for at least that much more. I don't see any reason why we can't break ground in the next six to nine months. Are there any questions?"

In other words, the entire campaign is completely stalled! Although the development officer received one large gift to start the campaign, and has picked up a few respectable donations and some promises in the succeeding year, he offers no plans for raising the last $2.5 million for the building.

What is the true time frame for investing the $875,000 that is in the door? Well, it sure is not six months, which is how the funds are being invested presently—rolling six-month CDs at the bank. The true time frame is probably five years and maybe longer. Not quite long enough perhaps for an allocation to equities, depending on the mettle of the board, but certainly long enough to improve upon rolling six-month CDs.

This is a very common situation. Capital campaigns invariably take longer than everyone expects. In the meantime, the initial funds are invested on a short-term basis in the expectation that ground breaking will occur as originally planned.

RETIREMENT FUNDS

The two broad categories of funds set aside for the retirement of employees are pension plans and profit-sharing plans. Until recently, profit-sharing plans did not exist in the nonprofit community. As of 1996, charitable organizations are permitted to establish 401(k) plans, which the for-profit world considers a type of profit-sharing plan.

Some charitable organizations maintain what are best described as quasi-retirement plans. They include any arrangement whereby the organization reserves sums for retirement from an employee's compensation. Due to the lack of regulation under which most of these quasi-plans operate, it is impossible to categorize them with any specificity in terms of investment time frames, tax characteristics, investment restrictions, or the like. These things will vary from fund to fund. Therefore, we will simply toss these quasi-retirement funds into the general pension and retirement plan pot on the assumption that many of the same concerns will exist for these funds.

In true pension plans, it is reasonably easy to determine the anticipated term of the funds and future cash flow requirements. The calculations are based on the anticipated retirement ages of the participants at which time they will either withdraw their funds entirely or annunitize them into an income stream according to the plan's provisions. Most organizations that maintain true pension plans are large enough to hire pension plan administrators who provide calculations of the organization's future liabilities. Armed with such a liability study the organization can set policy appropriately for these funds.

With 403(b) and 401(k) plans, the organization is usually not involved in the investment process. Rather, there is a range of permitted investments provided by the plan sponsor. At one time, this area was almost "owned" by major insurance companies. Increasingly, however, securities brokers, mutual-fund sponsors and others have offered such plans with a full range of investment options.

PLANNED-GIFT ASSETS

A variety of planned-gift assets cause a charitable organization to have funds under management. The most common are charitable remainder trusts, gift annuities, and pooled income funds. The determination of the time horizons of such funds and the range of permitted investments for these instruments is so complicated—and so potentially rewarding—that a considerable portion of Chapter 8 concerns this topic.

PERMANENT FUNDS

The final category is considered permanent funds. They are often referred to as endowments but many other terms, including trust funds, are also used. The terminology confusion results from the fact that an endowment is not a defined legal entity like a partnership, trust, or corporation. In the case of partnerships and corporations, uniform acts adopted by all 50 states define the characteristics of each. Because there is no such body of defining law for an endowment, the exact character of each can vary from fund to fund even within a single charitable organization.

There is, however, growing language consistency in the use of the terms *endowment* and *quasi-endowment*. Generally speaking, an endowment refers to funds that are subject to either donor-imposed or an institutionally-imposed restrictions on the invasion of principal, which cannot be evaded merely by board action. A quasi-endowment is any fund treated as an endowment whose restrictions are temporary or terminable. In both cases, the funds are typically considered permanent or long-term, and therefore boards can make investment decisions and establish asset allocation policies from that perspective.

Conducting an Investment Policy Audit

One of the most important steps a charitable organization can take in developing appropriate investment policies is to ask, "What assets do we have to manage?" The task of identifying manageable assets is more complicated than one might suppose. It is not just a matter of identifying amounts of money. Rather, the organization needs to know the investment management characteristics of that money. Such characteristics include the purpose for which the money is being maintained, the length of time for which it will be held, the amount of income or distributions required, the amount of principal risk that can be taken, the tax character of the fund, and the history of the fund. Collectively, these factors determine what investments are appropriate for each fund. Consequently, each factor must be understood before one can craft and implement appropriate investment policies.

Surprisingly, even large organizations frequently do not know either the extent or the character of the funds under their care. One agency with which I worked, for example, had operating reserves which fluctuated by millions of dollars but never dropped below $4 million. Because they were unaware of that fact, however, the funds were always invested on a much shorter term basis than was necessary.

Even more commonly, organizations with substantial planned gift assets are surprised by the extent of these holdings. Having once fallen into the habit of managing these funds trust by trust, they rarely step back and consider the whole. So while they "know" the amount, they do not know the amount in a manner that permits them to consider managing these funds in the aggregate.

And so it goes. Of all the thoughts and suggestions contained in this book, the idea of completing the questionnaire contained in Appendix D entitled "Internal Self-Guided Investment Management Assessment Form" may be the most valuable. The remainder of this chapter consists of a detailed explanation of the use of this form.

Who Conducts the Study?

Most of the time, the chief financial officer will be primarily responsible for conducting this review. That does not mean that she should do all the work. Rather, she is a coordinator of the overall process and, most important, a recruiter of the other participants.

The investment assessment is divided into five sections:

    I.   General information
    II. Development (fund-raising) information
    III. Investment accounting, gift administration, and reporting
    IV. Investment philosophy and objectives
    V. Fund information.

Each section can be completed separately by one or more individuals, depending on the organization's structure and size. The form itself calls for those sections to be completed by the executive director (I), the senior development officer (II), the CFO or treasurer (III), the investment policy committee or an appropriate group of board members (IV) and, finally, the CFO again for part V. In very large organizations with multiple staff in development and finance, others in addition to the senior officers just mentioned may well be involved.

The inclusion of the development staff is intentional. A common problem in the nonprofit community is the great information gulf that exists between development officers who are charged with bringing the gifts in the door and financial officers who are responsible for administering the gifts once they arrive. Frequently, the right hand does not know what the left hand is doing. This expresses itself in many ways, all of which are bad.

One of the more common expressions of this problem is an organization with buckets full of problem trusts. The trusts might be net income trusts with very high pay-out ratios—8, 9, 10 percent or more. The trusts might be very small, some in the $5,000 or $10,000 range. Or, the trusts might be funded with real estate or other difficult-to-sell assets. In each case, there is a "gift" that someone made to the organization, but in each case the organization is not making money and may even be losing money when administrative costs are considered. This happens in part because the development officers and the financial officers are not pulling on the same oar.

Therefore, it is very important to include the development officers in the process of identifying investment management assets and of crafting the resulting investment policies. There are a number of questions that they are uniquely capable of answering and that bear on both the creation and implementation of investment policies. In addition, if their contribution is solicited, accepted, and valued, they will tend to think well of the results they helped create. This is a situation in which the process is as important as the outcome. The goal is to build support for investment policies from the beginning and to share the results with everyone who participates.

There is a footer on each page that calls for the name of the person who completed the page and the date the page was completed. This anticipates the involvement of many people who are perhaps working at different times. The footer will quickly tell all involved the source and timeliness of the information (see Exhibit 5.2).

Part I: General Information

The information on the first page will give all those involved a good feel for the general operation of the organization. Some of the questions are obvious. Others may take a little digging. What is certain is that just this information—in one place and made available for the use of those who will create investment policies and manage the funds—is a more complete description of a nonprofit organization than has ever been handed to me in an initial meeting with a prospective client. You are starting down the path of being prepared and therefore helpful to your outside service providers. This will save time and money and ultimately produce better results.

The ten questions in Part 1 are intended to identify quickly the nature of the organization and some of its salient features. The form purposely calls for completion by the executive director to involve him or her in the process. The first question asks for the name of the organization (see Exhibit 5.1 for questions 1–4). Question 2 calls for identifying the senior staff members and their phone numbers. If there is no investment policy committee, substitute the name and phone number of the board member most involved in overseeing finances. The reason for names and phones numbers is to create a working document that all those involved in the process can use for their own purposes and for follow-up tasks required to create and implement your investment policies.

Question 3 identifies the type of organization and question 4, its business structure. There are many forms of business; only the most common are identified. For nonprofit corporations in California, the answer may be public benefit, mutual benefit, or religious. Because slightly different code sections and rules apply to each, this information might be important for your subsequent work.

Questions 5 through 10 are intended to provide an overview of the organization by asking for a copy of the mission statement, the size of the annual budget with financial statements, information about the organization's origin, and the state of incorporation (see Exhibit 5.2 for questions 5–10). Since most laws that apply to for-profit and nonprofit organizations are enacted at the state level, the state of incorporation and of corporate residency (usually the headquarters) is significant. Typically, the laws of the state of incor-

EXHIBIT 5.1. Assessment Form, Part I, 1–4

Part I: General Information
(This portion is to be completed by the Executive Director)

1. **Institution:** _____

2. **Senior Staff:**   **Name**   **Phone**

Executive Director _____   _____

Senior Devel. Off.   _____   _____

CFO   _____   _____

Board Chairman   _____   _____

Invest. Comm. Ch. _____   _____

3. **Type of Institution:**   School or College   Retirement Home
                                        Hospital   Church
                                        Pension Plan   Other Religious Organization
                                        Public Foundation   Social Service Agency
                                        Private Foundation   Other Public Charity

4. **Business Structure:**   Unincorporated Nonprofit Association

                                       Nonprofit Corporation (Type) _____

                                       Limited Liability Company (Type) _____

                                       Other _____

poration will control most corporate actions—board meetings, mandatory officers, and the like—but any state that has a substantial contact with the organization may attempt to assert jurisdiction. Most states also apply their laws to corporations doing business in the state when necessary to protect the residents of that state.

Consequently, these questions (while not exhaustive by any means), are intended to give your advisors some preliminary information on who among the states is most likely to regulate investment matters. Here, as in many places in this form, specific problems may at some point need more specific answers than this form is intended to provide. The goal is to get the big picture first and deal with specific problems later.

Part II: Development (Fund-Raising) Information

Part II is to be completed by the senior development officer. The purpose of this section is threefold:

1. Identify the current status and emphasis of the development program

EXHIBIT 5.2. Assessment Form, Part I, 5–10

5. Mission Statement: (Attach copy or brief narrative description)

6. Approximate Annual Budget: $_____
(For reference purposes, please attach a copy of your most recent financial statements)

7. Origins: Founded By: _____   Date: _____

Founded in (City, State & Country) _____

8. Incorporation: State: _____   Date: _____

9. Address of Corporate Headquarters: _____

10. Geographic Service Area: (Describe and also list states in which you have at

least one full-time employee and a physical location) _____

This Page Completed By (Name)	Date Completed

2. Articulate the program's future direction
3. Create a basis upon which to identify those places where the development officer's perception differs from that of the administrative staff.

The first question focuses on the staffing of full-time professionals and support personnel (see Exhibit 5.3 for questions 1–4). This question also asks the development officer to identify others who spend some of their time in fund raising and to estimate the percentage of each person's time so spent. The concern that organizations raise money "efficiently" and thereby deliver dollars raised to the actual projects for which they are solicited has led to inaccurate accounting of the true costs of fund raising. Many organizations do not, for example, classify the executive director's salary or employment-related costs as fund-raising expenses. Yet in any successful charitable organization, the executive director, chief executive officer, or president is almost always regularly and intimately involved in fund raising. While it may be good press to claim that you only spend 3 percent of total revenues on fund raising, it is not helpful in the effort to gauge the true commitment of the organization's resources to that effort.

Questions 3 and 4 are intended to identify the age of the program, since that could be a clue to judging its effectiveness. A young program with a lot of money is clearly doing something right. A 50-year-old program with

EXHIBIT 5.3. Assessment Form, Part II, 1–4

Part II: Development (Fund-Raising) Information
(This portion is to be completed by the Senior Development Officer)

1. Current staffing of development program:

Full-Time Development Staff	Number of Professionals	Number of Support Staff
Other Staff (Names) who spend some time in Development	**Regular Position**	**% of Time Spent in Development**

2. What percentage of your organization's total income comes from donations (gifts as opposed to fees for services, sales of products, etc.)? _____

3. When did you start a full-time fund-raising program? _____

4. When did you start soliciting and/or accepting planned gifts? _____

no endowment, three small trusts, and a shortfall in the annual campaign is another story.

Question 5 focuses on the sources of gift income (see Exhibit 5.4). Some development officers will be able to answer question 5 with specificity but many will not. For those who cannot, the three-year time frame in questions 5 and 6 is arbitrary. It is a way of saying "recently," since the development officer's best guess of longer-term averages is likely to be more accurate than a more focused question such as "the last fiscal year." Obviously, the more disciplined programs will have this information at hand.[2]

Question 6 moves from documenting the current status of the program to looking forward to the development office's goals for the program (see Exhibit 5.5). This is important information from an investment management and administrative standpoint. An organization that emphasizes planned giving, for example, needs much greater administrative and investment management muscle than does one that intends to rely solely on cash gifts and bequests. Question 5 sets up question 6—by providing a basis on which

---

[2] The form does not deal with pledges or other expectancies on the theory that such funds are not manageable until received. For organizations with substantial pledges, however, the information may be important and can be added to the form.

EXHIBIT 5.4. Assessment Form, Part II, 5

5. Please indicate the composition of gift income by category over the last 3 years.

	Average Annual %, past 3 years	Highest Annual % in last 3 years	Lowest Annual % in last 3 years
Individual Contributions			
Corporate Gifts			
Grants			
Bequests			
Lifetime Planned Gifts			
Special Events			
Gifts in kind; sponsorships			
Other			

EXHIBIT 5.5. Assessment Form, Part II, 6

6. Of the categories listed in the above table, which do you believe are most likely to increase or decrease as a percentage of total annual gift income over the next 3 years?

Most likely to increase   _____   _____   _____

Most likely to decrease   _____   _____   _____

to gauge the likelihood or probable accuracy of the development officer's go-forward estimates with a solid sense of development history.

Question 7 seeks to determine the intended emphasis of the development program for the coming year (see Exhibit 5.6). By asking the development officer to rank the priorities for different types of fund-raising activities and to indicate the rough percentage of time to be spent on each, one should get a good idea of what matters most.

Question 8 focuses a bit more on planned gifts and is another way of gauging the status and maturity of the development program (see Exhibit 5.7). The first column asks if the organization accepts standard planned gift instruments. The second and third columns address gift acceptance policies. If the answers to this question indicate that the program accepts all these instruments but does not have established minimum ages or minimum dollar amounts, that may be an indication of a young and relatively unsophisticated program. Conversely, answers that indicate relatively high ages in each category and large dollar amounts suggest a more mature program.

Question 9 is a chance for the development officer to say anything else

EXHIBIT 5.6. Assessment Form, Part II, 7

7. Please rank each of the following areas to indicate your fund-raising priorities in terms of the allocation of development staff time for the coming year.

Fund-Raising Categories	Rank (1st–5th)	Allocable % of Staff Time
Current Annual Giving		
Planned (Deferred) Giving		
Capital Campaign		
Events; Sponsorships		
Corp./Foundation Grants		

EXHIBIT 5.7. Assessment Form, Part II, 8

8. What are the types, ages, and minimum dollar amounts of the deferred gifts and trusts which your organization accepts?

	Accepted (Y/N)	Minimum Age	Minimum $ Amount
Gift Annuities			
Charitable Remainder Trusts			
Charitable Lead Trusts			
Pooled-Income Fund			
Donor-Advised Fund			
Life Interest Agreements in Real Property			
Life Insurance			
Other			

he or she thinks is important (see Exhibit 5.8). Again, keep in mind that the goal is to encourage the development officer to "buy into" the need to create and implement investment policies. The opportunity for unstructured comments is part of that process.

The purpose of asking the development staff to complete the table in question 10 is to identify existing outside resources (see Exhibit 5.9). Those people and organizations the operation relies on are indeed resources. This table will be repeated later in the questionnaire for other officers or groups within the organization because it is not uncommon for different staff members to use different service providers. If that is the case, you need to know them all.

EXHIBIT 5.8. Assessment Form, Part II, 9

9. Please briefly describe the additional staff support, funding, administrative support, or other assistance, if any, that you believe would permit you to more effectively raise funds for your organization over the next 3 years.

_____

_____

_____

_____

_____

_____

Part III: Investment Accounting, Gift Administration, and Reporting

This section is to be completed by the chief financial officer or a member of his or her staff. While accountants usually strive for precision when it comes to numbers, the concern for now is with getting the big picture. Many organizations have discovered, for example, that their charitable remainder trusts cannot be administered in a cost-effective manner by an institutional trustee on a free-standing basis. The trusts are usually too small to generate an adequate fee for a trust company. But if an organization has endowment funds or gift annuity reserves, it is often possible to make a package deal. The institutional trustee agrees to administer the trusts at what to them is a money-losing price, in exchange for being allowed to also manage other assets. An organization cannot think about making such deals unless it knows what assets it has under management. With the big-picture goals in mind, I would encourage the financial officer to relax and enjoy working on something where close is good enough. When precision is needed, you can get it later (see Exhibit 5.10 for question 1).

As a brief aside, this questionnaire may not be extensive enough for some organizations as it focuses heavily on fund-raising assets. Certain types of retirement homes, for example, maintain substantial reserves that are tied directly to the core business of providing lifetime care to residents. Other organizations have benefited from state-guaranteed bond financing and must, as a result, maintain substantial "sinking funds" with which they will eventually repay their bonded indebtedness. In all such cases, the particular funds are beyond the scope of a current fund-raising focus and may, in a sense, be beyond the scope of our thinking when it comes to the issues we are discussing.

It is common, in my experience, for such specialized funds to be professionally managed already under strict and often times legally mandated

EXHIBIT 5.9. Assessment Form, Part II, 10

10. Which of the following outside service providers do you currently use in development?

	Organization	Key Contact	First Service (Date)	Address (City, State)	Phone
Fund-Raising Consultants					
Collateral Material Services					
Securities Broker/Consultant					
Bank or Trust Company					
Investment Advisor					
CPA					
Attorney					
Insurance Agent or CFP					
Other					

EXHIBIT 5.10. Assessment Form, Part III, 1

Part III: Investment Accounting, Gift Administration and Reporting
(This portion is to be completed by the Chief Financial Officer.)

1. What planned gifts, endowments, or other funds does your organization currently have?

Type	No. of gifts	Total Dollar	Median Size	Oldest Donor	Youngest Donor	Largest Gift—$	Smallest Gift—$
Gift Annuities							
Pooled-Income Funds							
Remainder Trusts							
Revocable Trusts							
Operating Reserves							
Endowments							
Retirement Plans							
Capital Campaign Funds							
Other							

guidelines. Consequently, there is some tendency for boards to put those funds almost beyond the range of *their* thinking even though, frequently, the organization remains in control of the funds and of their investment management. To the extent that your organization has such specialized funds, include them on the form. Even if the organization treats those funds as "not theirs," they must still be subject to investment policies. In addition, allowing the right organization to manage such funds—even within the legally directed guidelines—might be the key to solving all kinds of other investment management and gift administration problems.

The purpose of question 2 is to identify the cost of administering your planned gift and other investment management assets (see Exhibit 5.11). The table in question 2 can be replicated and used for accounting costs, tax returns, and investment management costs. I suggest this because there is so much information in each category that it would be difficult and confusing to lump them together. In all these areas, there may be a mix of staff people and outside service providers. The middle column of question 2 is intended to identify who is doing the work. For internal costs, the person completing this form should guess what percentage of the total accounting department budget is consumed by these expenses.

Here the questionnaire may be too detailed. It may not always be necessary or helpful, for example, to allocate your accurate accounting department budgetary number between the categories of gift instruments. Further,

EXHIBIT 5.11. Assessment Form, Part III, 2

2. How much do you spend administering planned gifts, endowments, or other reserves in each of the following categories: Accounting, Tax Returns, and Investment Management?

	$ Cost	Inside or Out	Service Provider or System Used
Gift Annuities			
Pooled-Income Funds			
Remainder Trusts			
Revocable Trusts			
Operating Reserves			
Endowments			
Retirement Plans			
Capital Campaign Funds			
Other			

if the organization is large enough to have a trust administration department that does all the accounting work, then one can tell from the trust department's annual budget what this administration costs. Completing one version of this form for the tax returns and another for investment management would, when added to the administrative budget, give the total cost.

The purpose of the third question is to identify who is actually paying the freight for these administrative services (tax, accounting, and investment management). With a possible mix of employees and outside service providers and the ability to allocate expenses of some trusts to either income or principal, the picture of who is paying for the universe of investment asset administrative expenses can be complex. It is worth identifying where these expenses are being charged (see Exhibit 5.12).

There is a tremendous potential benefit (unused by a great many nonprofits) in the form of potential reimbursements or allocation of expenses to gift instruments. In the absence of such allocations, the charitable organization frequently ends up bearing all of the costs of planned gift administration as a direct, budgeted expense. Costs and fees that in truth ought to be shared by both income and remainder beneficiaries end up being allocated, by default, entirely against the ultimate charitable gift. There is potentially an opportunity to change the way the organization does business and allocate some of those costs to others in the future. Before you can even think about that, however, you must first know what costs you are incurring and who is paying them now.

EXHIBIT 5.12. Assessment Form, Part III, 3

3. How do you allocate administrative expenses for each of the following investment instruments (express on a percentage basis)?

	Operating Budget	Charged to Trust or Fund	Comments
Gift Annuities			
Pooled-Income Funds			
Remainder Trusts			
Revocable Trusts			
Operating Reserves			
Endowments			
Retirement Plans			
Capital Campaign Funds			
Other			

Finally, take some time to understand what investment management expenses you are currently paying. Many people believe that by investing in no-load mutual funds, they avoid all investment management expenses. That is simply incorrect. The average no-load equity fund's annual internal fees and expenses are about 1.25 percent. While mutual funds are tremendously helpful instruments in many investment management situations, as dollar amounts increase—and especially as the size of discrete pieces increases—mutual funds' internal fees become more expensive than direct investment management. That difference can be a lost resource to your organization.

Question 4 focuses on the administration of planned gifts and other assets (see Exhibit 5.13). For most, some form of reporting and income distributions to donors is required. This table will give you a picture of how frequently distributions are being made, who is serving as trustee, and the level of reporting. In evaluating the magnitude of the task of managing these assets, this information is important.

Question 5 is intended to solicit the CFO's view of investment policies (see Exhibit 5.14). It is merely a precursor to the more extensive questions directed at the investment policy committee later.

Questions 6 and 7 are checklists designed to identify current service providers and internal officers (see Exhibit 5.15 for question 6 and Exhibit 5.16 for questions 7 and 8). Question 8 attempts to identify which, if any, of your outside service providers is helpful in managing the peripheral problems associated with running a planned giving program. Sometimes the answers to this question are helpful and other times the question merely serves to

EXHIBIT 5.13. Assessment Form, Part III, 4

4. For each of the following instruments, how frequently do you make income distributions and send reports? Who serves as trustee on the trusts and what information do you provide when reporting?

Key: Frequency: Q = quarterly, M = Monthly, A = Annual;
Reports: 1099, K-1, IP (Investment Performance)

	Trustee	Income Distributions Frequency	Reports—Frequency and Content
Gift Annuities			
Pooled-Income Funds			
Remainder Trusts			
Revocable Trusts			
Operating Reserves			
Endowments			
Retirement Plans			
Capital Campaign Funds			
Other			

EXHIBIT 5.14. Assessment Form, Part III, 5

5. Do you have established investment policies for your managed funds? (Y/N) _____

Who sets the policies? _____

Are the policies disclosed to your donors? (Y/N) _____

get everyone thinking about new and creative ways to work with outside advisors.

Questions 9 and 10 address gifts of noninvestment assets (see Exhibit 5.17 for questions 9–11). The existence of such gifts usually creates an investment management problem because specialized skills are required to preserve, protect, and obtain value from these assets.

The last question (11), again, is an opportunity for open-ended and unstructured comments.

Part IV: Investment Philosophy and Objectives

This section is intended to be completed by the investment policy committee of the board, if there is one. It is probably best if the chief financial officer

EXHIBIT 5.15. Assessment Form, Part III, 6

6. Which outside service providers do you currently use in administering your planned-gift and investment management assets?

	Organization	Key Contact	First Service (Date)	Address (City, State)	Phone
A) Securities Broker/Consultant					
B) Bank or Trust Company					
C) Investment Advisor					
D) CPA					
E) Attorney					
F) Insurance Agent or CFP					
G) Other					
H) Other					
Other					

EXHIBIT 5.16. Assessment Form, Part III, 7 and 8

7. Who in your organization is responsible for supervising each of the following areas?

	Name	**Phone**
Trust Administration		
Investment Management		
Donor Reporting		
Financial Accounting		
Regulatory Compliance		
Tax Compliance		

8. Please indicate which of the service providers, if any, listed in question 6, above, assist you in the following areas. Write the letter for each provider (see #6) in the space provided.

Communicating investment options to prospective donors? _____

Establishing investment objectives and policies? _____

Constructing planned-giving presentations for major donors? _____

Matching return expectations to spending needs and obligations? _____

Reporting investment results to donors and management? _____

Providing information for trustee decisions on risk/return relationships, asset allocation, and other similar issues? _____

Analyzing investment performance for the benefit of donors and management? _____

Segregating charitable remainder trust funds for independent management based on category of trust (e.g., Income Only, Income Only with Makeup, 5%, 8%, etc.)? _____

EXHIBIT 5.17. Assessment Form, Part III, 9–11

9. Do you accept gifts of illiquid assets, such as real estate and collectibles? _____

10. Who helps with the management and/or liquidation of such assets?

11. What are the most pressing problems you face in the areas of trust administration, investment management, or planned-gift administration?

or the executive director meets with the committee to elicit their responses. In the absence of such a committee, the form could be completed by those board members who are most involved in the organization's financial matters.

The purpose of these questions is to identify the attitudes of the board members toward investment goals and objectives, risk, and delegation. This information, though necessarily somewhat vague, is nonetheless essential. If, for example, you advise the board that the best approach to managing the endowment fund is to create a multiclass asset allocation model optimized on the basis of 10-year historic returns for the various classes after adjusting return expectations for the current interest rate environment, and the board responds by asking if that would be as "safe" as a CD at the bank, then you are dead in the water. The proposed "ideal" solution is hopelessly beyond the level of sophistication and risk tolerance of the board. While these attitudes can and will change, particularly with a conscious effort at educating the board, there is no point in attempting elaborate investment strategies in the meantime. Understanding current attitudes and beliefs is critical background information.

GOALS AND OBJECTIVES

Broadly speaking, there are three ways in which goals and objectives are described for investment policies. Each way is reflected in the four questions under this subheading (see Exhibit 5.18). The first characterizes the goals and objectives in terms of either growth of the portfolio's value or the generation of maximum current income on a continuum from one end of that spectrum to the other. The choices in question 1 show the characterizations and the continuum.

The second method (question 2) is to state goals and objectives in terms of an absolute return on either a gross or a net of inflation basis. The third approach (question 3) is to state investment goals and objectives on the basis of performance relative to the broad market, usually as measured by an index such as the S&P 500. This is the direction in which most professional investment management has been moving in recent years.

The movement toward relative standards is occurring because managers are recognizing their inability to guarantee a particular level of absolute performance if that level is not supported by the markets in which they are invested. Part of the movement toward relative standards is therefore occuring not because it is the best way to measure portfolio performance but because it is easier for those charged with managing the funds. Their goal is to stay within a foot of the market and hopefully a foot on the high end of the average. That does not necessarily mean, however, that the board is ready to embrace that standard for its funds or even that relative standards are appropriate standards for all of the funds an organization maintains.

EXHIBIT 5.18. Assessment Form, Part IV, 1–4

Part IV: Investment Philosophy and Objectives

(To be answered by the Investment Committee of the Board or by the full Board if there is no committee. For those organizations that maintain multiple funds, these questions should be answered with regard to the endowment or other perpetual or long-term funds.)

Goals and Objectives

1. How would you categorize your overall investment objectives? Choose one.

   _____ Growth—maximum growth of capital with little or no income consideration

   _____ Growth with income—primarily capital growth with some focus on income

   _____ Balanced—equal emphasis on capital growth and income

   _____ Income oriented—primary emphasis on income

   _____ Capital preservation—preserve original value regardless of income or growth

2. What average annual "absolute" rate of return, if any (as opposed to a return "relative" to a market index) do you consider appropriate for long-term investments?

   _____ % per year   _____ % per year above inflation (CPI)

   _____ Prefer a relative standard

3. Relative to popular stock market indexes (such as the S&P 500), rank your preferences for portfolio performance; 1 is your strongest preference and 5 is what you least prefer.

   _____ Outperform the market in UP market years

   _____ Decline less than the market in DOWN market years

   _____ Outperform the market on average over an extended period, without regard to individual years

   _____ Match market performance over an extended period

   _____ Ignore relative performance and focus solely on the absolute return goal(s) identified in question 2, above.

4. Please rank your preference for the following investment performance reporting options from 1 to 5, with 1 being your strongest preference.

   _____ Measuring current return or yield relative to required distributions

   _____ Comparing account returns to an "absolute" percent return target

   _____ "Relative" comparison (comparing the account returns to various market indexes)

   _____ Comparing to a "real" return (i.e., exceeds the inflation factor by X%)

   _____ Using "absolute" and "relative" total return measures without regard to yield.

The fourth question in this section ties performance reporting to the different ways of stating goals and objectives. It is intentionally repetitive. The board is getting a second chance to express their preferences.

In that same spirit, the fifth and final question is an opportunity for the board to describe specific return requirements or other concerns in their own words (see Exhibit 5.19). When I have conducted surveys like this, I have frequently found that the canned questions missed the mark. By the time we get to the open-ended questions, however, the canned questions have stirred the pot of the interviewee's thinking. I then end up flipping the page and taking notes like mad on the back, as the person gives me the best of their then wide-ranging thinking. If you, as a CFO, development officer or key board member "conduct" an interview of your board using this form, you may have similar experiences.

RISK

Questions 6 through 9 pertain to notions of risk (see Exhibit 5.20). Question 6 asks the board to rank risks in order of concern, with the range of choices intended to help characterize the board as safety-conscious or long-term-growth conscious. Questions 7 and 8 focus on the amount of decline in the value of a portfolio that the board could tolerate. The first is expressed in absolute terms and the second in relative terms. The reason to ask both is to develop some sense of whether the board thinks in relative or absolute terms.

The discussion of risk concludes with another open-ended question. All of the earlier comments on the value of interviewing the board apply in spades to any discussion of risk. One almost has to watch for body language and expressions to get a real feel for the intestinal fortitude of the group on whose staying power the success or failure of the investment program may depend. Take your time!

INVESTMENT ADVISOR

The primary focus of the investment advisor questions (10–12) is again to identify existing attitudes, in this case toward delegation (see Exhibit 5.21). Like the two preceding sections, this section concludes with an open-ended

---

EXHIBIT 5.19. Assessment Form, Part IV, 5

---

5. Please describe any specific return requirements or performance-reporting concerns that have not been addressed by the preceding questions.

EXHIBIT 5.20. Assessment Form, Part IV, 6–9

Risk Questions

6. Please rank the following risks in the order of greatest concern (1 being the highest concern, then 2, etc.).

_____ The failure to generate enough current income to cover required distributions

_____ The possibility of not achieving an intended rate of return

_____ Decreasing purchasing power due to inflation

_____ Wide swings in the value of our investments over 3 to 5 years

_____ A large drop in the value of any one or more investments, wholly apart from overall portfolio performance

_____ Other (Please specify) _____

7. What is the maximum loss you could tolerate in your most aggressively invested portfolio over the following time frames?

_____ % per quarter   _____ % in any two-year period

_____ % per year   _____ Other (Please describe) _____

8. Compared to a broad stock market index such as the S&P 500, how much fluctuation can you tolerate in the equity portion of your portfolio in any given year?

_____ Much more fluctuation than the market

_____ Slightly more fluctuation than the market

_____ Approximately the same fluctuation as the market

_____ Slightly less fluctuation than the market

_____ Much less fluctuation than the market

9. Please describe any risk concerns that the preceding questions have not addressed.

_____

_____

_____

question (13) and a table (question 14) for identifying current advisors (see Exhibits 5.22 and 5.23). Here the open-ended question is a bit more directed in an effort to determine what the board thinks is working well and what they are worried about. While their perceptions are not necessarily correct, they are certainly important.

When asking the investment policy committee or the board to complete this table, I would also ask them to complete a second copy, listing people they know who might be helpful advisors but who do not currently have a

EXHIBIT 5.21. Assessment Form, Part IV, 10–12

Investment Advisor Questions

10. Which statement best reflects your opinion as to how managers should implement your investment goals?

_____ We should establish overall objectives for the plan and allow the manager complete discretion regarding implementation.

_____ We should establish asset allocation parameters with the investment manager and then allow the manager discretion in selecting investments within those parameters.

_____ We should establish asset allocation parameters with the investment manager and then actively participate in and/or supervise the day-to-day selection of investments.

11. How do you feel about giving investment discretion to a third-party investment management firm? Choose one.

_____ Very comfortable   _____ Somewhat uncomfortable

_____ Somewhat comfortable   _____ Very uncomfortable

12. Select the statement that best describes how you currently make investment decisions.

_____ We collect and analyze the facts and make decisions on our own.

_____ Others advise us and we make decisions based on their advice.

_____ Our advisors make the decisions.

EXHIBIT 5.22. Assessment Form, Part IV, 13

13. Please briefly list or describe those aspects of your current investment management process that are working well and those which you believe have problems or could be improved. (Examples include performance, performance reporting, asset allocation, etc.)

Working Well: _____

_____

_____

_____

Concerns—May Need Improvement: _____

_____

_____

_____

EXHIBIT 5.23. Assessment Form, Part IV, 14

14. Which of the following outside service providers presently provide your organization with investment management assistance?

	Organization	Key Contact	First Service (Date)	Address (City, State)	Phone
Securities Broker/Consultant					
Bank or Trust Company					
Investment Advisor					
CPA					
Attorney					
Insurance Agent or CFP					
Other					
Other					
Other					

relationship with your organization. When the time comes to hire new advisors, some of these folks will be initial contacts.

Part V: Fund Information

The final portion of the questionnaire is to be completed by the chief financial officer for each fund the organization maintains. If the organization serves as trustee or otherwise administers charitable trusts, it is necessary to complete this information for each trust or, if there are many trusts, for each category of trust.

The first question identifies the general objective of the fund within the income-to-growth continuum used earlier (see Exhibit 5.24 for questions 1 and 2). Question 2 identifies the investment time horizon most appropriate for each portfolio. There can be more science to the question of appropriate time horizons for a portfolio than one might think. For example, some consultants conduct liability studies that attempt to characterize exactly what withdrawals and other distributions can be reasonably anticipated from a particular fund. This can be important and helpful.

If the organization is currently engaged in a capital campaign for a building that one believes will be constructed in six years, the liability for this fund could be described as follows: net additions for each of the first five years with a complete liquidation at the end of the sixth. Therefore, funds contributed in year one have a six-year time horizon, in year two, a five-year time horizon, and so on. If, as is frequently the case, one can earn a significantly greater total return in five- to seven-year government and corporate bonds than in cash, then in the absence of some unusual restriction or special reason to the contrary, it would be sensible to use such investments and not leave the funds in a money market account. Without significant principal risk, one could earn the greater return by investing those funds in a manner appropriate for their likely duration.

Question 3 asks for target rate of return appropriate for each fund (see Exhibit 5.25 for questions 3–5). Information about the target rate of return can be factored into most optimization software where it affects the recommended mix of assets.

Questions 4 and 5 are now familiar efforts to characterize tolerance for risk, in this instance as it applies to each particular fund.

Questions 6 and 7 on the tax status of the fund can also be important for investment management purposes (see Exhibit 5.26 for questions 6 and 7). An investment management approach that minimizes the realization of capital gain can significantly enhance the total returns of a taxable fund on a net after-tax basis. Even in the nonprofit world some funds, such as charitable remainder trusts, are affected by tax consequences.

Question 8 rounds out the picture of particular fund requirements by asking if there is an annual yield requirement and if the fund otherwise

EXHIBIT 5.24. Assessment Form, Part V, 1 and 2

Part V: Fund Information (To be completed by CFO)
Please answer a set of questions for each fund identified in Part II of this questionnaire.

Name of Fund: _____ Type of Fund: _____

1. General Portfolio Objective: (Select one.)

_____ **Capital Preservation**—the preservation of capital with returns exceeding risk-free investments. Accordingly, the risk level should be low with minimal price volatility.

_____ **Income**—modest growth of capital with the generation of income as the primary objective.

_____ **Growth and Income**—primarily oriented toward growth of principal with a minor emphasis on portfolio income. Investments could include equities, debt instruments, and cash or cash equivalents for diversification and risk management.

_____ **Growth**—growth of capital. The portfolio will exhibit increased volatility while expecting to outperform equity indexes over a market cycle.

_____ **Aggressive Growth**—aggressive growth of capital is the primary objective. The portfolio may accept higher volatility associated with aggressive growth while expecting to outperform equity indexes over a market cycle.

2. Investment time horizon most appropriate for this account: (Select one.)

_____ Ten years or more

_____ Five to ten years

_____ Three to five years

_____ Less than three years

---

anticipates contributions or withdrawals (see Exhibit 5.27). The yield requirement is an interesting one. The wrinkle that it creates is that most optimization software works exclusively with total return figures. So it is frequently more difficult to optimize a portfolio around a required level of yield than one might imagine. This is discussed in greater detail in Chapter 8.

In answering the rest of question 8, one may also need to characterize the source and the certainty of anticipated contributions. A gift-annuity reserve fund that is raising more money each year in new annuities than it is distributing from maturing gifts is essentially a perpetual fund. But before investing on the basis of that assumption, one would want to know how much money has been raised in each of the last three to five years. To the extent that an "anticipated annual contribution" is from a variable source such as fund raising, make a note of it when filling in a number on the form.

EXHIBIT 5.25. Assessment Form, Part V, 3–5

3. Target rates of return: 1 year: ___.___%   3 years:___.___%   5 years:___.___%

4. What is the current relative risk tolerance for this fund?

_____ More fluctuation than the market

_____ Approximately the same fluctuation as the market

_____ Less fluctuation than the market

_____ Relative performance measures are inappropriate for this fund

5. What is the maximum loss you could tolerate in this fund over the following time frames?

_____ % per quarter

_____ % per year

_____ % in any two year period

EXHIBIT 5.26. Assessment Form, Part V, 6 and 7

6. Is the fund taxable?   _____ yes   _____ no

7. If the fund is taxable, give the following:
Income Tax Rate: _____._____%   Capital-Gains Tax Rate: _____._____%

EXHIBIT 5.27. Assessment Form, Part V, 8

8.   Other information

Minimum Required Annual Yield (Div. & Interest): $ _____

Anticipated Annual Contributions: $ _____

Anticipated Annual Withdrawals: $ _____

Questions 9 and 10 are intended to determine how the fund is presently invested by asset category (see Exhibit 5.28). The classes in question 9 are quite broad and some might say simplistic; most of the time one will see stocks, bonds, and cash in response to this question. While the list of asset classes in question 10 is far more extensive, it is worth remembering that billions of dollars are still managed nationally in two- and three-asset-class models.

My own opinion is that the eight classes listed in question 10 probably encompass 95 percent of the degree of differentiation in most managed portfolios nationally. Admittedly, there are many ways to slice and dice asset allocations, so this list reflects my prejudices as to the categories that matter most. The most glaring omission, arguably, is the failure to differentiate U.S. equities by style such as value or growth. The use of such categories is very common within the investment management industry. Thus, their omission

EXHIBIT 5.28. Assessment Form, Part V, 9 and 10

9. Please list the existing assets and attach a current portfolio statement, if available.

Asset Class	Percent Allocated	Dollar Amount
Cash/Cash Equivalents (includes mutual funds)		
Equities (includes mutual funds)		
Bonds (includes mutual funds)		
Real Estate (includes mutual funds, REITs, etc.)		
Private Placements (includes personal business)		
Other Investments (includes mutual funds)		

10. Indicate the current asset allocation percentages and the permitted range if such targets exist. If a category is prohibited, indicate with a "0" maximum percentage. If a category is required, indicate by stating the same percentage for minimum and maximum.

Asset Class	Current	Minimum	Maximum
Cash/Cash Equivalents			
U.S. Stocks			
Foreign Equities			
U.S. Investment Grade Bonds			
Junk Bonds			
Foreign Bonds			
Real Estate (includes mutual funds, REITs, etc.)			
Private Placements (includes personal business)			
Other Investments (includes mutual funds)			

represents a bias that style differentiation is not as important as many consultants believe. If your organization's operation is already this sophisticated and your consultant believes in style differentiation, then it is easy enough to correct my form by substituting the asset classes you are already using or the classes that your consultant recommends. In fact, your consultant will probably have his own more extensive form to use in place of this one.

The final question, number 11, asks for a narrative description of special problems or restrictions (see Exhibit 5.29). These would include social, moral, or organizational issues, assets that someone has determined may

---

EXHIBIT 5.29. Assessment Form, Part V, 11

---

11. Please describe on an attached page the purpose of this fund, any special income or other requirements, any restrictions on investments, and any special reporting requirements.

---

not be sold, odd distribution dates for income, and the like. While these things are usually minor, odd quirks of trusts in particular tend to be the place where the investment managers, administrators, and development officers get in trouble with donors.

Back at the ACO . . .

SURPRISING REVIEW

"Wow—I never knew we had that much!" Surprise and wonderment are common reactions to an investment management review. Even though the ACO board members know, in the aggregate, that the organization annually raises and spends $3 million, they are still surprised to learn that they usually have a cash balance of at least $500,000, due to the prudent management of expenses by their CFO. This does not count the $875,000 they just realized is sitting in their capital campaign account. In addition, they were stunned to discover that they now have more than $5 million in the several trusts they have been administering. Since they never see the income from those trusts and have not until recently even reflected those amounts on their financial records, in a very real sense they just never knew how much money they actually controlled. Completing the form was not only an eye opening experience, but one that stirred the pot in other ways as the board began to consider just what they have been doing with the funds under their control.

Conclusion

Overall, completing the self-assessment form and involving all the players may do more for equipping an organization to create and implement investment policies successfully than anything else recommended in this book. To everyone's surprise, organizations frequently do not know what they have to manage, what costs they are incurring investing assets, or how much time and effort is spent administering gifts. This is not a problem that is limited to small, unsophisticated organizations. Rather, even in large organizations, these issues have simply grown over time, piece by piece, in response to the then-current problems. The process of completing the form will provide an organization with much of the information it needs to make decisions, discuss investment opportunities with outside advisors, and go forward successfully.

▼ 6 Hiring Help

At the ACO . . .

"SHE'S ALWAYS DONE RIGHT BY ME"

"My broker's always done right by me." This time it was not one of our bankers on the board who was speaking, but another member. The subject was who to hire to manage the money. After having been so conservative with their funds for so long, it seemed surprising that nearly every board member had an opinion or recommendation as to who to use. Since the funds are all on deposit at the bankers' banks, they both kept pretty quiet as anything they might say would appear self-serving. But the rest of the board members mixed it up.

"Like I said," repeated one, "My broker's always done right by me."

"Yeah, but she's only with a regional firm. If we're going to use a broker, I think we ought to use one of the big players."

"The big player's fees are too high. Let's use a discounter."

"But the discounters don't know anything about picking stocks."

"You think the regular brokers do?"

"None of them do. Let's hire an investment manager."

"We don't have enough money for one of those guys. They all require at least $10,000,000."

"And they don't necessarily do any better. Let's just use mutual funds."

"Which funds?"

"I don't know. Maybe someone can help us pick them."

"How about my broker," chimes in the first director to have spoken. "She's always done right by me."

Hiring Help, Part 1—Too Many Choices

Probably the most difficult task in the world of investing is finding the right help. Incredibly, the problem is one of too many choices. These days, even a Manhattan cabby is likely to have a favorite "hot" stock. Everyone, it seems, wants to be in the investment management business.

One reason that so many organizations want to manage money is that it pays very well. This is true both at the macro level (meaning the fees earned by various categories of institutions for managing funds) and at the level of the individual who is employed in the industry. Both collectively and individually, managing other people's money is a lucrative business. Knowing that will not make it any easier to hire investment professionals, but it does explain why there are so many people from disparate parts of the financial world who are trying to bring assets under management.

And that—the effort to bring assets under management—is one of the two great themes that run through the entire area of trying to hire appropriate help. All of the players—the banks, brokers, investment advisors, and even insurance companies[1]—are trying to use their expertise in one or more areas to bring assets under management. We will see this most clearly when examining the area of custody (the safe keeping of assets), which is the most mundane of tasks. Unglamorous and low-paying though it may be, everyone wants custody of assets.

The second great theme is the desire to be in charge. More specifically, it is the desire of every service provider to have that relationship with the client, which controls all of the other relationships. It is the desire to be the primary, or at least the first, advisor. That desire in turn has led virtually every would-be advisor to become, or at least claim to be, a "full service provider."

Thus, no matter how far removed a task might be from whatever it was that the service provider did historically—for example, loaned money, bought and sold stock, gave investment advice for a fee, sold insurance—that task is now part of the package of services that each provider offers. To add to the confusion, most of the providers now use the same titles. Thus, insurance salesmen, stock brokers, Securities and Exchange Commission (SEC) registered investment advisors, and bankers all commonly refer to themselves as "investment advisors" or "financial consultants."

The complexity that results has become so daunting that a new generation of consultants has emerged whose only job is to hire the people who actually do the work. Such consultants (who might themselves be licensed as a bank, broker, or investment advisor) might never buy a stock or bond, hold money in an account, make a trust disbursement, clear a check, or issue a custodial report. Yet, by helping to tie all the pieces together, such consultants often provide a valuable service.

In an effort to reduce the complexity, the following discussion begins by breaking down the concept of investment management into its component parts. Once we understand that investment management includes only a few core services, it becomes easier to find appropriate providers for each task.

[1] Insurance companies have not been listed as a category of service provider in the exhibits that follow nor have they been referred to as such in the materials. The reason is that when insurance companies offer investment products, it is typically in reliance on securities brokerage licenses through affiliates or subsidiaries. The large insurance companies with investment operations would be included with the securities brokers.

Investment Management: A Functional Analysis

Exhibit 6.1 is entitled "Function/Provider Matrix." It is an effort to summarize on a single page the tasks that need to be performed and the list of potential service providers that are available to perform them. On the left side of the chart is a list of the functions that need to be performed, which collectively constitute "investment management." The five key functions are custody, asset allocation, investment selection, securities brokerage, and performance evaluation and reporting.[2]

Moving from left to right across the top of the chart is a list of investment management service providers—types of organizations that offer one or more of the services. The service providers are securities brokers, banks (which includes trust companies), investment advisors, and consultants. The consultant category is slightly different than the first three in that it does not represent a separate legal licensing category. Rather, calling someone an investment consultant is merely an acknowledgment of the role that they are playing. In the world of investment management, the consulting function might be provided by someone who is licensed and regulated as a securities broker, a registered investment advisor, or a bank.

The discussion that follows examines four of the five functions—custody, asset allocation, investment selection, and securities brokerage—as a prelude to discussing the various combinations of service providers that might be retained to perform those functions. Performance evaluation and reporting is the subject of its own chapter (Chapter 7).

CUSTODY

When investment professionals talk about custody, they usually mean a collection of services provided by a bank, trust company, or brokerage firm involving the safekeeping of investment assets. In addition to keeping physical possession of the securities, those services usually include collecting dividends and interest, sweeping such funds into a money market or other interest-bearing account, dispersing funds both regularly and on request, and issuing reports, usually monthly, detailing the securities held and the transactions or events that have occurred in the preceding month.

---

[2] A number of other tasks, though not usually considered part of the investment management process, are nonetheless quite important. Those tasks include fund accounting, regulatory reporting and compliance (such as that required of organizations licensed to issue gift annuities), tax reporting and compliance, disbursement of funds, budgeting, and cash flow analysis. These activities are not often thought of as part of the investment management process but are rather considered part of the accounting function. Nonetheless, they deserve acknowledgment here if only to remind us that our investment management function ultimately needs to be integrated with these other functions or tasks.

EXHIBIT 6.1. Investment Management Options—Function/Provider Matrix

Function	Securities Brokers	Banks	Investment Advisors	Consultants
Custody	Brokers have traditionally provided custody without charge as part of the securities brokerage function.	One of the banks' primary historic roles is to hold assets.	Many, perhaps most, pure investment advisors do not provide custody. Rather, a bank or securities broker holds the assets. Some investment advisors offer custody through affiliates.	Consultants rarely provide custodial services and do so, if at all, through affiliated entities.
Asset Allocation	This has not been a traditional, separately offered service until recently (e.g., last 10 years). Increasingly, brokers provide asset allocation in conjunction with other services.	Banks have traditionally provided high-end investment "advice" for wealthy individuals through so-called Private Client groups. In recent years, these groups have added asset allocation and related services.	Yes	Consultants typically are either securities brokers or registered investment advisors who specialize in providing asset allocation, manager searches, and performance-reporting services.
Investment Selection	Brokers have always helped clients "pick stocks." Brokers today still select investments but far more commonly "hire" expert advise through mutual funds or investment managers.	Not a traditional primary service outside of trust departments, which historically (and still) utilize common trust funds.	Investment selection is the primary historic function of investment advisors.	Consultants do not select investments but will often help select investment advisors whose work they subsequently evaluate for the client for a fee.

(continued)

EXHIBIT 6.1. Continued

Function	Securities Brokers	Banks	Investment Advisors	Consultants
Brokerage	Brokers' primary, historic function has been buying & selling securities on exchanges.	No	No	No
Performance Reporting	As brokers have moved toward supervision of mutual funds or investment management, they have increasingly provided performance reporting, sometimes through consulting units or subsidiaries.	Not a traditional service. Offered today through private banking or investment affiliates.	yes	Primary historic function

ASSET ALLOCATION

As you may recall from Chapter 3, asset allocation is the process of choosing the types of investments that will be made and the percentages of the portfolio to be invested in each. There is a growing belief within the investment community in the importance of the asset allocation decision. This is based largely, but not exclusively, on portfolio theory.

The increase in importance of the decision is also due, in part, to the growing number of choices that can be considered asset classes. Those choices exist in a more meaningful way today than they did 20 years ago due to the widespread availability of better reporting information.[3] In the earlier days of portfolio theory development, there were relatively few sources of essential data. In addition, much of the computer software needed to optimize portfolios was proprietary and expensive.

Neither of those conditions continue to exist, as many established collectors of data now offer inexpensive asset allocation computer software together with enormous quantities of historical data. That data includes all of the important market indexes and numerous other compilations of economic statistics, currency information, and investment manager performance numbers. Armed with these programs and the related data, virtually anyone in the industry can provide asset allocation services, at least to the extent that such services are based on historical data.[4]

That is, in fact, one of the dominant forces at work in the industry. With the asset allocation decision leading to the subsequent decisions—that is, which investment managers to hire for each class of asset, where to custody the assets, and where to execute trades—virtually everyone who can wants to become an asset allocator.

INVESTMENT SELECTION

With all the emphasis being placed on portfolio theory, it's easy to forget that someone has to actually pick stocks. In the world of institutional in-

---

[3] While it may seem self-evident, you cannot rationally decide to invest in a certain category of assets unless you have some reason to believe that doing so enhances your portfolio's likely performance on a risk-adjusted basis. Since the beginning point for all projections is an adequate historical record, without that record you simply cannot make the allocation, at least not for quantifiable reasons.

[4] A remaining distinction between consultants is between those who change the inputs based on economic projections and those who do not. Many of the "pure" consulting firms have a strong economics bent and will in fact adjust the inputs, that is, projected rates of return for various asset classes, based on their own econometric forecasting. Even many broker-consultants do the same thing if only by adjusting the risk-free rate of return to reflect current rates. Everyone has some temptation to lower projected returns for those asset classes that have performed better in the time frame being used, for example, the S&P 500 over the last 15 years, than that same index has performed over 50 years or longer.

vesting, stock and bond selection, the actual decision making on which securities to buy and sell and when to do so, is usually performed by registered investment advisors.[5] These advisors select securities for either mutual funds or for individually managed portfolios. In either case, the securities selection techniques that the manager follows will be the same: the vehicle—fund or account—is chosen by the client based primarily on the amount of money involved. Larger amounts tend to be separately managed and smaller amounts tend to be invested in funds.

SECURITIES BROKERAGE

The next investment management task is the actual purchasing and selling of securities. On the major exchanges of the world, the New York Stock Exchange being the largest, that which people are willing to pay and for which people are willing to sell moves quickly and almost seamlessly to a constantly changing equilibrium price. A particular type of broker called a "specialist" facilitates this process by gathering together the buy and sell orders for the securities of particular companies, matching them in a way that assures a continuous market.

In the over-the-counter market, actual bids and asks are displayed electronically through a vast computer network. In a very real sense, the parties find each other. In both situations, the pricing is so rapid and the market so efficient that there are relatively few opportunities to gain a significant advantage in the buying and the selling of the shares. For the purposes of institutional investment management, the advantage that any one broker can bring to the table over another—just in the trading of shares—is usually so modest that it is no longer a reason to choose one broker over another.[6]

As we will see in just a moment, therefore, where shares are actually traded ends up being a secondary consideration most of the time. Whichever service provider we end up relying upon as our "general contractor," a concept we will examine next, will end up effectively selecting our securities brokers or at least selecting those who actually direct the trades.

---

[5] Registered investment advisors are so-called because they are licensed by the SEC to sell advice on selecting securities under the Investment Advisors Act of 1940. Currently, there are more than 20,000 registered investment advisors in the United States and more than 500 of those manage $1 billion or more.

[6] This conclusion applies to major markets of actively traded shares. There are places, even in the United States, where one brokerage firm has sufficiently greater expertise, market share or other advantage that it can be beneficial to do business with that firm. Particularly where large brokers actually make markets in-house, the brokers have the opportunity to save money for their clients. But much of the time, the pure trading of shares on exchanges need not be a basis for selecting a stock broker.

Investment Advisors

Investment advisors increasingly classify themselves by asset classes and styles. They define themselves, in other words, by the type of investments that they make. There are so many "systems" or theories that have been used over the years for selecting stocks that it is very difficult to categorize managers (or, in the case of mutual funds, the funds which the managers direct) in a rational or systematic way. But it is not completely impossible as the more common categories necessarily include the vast majority of the managers.

EQUITY MANAGERS

Exhibit 6.2 is an effort to summarize the world of equity managers based on the markets in which they invest, segments of the market, whether they are active or passive, portfolio style, portfolio construction and research techniques. The problem here is that something I am calling a "market segment" others would consider a "management style." While all the words in the chart are commonly used and generally understood within the industry, they are not precisely defined.

Markets
Managers tend to invest either domestically or in foreign markets. Within the international arena the major markets are those included in the Morgan Stanley EAFE Index (Europe and the Far East) while the markets of the rest of the world are considered "emerging."

Market Segment
Managers tend to concentrate on large companies or smaller companies. In doing so they refer to themselves as "large cap" or "small cap" managers. By "cap" they mean "capitalization" which is the total value of all of the outstanding securities of a particular company. If ABC Manufacturing, Inc., has 100 million shares outstanding that are currently trading for $40 per share, then it has a market capitalization of $4 billion ($40/share times 100 million shares). That would be a large cap company. And of course there is no precise definition of where you draw the line! Some managers (and some consultants conducting manager searches) have a "mid-cap" category. Generally, anything under $500 million is considered small cap, anything over $2 billion would be large and the things in the middle, mid-cap.

Management Style
Active managers select securities in a conscious effort to enhance returns. Passive managers maintain portfolios which track an index. Among managers, the passive approach was long scorned and is only now coming into

EXHIBIT 6.2. Equity Managers

Markets	Market Segment	Management Style	Portfolio Style	Portfolio Construction	Research
U.S.	Large capitalization	Active	Value	Bottom up	Fundamental analysis
Major foreign	Small capitalization	Passive	Growth	Top down	Technical analysis
Emerging markets			Market timing		Macro economic analysis
			Sector rotation		

widespread prominence because the so-called index funds have performed so well. Passive management requires less infrastructure (i.e., no research) and so the fees are lower. That is part of its advantage. Passive management tends to exist only in major markets with well established indices.

Portfolio Style
There are a great many investment management styles; only the more common ones are named here. The big categories are "value" and "growth." Value managers are essentially price-driven. They believe that companies have a "value" that can be determined by careful analysis of balance sheets and the like, which they sometimes call "intrinsic value." Obviously, if there is such a value, then whenever the shares were trading below that value one would be getting a good buy. Most value managers talk about buying shares "at a discount." Shares purchased by value managers will usually have a lower price to book (p/b) ratio, lower price to earnings (p/e) ratio and higher dividend yield than the market as a whole. (See Exhibit 6.3).

Growth managers look for companies they believe are likely to grow their sales and revenues more quickly than the average company in the market. In recent years, many growth managers have invested heavily in technology stocks. Growth managers are not concerned about low p/e or p/b ratios. Their concern is with high growth rates. So the characteristics of their portfolios might look like Exhibit 6.4.

There are many other investment styles. Among the better known are market timers and sector rotators. Market timing is the effort to move in and out of the market based on whether the market is going to go up or down. It is notoriously difficult to do, but the idea is so appealing—buy right before a big run or sell right before a big drop—that people, and some managers, continue to try. The usual result is higher commissions from moving in and out of positions.

Sector rotation is a similar, though perhaps a more reasonable discipline. Sector rotators invest more heavily in certain portions of the market than others, based on their assessment of the relative prospects of those sectors.

Portfolio Construction
Managers tend to either pick stocks according to some discipline, in which case they are building portfolios "bottom up," or make broader economic decisions and then implement those decisions by purchasing groups of securities. The latter approach is called "top down." As one might imagine, most value managers take a bottom up approach. They are looking for good deals, stock by stock. Most international managers, on the other hand, are top down. They are surveying the world, and when they decide that "Spain is under-priced" or that "India has great growth prospects," then they purchase shares of companies in those markets.

EXHIBIT 6.3. Portfolio Style: Growth Managers

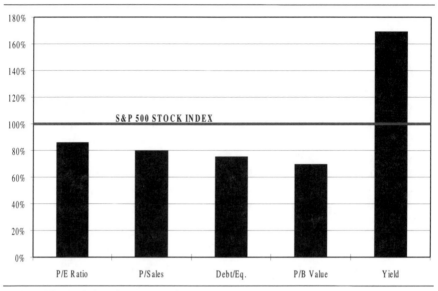

Produced by Capital Markets Research

EXHIBIT 6.4. Portfolio Style: Value Managers

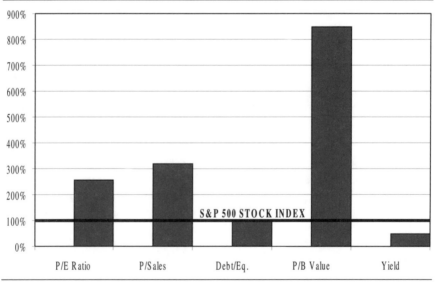

Produced by Capital Markets Research

Research

While all sorts of research techniques are pursued in financial circles, they tend to fall into three basic areas: fundamental analysis, technical analysis, or economic analysis. The first is research at the company and industry level. How much money are they making? What are their growth prospects? Where do they rank in the industry? How strong is their balance sheet? All of that is considered fundamental analysis.

Technical analysis is the study of the movements of markets. In its most defensible form, it is an effort at trying to analyze the psychology of the markets. As practiced by chartists and others, it is of questionable value.[7] The third broad category is economic analysis, with which we are all at least somewhat familiar. This is the study of an entire economy. Here, interest rates, inflation, job growth, and a myriad of numbers used to measure the economy are the coin of the realm.

Summary

It will always be difficult to select advisors. But to be a good supervisor, it helps to understand the language of the industry. The purpose of Exhibit 6.2 is to provide a basic familiarity with that language by defining the words and describing the ways in which equity managers use those words to describe themselves.

One group of managers, for example, might describe themselves as follows:

> We are U.S. value managers with a large cap orientation. We actively select shares we believe to be trading at a discount relative to their intrinsic value as determined by our own fundamental research. We pursue a disciplined bottom up style of portfolio construction and do not attempt to time the market.

That is a reasonable description of a large cap value manager.

Another group of managers might say:

> We invest in both major foreign and emerging markets. We actively seek growth opportunities throughout the world. Frequently, the best opportunities are among smaller companies. While we try to pursue a bottom up approach for actual stock selection, we concentrate our efforts in those countries or regions of the world that our economic analysis leads us to believe are the most promising.

This is an international manager with a small cap—growth orientation.

---

[7] For a good critique of both fundamental and technical analysis, see Burton Malkiel, *A Random Walk Down Wall Street* (New York: W.W. Norton and Company, 1996), Chapters 5–7 and the studies cited there.

FIXED-INCOME MANAGERS

The world of fixed-income management is divided among managers in a similar way to the equity side of the house (see Exhibit 6.5). In some respects, fixed-income investing is more straightforward than equity investing as fixed-income strategies are usually related to the characteristics of the instruments in a more understandable manner. In this world, in addition to markets and market segments, the key characteristics tend to be credit quality and maturities. Research, in turn, tends to focus on different types of risks.

Markets
The choice of which fixed-income markets to invest in is the same as for equities. There is, however, one significant difference. All fixed-income markets—even the market for U.S. treasury obligations—are now effectively international. There really is no such thing any longer as an exclusively domestic fixed-income market. Why is that?

Quite simply, since the enormous increases in U.S. debt-financing of the government, many of the largest purchasers of those bonds are foreign governments through their central banks. Consequently, changes in the interest rates in Germany or the exchange rates for the yen are frequently as important to domestic bond markets as the action of our own central bank, the Federal Reserve Board. So venturing into international investing is not the great leap that one may think.

Market Segments
The most important market segments are government and corporate bonds. In theory, government bonds represent no credit risk since they are guaranteed by the full faith and credit of the United States. They are the ultimate AAA obligation.

In both areas, governments and corporates, there are submarkets. The government issues both collateralized mortgage obligations and various types of agency bonds. These are guaranteed by the government but are not direct obligations of the government, as are treasuries. Consequently, they frequently offer a few basis points of incremental yield.

Credit Quality
On the corporate side, the great divide is under credit quality, the third column in Exhibit 6.5. Investment grade obligations are those rated BBB or higher. After that, from a ratings perspective, everything rated BB or lower is considered "junk bonds." Managers who invest in junk bonds tend to specialize in that area, so it can be a legitimate specialized area of expertise.

Maturities/Durations
The next important concept is that of "maturities." Investing in very short-term fixed-income instruments is usually called "cash management." Be-

EXHIBIT 6.5. Fixed-Income Managers

Markets	Market Segment	Credit Quality	Maturities	Management Style	Research (Risks)
U.S.	Government bonds	Investment grade	Cash management under 1 year	Active	Credit risk
Major foreign	Corporate bonds	Below investment grade	Short term 1–3 years	Passive	Interest rate risk (yield curve)
Emerging markets	Collateralized mortgage obligations		Intermediate term 3–10 years		Reinvestment risk
	Government agencies		Long term 10+ years		Currency risk
	Municipal				Duration risk

cause of the effectiveness of money-market mutual funds, one rarely sees fixed-income managers actually managing cash in separate portfolios in amounts less than $10 million. Below that it is usually not possible to add value over the funds.

As the maturities extend, the possible investment techniques and the risks increase. Among professional fixed-income managers, once you get past cash management, they actually tend to focus more on "duration" than on maturities. It is a related but slightly different concept:

> DURATION [is a] concept first developed by Frederick Macaulay in 1938 that measures bond price volatility by measuring the "length" of a bond. It is weighted-average term-to-maturity of the bond's cash flows, the weights being the present value of each cash flow as a percentage of the bond's full price. For working purposes, duration can be defined as the approximate percentage change in price for a 100 basis-point change in yield. A duration of 5, for example, means the price of the bond will change by approximately 5 percent for a 100-basis point change in yield.[8]

Research

Finally, fixed-income managers focus their research areas by the risks with which they are dealing. Credit risk is the risk of default in the payment of interest or principal. This research is very similar to the fundamental research conducted by equity managers. Not surprisingly, some junk bond managers—those who are actively dealing with credit risk—are also equity managers.

Duration, discussed above, is both a concept and a technique for assessing interest rate and reinvestment risk. Virtually all professional fixed-income managers deal with these concepts. Finally, managers of international fixed-income investments must also deal with currency risks. Here, they usually have the opportunity to invest internationally on either a hedged or unhedged basis. To be hedged simply means that they are purchasing or selling some sort of currency future so as to protect themselves against possible currency fluctuations.

Consulting—Who Gets to Be in Charge?

We have briefly examined each of the pieces—custody, asset allocation, investment selection, and securities brokerage—and met the players—the securities brokers, banks, and investment advisors. Now it is time to see

---

[8] Quoted from *Barron's Finance & Investment Handbook*, 4th Edition, 1995

who is in charge. Most commonly, the person or organization making the asset allocation decision will be the leading decision maker. They are, essentially, the "general contractors," the ones who supervise the other service providers while no one (except the client) supervises them. Given that dynamic, almost everyone in the investment world with a client relationship would, if they could, become an asset allocator.

INSTITUTIONAL CONSULTANTS

At the institutional level, a whole new generation of service providers known as consultants has emerged. Consultants typically prepare asset allocation models for their clients, screen and select managers whose styles are consistent with the various asset classes, report on the performance of the managers, and make periodic rebalancing recommendations. There are a number of firms that act in this capacity.

Institutional consultants are usually compensated on either a percentage fee basis, similar to an investment manager, or on a hard dollar basis. On "smaller" relationships, those under $100 million, the consultant is more likely to be paid on a percentage basis, which might range anywhere from 10 to 50 basis points of the assets under management. On larger accounts, the organization is more likely to simply pay the consultant a fee for the services being performed. Most charitable organizations with investment assets of more than $100 million utilize the services of a consultant.

At the other end of the spectrum, consultants are rarely used for accounts of less than $5 million. Even at the $10 million level, their presence is limited. There are two reasons for this. First, the work being performed is largely unaffected by the total amount of money involved. Asset allocation models are constructed on a percentage basis from a combination of historic performance information and anticipated returns by asset class. So the modeling process and the work involved in doing it is identical, whether applied to a $10 million fund or a $10 billion fund.

Assume, for example, that a consultant wishes to charge $50,000 for creating an initial asset allocation model and a smaller amount for reviewing and rebalancing the model in future years. On a $10 billion portfolio, a $50,000 fee is inconsequential—less than one basis point. But on a $10 million portfolio, a $50,000 fee is one-half of one percent, or 50 basis points. The primary reason, therefore, that consultants are not present in the low-dollar end of the market is that it is not economical for them to do so.

A secondary reason is that smaller funds cannot be divided into multiple pieces for style-specific investment management without increasing costs. One might expect a $5 million balanced portfolio of U.S. securities to be managed for 1 percent plus another 50 basis points for trading costs and expenses: total cost, 1.50 percent. Divide that $5 million into five $1 million pieces and you will likely have a 1.25 percent management fee on each of the

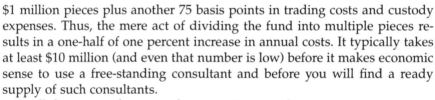

$1 million pieces plus another 75 basis points in trading costs and custody expenses. Thus, the mere act of dividing the fund into multiple pieces results in a one-half of one percent increase in annual costs. It typically takes at least $10 million (and even that number is low) before it makes economic sense to use a free-standing consultant and before you will find a ready supply of such consultants.

In all these areas, be aware that my estimates of investment management fees and expenses are broad generalizations, not hard and fast industry standards. The fact that it does not cost more or take more time to produce asset allocation models for billion-dollar portfolios than it does for small portfolios is likely to be an abiding truth. Fees charged by consultants and investment advisors, on the other hand, are changing minute by minute. Consequently, it is much more important to understand the relationships. Armed with such an understanding, you will be able to research current fees in your geographic location and make a good decision on your own.

BROKER-CONSULTANTS

In the lower reaches of the market, clients are not foregoing asset allocation decisions. Rather, they are acquiring and paying for that help in other ways. In the retail market, all major securities brokers offer "wrap programs." These are agreements that provide custody, security brokerage, and professional investment management for a single fee. In addition, many pure mutual fund companies are giving away simple versions of asset allocation software that help their customers select mutual funds. In both cases, assistance with asset allocation is an important component of the product or service.

For the smaller institutional client, there are multiple sources of help with asset allocation decisions. Probably the most common are "broker-consultants." Broker-consultants are in fact "stockbrokers," which means that, legally, they are registered representatives or registered principals of an SEC-licensed broker-dealer. The broker-dealers with the largest consulting operations are Merrill Lynch, Smith Barney, Prudential, Dean Witter, and Paine Webber. There are also, still, a fair number of smaller, regional firms with the same licensing. Within this arena, the broker-consultants fall into one of two categories, formal and informal. Formal broker-consultants are organized within the large companies as separate operations. Such relationships are functionally identical to the independent consultants described above. The only real difference is the potential for conflicts of interest if the broker-consultant is using its own firms for other services.

Concerns about such conflicts are frequently overstated to some extent. The answer to a conflict is disclosure. Buying multiple services from one provider is not the problem; not knowing that one is buying multiple services is a problem. Moreover, the major "pure" consulting firms are probably not as independent as they claim. Scratch the surface and, at the least, one finds cross-referral relationships between consultants and their favorite managers. None of that is necessarily bad. It merely means there is no sub-stitute for monitoring who is selling what to whom.

Informal broker-consultants are brokers (financial consultants) who choose not to pick stocks. When they help their clients invest, they do so by using mutual funds, wrap programs, or by placing money directly with investment managers outside the wrap programs. In that case they generally retain custody and brokerage commissions, on larger accounts at institutional rates, and may or may not have some other fee arrangement to provide compensation for asset allocation services.

This is a difficult area in which to characterize the quality of the services being rendered or even to describe the ways in which the service providers are paid. Many broker-consultants are outstanding service providers who meet their clients' needs efficiently and also have time for customer service and marketing. Those with larger client and asset bases frequently deliver their services for an effective charge of less than one-half of one percent. Occasionally, those fees are paid directly on a consulting fee basis. More commonly, the "fees" are the result of brokerage transaction commissions as described above or, on smaller accounts, the internal marketing fees on proprietary products, mutual fund fees (known as 12(b)(1) fees), or a portion of the wrap fee that does not go to the outside investment advisors.[9] Among these informal broker-consultants, when the fee to them is in the one-half of one percent range or less, then they are undoubtedly in control of very large sums of money.

Hiring Help, Part 2—Putting the Pieces Together

The heart of the problem of finding the ideal consultant, broker or other-wise, is that it is hard to tell the difference between registered representa-tives who function as sophisticated investment consultants and those who claim they do. There are too many similarities in terms of licensing, location, and the other traditional ways of evaluating service providers. The conclud-ing section of this chapter will discuss how to find investment help by focus-ing on each of the key functional areas of investment management. Here, again, the two main forces—the desire to bring assets under management and the desire to be in charge—affect *our choices* when it comes to hiring help.

---

[9] Wrap fees are programs in which the customer pays the brokerage firm a single fee for both transactions and investment management services. The customer typically selects one or more investment managers with whom the firm has negotiated agreements to participate in the pro-gram. Out of the single fee, the broker then pays the investment manager. It is a good system except for the fact that the fees have been too high, especially off the rate sheet. When first introduced, wrap fees started at 3 percent on smaller accounts. Competition worked its magic, however, and the fees more commonly charged today are considerably lower.

CUSTODY: A TOOL FOR GATHERING ASSETS UNDER MANAGEMENT

The area of custody illustrates in a microcosm the paradox of the forces at work in the investment management world. Relatively speaking, there is no money in custody since the fees are very low. Yet, everybody wants to have custody. Recently in California, for example, a major national bank was awarded the custody work on a huge government pension plan for California state employees. If the numbers reported in the newspaper are correct, they bid only $1.8 million for providing custodial services on a $60 billion plan. No matter how sophisticated the computer systems and how expert their staff, such a fee for the amount of work involved in reporting all the securities positions, the dividends received, the monthly changes in value, and so on, seems like a losing proposition. What is going on? Why are they doing this?

The answer is that the bank believes that with custody of those assets, they have an inside track on providing the pension plan with other fee-generating services. They will be in a position, for example, to monitor the performance of the pension plan managers.[10] Since the bank also has a large investment management operation, if they spot a manager who is underperforming relative to its style or, better still, relative to the bank's manager or management group for that investment style, they are in an enhanced position to bid on that business. Consequently, the bank wants to get the assets in the door and worry about how to make the business profitable later.[11]

While the last statement may be a slight overstatement (and one with which the bank may take exception), it nonetheless characterizes the attitude in the industry. Get the assets in the door and sooner or later we will make some money. This theory is as true at the smaller account level (which for the purpose of this conversation are pools of funds of $100 million or less) as it is for the largest pension plans or endowments.

WHAT ARE THE CUSTODY CHOICES?

Banks, trust companies, and securities brokers all offer custodial services. Banks and trust companies charge for the services directly. In the southern

---

[10] By having custody, the bank can track beginning values and changes in value, net of additions and distributions. From this data, calculating investment performance is a straightforward, spreadsheet function of no particular difficulty. If the funds are segregated in various ways in order to permit different managers to direct portions of the fund, the custodian is in a position to track performance for such portions as well.

[11] Later is not necessarily that far away. Custodians can be allowed to "lend" securities to others, for example, for short-selling purposes (selling shares you do not own). The lender of the shares earns interest or fees when doing so. Securities lending is now itself a billion dollar per year business.

California market the major banks charge smaller accounts $400–$1,000 per year plus $20–$25 per transaction for holding the securities, collecting dividends and interest, pricing the securities each month, and issuing a monthly report. By comparison, virtually all major brokerage houses provide custody on such accounts for free.

On large pension plan and endowment accounts, express custody charges by major banks are now commonly less than 5 basis points. For these accounts the brokerage firms either match this type of fee or, more commonly, place custody at a custodial bank or make some other arrangement that takes advantage of their normally free custody as part of a package of services. So the differences between free broker custody and bank custodial charges occur mainly in the under $100 million market.

Why the difference? There are a number of forces at work here that explain the disparity between express custody charges at the bank and the "free" custody at the brokers. Part of the story is that securities brokers, like the bank in the earlier example, know that if they get assets in the door, they will eventually make money on those assets. Because they currently have so many more ways in which to make money on investments assets than do the banks, they can afford to give away some services. For banks, by comparison, on the under $100 million accounts custody *is* the service and not just a loss leader. But there is also more to the story.

MONEY MARKET ACCOUNTS

One of the services that all custodians offer is the daily sweeping of available cash into a money market fund. At the end of each business day, the custodian's computerized record-keeping system checks for any cash additions made to the account as a result of deposits, dividends, interest, or sales proceeds received. Amounts of available cash down to the even dollar are used to purchase shares of the custodian's money-market mutual fund. The result is that the only cash left in the account is less than one dollar.

Money market mutual funds are very useful instruments. They were first created in the mid-1970s as an alternative to bank demand accounts or certificates of deposit. Such an instrument is an open-ended mutual fund regulated under the Investment Advisors Act of 1940. When an investor purchases units in such a fund, he or she is purchasing new units issued by the fund. When the investor withdraws money, the fund redeems units for cash.

Money market funds have certain unique characteristics that are at the heart of their utility. First, the funds are managed in such a way that the net asset value (NAV) of a unit is always $1. This is achieved primarily by restricting fund investments to U.S. government and high-grade corporate debt instruments of short maturities. Typically, the maximum permitted maturity of an instrument in such a fund is one year, and the weighted-average maturity is usually 90 days or less. While that investment strategy provides

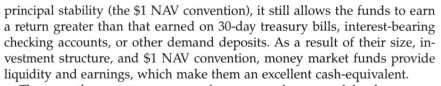
principal stability (the $1 NAV convention), it still allows the funds to earn a return greater than that earned on 30-day treasury bills, interest-bearing checking accounts, or other demand deposits. As a result of their size, investment structure, and $1 NAV convention, money market funds provide liquidity and earnings, which make them an excellent cash-equivalent.

There are three common types of money market mutual funds: government funds, government and corporate funds, and tax free funds. The first invest only in U.S. government securities; the second invest in both government and corporate securities; and the third invest only in state or municipal debt instruments, the income from which is tax free for federal income tax purposes. In many of the larger states, such as California and New York, there are double tax free bond funds available. These are money market funds that invest only in the debt and securities of municipalities of that state. The interest income from such single-state funds is exempt from both state and federal income taxation for residents of the issuing states.

Of the three categories, charitable organizations do not normally invest in tax free money market funds because, as charities, they are already income-tax-exempt. As the municipal funds pay lower interest than either of the taxable funds, there is no reason to give up the incremental yield. There may be special circumstances, of course, such as particular charitable lead trusts where the charity as a trustee wants to generate tax-exempt income and would use such funds. That, still, is exceptional.[12]

AREN'T ALL MONEY MARKET FUNDS CREATED EQUAL?

Given the nature of money market fund investments, it is difficult to imagine that there is a great deal of disparity between funds. After all, how much relative investment management expertise can any manager bring to selecting very short-term U.S. government debt securities? And in fact the yields on most major money market accounts in each of the three categories tend to be quite close.

---

[12] Charities do not need to restrict themselves to pure government funds as many do. The incremental risk represented by short-term commercial paper, corporate repurchase agreements, and other corporate instruments commonly used in the government and corporate money market funds is insignificant. If a nonprofit can add 5 or more basis points of incremental yield by using such funds, it should do so.

This recommendation assumes, first, that all of the money market funds in which nonprofits participate are issued by major financial institutions. This is not a place to consider "Joe's Mutual Fund." The second assumption is that we are talking about "vanilla" money market funds and not some far riskier cousin. Based on those assumptions, the incremental risk is negligible because the only issuers of short-term commercial paper or corporate repurchase agreements used in the corporate money market funds of major issuers are large domestic corporations. Consequently, the chances of significant default occurring in a portfolio of A- or AA-rated corporate instruments maturing in 90 days or less is probably no greater than the chance of default by the U.S. government.

Further, the NAV convention and ready liquidity of such funds will not allow charging a 4 percent or 5 percent sales charge, even if the market would bear such a fee. Not surprisingly, there are no sales commissions or other upfront fees on money-market mutual funds. Instead, the fund sponsor (a mutual fund company, bank, or brokerage firm) charges an internal management fee against monthly fund balances, as do virtually all other mutual funds.

Consequently, much of the difference in yield for the government and government and corporate funds of the largest domestic banks and brokerage firms is attributable to the difference in internal fees. Add a 20 or 30 basis point fee differential between the most expensive fund and the least expensive fund to the current yield of the most expensive fund and the difference pretty much disappears. Since custodians normally sweep cash only into their own money-market mutual funds, one may properly view the cost differential of the more expensive money market funds as a custody expense. The ability to earn even a modest fee on funds in the money market account begins to explain why some firms are willing to provide custodial services without a direct charge. To the extent that an organization maintains very large sums in cash for either investment or cash-flow purposes, it should consider the incremental money market fund expenses in choosing a custodian. These fee differentials will rarely be significant enough to be the determining factor, but in fairness to the banks one might discover that their direct custodial charges are not any higher than the incremental cost of brokers' higher money market fees.

PURCHASING FIXED-INCOME INVESTMENTS

A final factor in making the custody decision turns on whether the account will include a significant percentage of fixed-income investments. Fixed-income investments (particularly corporate and U.S. government bonds) are purchased and sold differently than equity securities. When trading equity securities on an established exchange or in the over-the-counter market, the broker's commission is stated separately from the price. For example, in a purchase of 100 shares of common stock at $40 per share, if the broker has a minimum commission charge of $75 versus 10 cents per share, the broker's confirmation for this transaction will state that $4,000 was paid for the securities and separately report the $75 commission plus several minimal amounts for exchange charges or other taxes, depending on the jurisdiction and exchange on which the transaction was made. If those ancillary charges total $6, the confirmation statement would show a total of $4,081, with the three categories of charges separately itemized.

In a purchase of government or corporate bonds, on the other hand, the broker's commission is usually buried in the price; the commission is rarely separately stated. The bonds are quoted on a percentage of par value basis.

The cost of a $1,000 bond trading at 100 is $1,000 or 100 percent of par value. A bond is said to be trading at a discount if its price is less than 100. A bond trading at 98, or 98 percent of par value, can be purchased for $980. Conversely, a bond traded above par value is said to be trading at a premium. A bond trading at 104 can be purchased for 104 percent of $1,000 or $1,040.

To purchase bonds, investment advisors or brokers call the bond-trading departments of major brokerage houses and ask for a quote. Whatever the price, it is quoted on a gross basis and includes the brokerage firm's commissions and/or markups. Because the quoted price includes the broker's commission, there is no way of knowing how much is commission or whether a better price is available elsewhere. The only way to get the best price on fixed-income investments is by comparing the prices of major bond-trading firms. If a fixed-income account is custodied at a bank, one is usually free to purchase bonds from any broker. In that case, the fixed-income investment manager can call the bond-trading desks at several firms to get the stated price for a particular security. Frequently, the manager will find a variation in quoted prices from $\frac{1}{32}$ of 1 percent to as much as $\frac{1}{4}$ of 1 percent or more, although such extreme differences are unusual.[13]

To do so, the account must be held by a custodian that allows you to purchase securities from outside brokers, which is why this is a custody issue. Major brokerage firms have historically not allowed "trading out" or "trading away," as the practice is called, on accounts custodied with them. Rather, they require that all trades be placed through their own traders. Thus, the only way to obtain best prices for bonds has been to use a bank custody account. This is still the case some of the time, although brokerage firms increasingly allow fixed-income trades on managed accounts to be executed through other firms.

CONCLUSION: CUSTODY RECOMMENDATION

Selecting an appropriate custodian is clearly more involved than choosing the least expensive alternative. The free custody offered by brokerage firms, while literally true, can include a number of additional expenses. So what is the best approach?

On accounts of less than $5 million, custody costs will rarely, if ever, matter. For small accounts, therefore, convenience and other factors are more important criteria. In the $5 million to $50 million range, custody costs (as we are defining them) for fixed-income accounts or for balanced accounts with a large fixed-income component begin to be significant. While custo-

---

[13] If the ability to receive the best price saves, on average, 1/32 of a point, that is only $0.3125 on a $1,000 bond. But on $1 million it's $312.50 and on $100 million it is $31,250. So as the amounts grow, placing custody so as to obtain the best price becomes much more important.

dial expenses decline on a percentage basis as the amount of the assets under management increases, at some point (probably on amounts over $50 million) the custodial fees are large enough that one will always want to explicitly negotiate for custodial services. Fortunately, as funds become larger, it is more common for the organization to negotiate a custodial arrangement for an agreed-upon fee as a result of which the major banks have a greater presence in the institutional custody market.

The larger the funds become, the greater the extent to which all components of the investment management process are customized to provide either additional services or lower fees. With larger amounts of money, it becomes less important to wrap services into affordable packages. So the most important point is simply to be aware that the custody decision can in fact be broken out and dealt with separately.

SECURITIES BROKERAGE

As noted earlier, on most major markets the area of buying and selling securities is not a place where brokers can often add a great deal of value. In addition, no matter how or where trades are executed today, the fees will be less than they once were so that cost concerns may not be a differentiating factor either. Lower brokerage costs are even more readily available in the institutional market of which most charitable organizations are a part. Large trades initiated at the direction of investment managers typically are executed at so-called institutional rates of between 6 and 8 cents per share. These rates are available from all major brokers on large institutional accounts and represent the range in which the vast majority of such shares are traded.

As it is increasingly difficult to differentiate brokers based on their stock-trading ability, and since fees are very low, the brokerage relationship will usually be selected based on other factors. Who ends up actually executing trades will largely be the result of who ends up in charge of the overall investment environment.

If that person is a broker, then the majority of the trades will usually be executed through the broker's own firm.[14] If the primary advisor is a consultant or an investment manager, then either the consultant will choose a brokerage relationship (possibly in combination with custody) or each investment advisor will execute trades wherever they can get the best service and price for securities within their asset class. In that case, you will

---

[14] Even this is not necessarily true. There are teams of financial consultants/stock brokers at more than one major national brokerage firm, all of whose funds are custodied away from their own firms (usually at custodial banks) and who execute only a small percentage of the trades through their own firms. They are true institutional consultants in the purest, general contractor role.

not choose the broker at all, but rather, the investment advisors will make that selection, and it won't necessarily be the same for all trades.[15]

Here, just as in the custody decision, the most important point is that securities brokerage can be a separately acquired and priced service. Even with a consultant and multiple advisors, if the broker your organization uses provides helpful service, then you may instruct your investment advisor to execute trades through that broker. This is commonly done in the industry.

When using a broker-consultant, trading alone, even at low rates, may cover all or a portion of the consulting service fees for which you might otherwise have to write checks. Numerous such relationships exist throughout the industry.[16] Consequently, in managing your investments, it is important to know what you are paying for trades and what services you are receiving. If you are trading in institutional volumes but not getting institutional rates, something is wrong. Even when trading at institutional rates, you should still be receiving good service. Ultimately, securities brokerage should be selected based on the services that the broker can provide to the overall investment management operation with price being only one component of the equation.

Finding Help

As we have now seen, there is an enormous amount of crossover by the various service providers in each of the five basic areas of investment function. The help that most organizations desire is that of a "general contractor" who can guide them through the entire investment management process: Such a person or organization can then bring in specialists (in essence, subcontractors) for each of the required functions. So how are we to find such help?

One way to begin the search for such an advisor is to spend a day or two calling the chief financial officers of a dozen comparable nonprofit organizations. Ask them who they use as their consultant, if they have one, their stock broker (if that person is different than the consultant), their investment

---

[15] While it can be a fine system to allow investment advisors to direct trades, one needs to be aware also of soft dollar arrangements. The major brokerage firms are important sources of investment research for the entire industry. They make the research available to their own people and then essentially sell it to others on a so-called soft dollar basis. The soft dollars are credits that the brokerage firms give to investment advisors who direct trades though them. The managers can then use these credits to purchase research services either from the brokers or from others. For many investment managers, soft dollars are an important source of revenue.

[16] I wish it were possible to be more specific and say, "You should pay Y cents per share for trades vs. X basis points as a total consulting fee," but the reality is that the universe of possible combinations of services over accounts of all sizes and compositions simply does not allow for a standardized approach.

managers, and where they maintain custody. In addition to names, solicit evaluations. The result will be a list of candidates to interview.

Continue your exploration by informally interviewing a number of the people identified through your initial calling. Ultimately, there is a fair amount to know about each potential service provider, some of which is reflected in the due diligence checklist in Exhibit 6.6. While the due diligence process is extremely important, the purpose of beginning with referrals and following that with informal interviews is to develop some sense of the character and compatibility of the potential service providers. The interviews, particularly of an informal nature, are not a substitute for due diligence in hiring help. Rather, they are a complement intended to help the organization's officers and directors attain a degree of comfort with the process.

Exhibit 6.7 shows a representative set of questions for a more formal Request for Proposal (RFP). Such requests, widely referred to as RFPs, are also commonly used by nonprofits in conducting investment manager and investment consultant searches. The final chapter of this book discusses the use of RFPs in greater detail.

KNOW HOW THE PROVIDER IS PAID

Several years ago, I was a speaker at a conference. I had already given my talk and was attending seminars offered by other speakers. While I was waiting for the next session to begin, an upcoming speaker introduced himself, and we got to chatting. His topic was something like "Maximizing the Benefit of Using Charitable Remainder Trusts."

"What do you do for a living?" I asked him.

"I give seminars," he answered.

"You give seminars!" I exclaimed questioningly. "How can anyone earn a living by just giving seminars?"

"Well, that's what I do," he said with a nervous chuckle.

"Really," I said, "the only people I know who appear to earn a living giving seminars actually sell life insurance."

"Oh, well," he admitted, "I also own a life insurance agency."

A few minutes later, I had attended enough of his seminar to be sure that no matter what the situation, the way to maximize returns from charitable remainder trusts was to purchase a wealth replacement life insurance policy outside the trust and to invest with a variable annuity contract inside the trust. In other words, there is no investment problem this gentleman would not solve by recommending more insurance or insurance industry products.

The real problem here is deceitfulness. If the man in my story had simply stated that he sells life insurance for a living, my first reaction would have been to ask for his card. If he had been willing to advertise his seminar as "Creative Uses of Life Insurance and Life Insurance Products in Charitable

EXHIBIT 6.6. Investment Manager—Due Diligence Checklist

1. Organizational History and Structure
   a) Ownership
   b) Affiliations
      e.g., Investment Counsel Association of America

2. Regulatory compliance
   a) Form of licensing
   b) SEC form ADV

3. Personnel
   a) Continuity
   b) Professional qualifications

4. Understanding of charitable world
   a) Existing clients (references)
   b) Related services

5. Assets under management
   a) Amount
   b) Types

6. Account requirements
   a) Minimum size
   b) Asset classes

7. Investment style

8. Research capabilities
   a) Sources
   b) Portfolio processes

9. Performance
   a) History
   b) Derivation of performance
   c) Industry reporting standards—Association for Investment Management and Research (AIMR)

10. Client relations
    a) Philosophy
    b) Frequency of contact

11. Fees

Remainder Trusts," I would have thought it just fine. Ironically, even though I generally am not enamored of life insurance products, the use of second-to-die wealth replacement insurance is actually an excellent device for many people, when coupled with a charitable remainder trust. My objection was not to the substance of his advice but to the fact that it presented the information in a deceitful manner. It is impossible to avoid all contact with deceitful people in the world of investing, but one of the easiest ways to identify

EXHIIT 6.7. Specific Questions for Investment Consultant Search

The notion of a "due diligence" checklist is also frequently reflected in a so-called Request for Proposal or RFP. The following 12 questions are an example of those that might constitute an RFP for an investment management consultant (the "general contractor").

1. Please provide a brief description of your firm, its history, ownership, and an organizational chart.

2. Please provide a summary that includes the firm's name, office address, name of contact person, phone number, and fax number.

3. List titles, responsibilities, and location of officers and other personnel who would provide services for our account. Describe their background and experience.

4. List total number of your consulting clients, along with the market value of their accounts, as of [most recent year-end date].

5. Provide a brief description of your proposed process and key criteria, including the client's involvement, for development of investment objectives and development of overall investment policy relating to specific asset classes.

6. Describe the process used for determining an asset allocation recommendation.

7. Briefly describe an actual asset allocation study prepared by your firm for a client.

8. When conducting a search, what is your source of manager candidates? If you use a search database, is the manager database maintained in-house or is it purchased?

9. Briefly describe the manager search process provided by your firm.

10. Briefly describe your reporting system and provide a sample report.

11. Please provide client references showing asset size, years with your firm, services provided, the client contact person and phone number for at least five clients of the firm who have been with the firm the past four years.

12. Please describe your fee schedule, with specific reference to (i) investment manager selection, (ii) development of investment policies, and (iii) performance evaluation.

them is to ask how they earn a living. It is a simple test. If you don't understand the answer, back slowly out of the room.

WHY IT IS IMPORTANT TO KNOW WHAT YOU ARE PAYING

Honesty is not the only reason one needs to know how service providers are paid. The other reason concerns something known in physics as "instrumentation effects." A simple example of an instrumentation effect is measuring the temperature of a small amount of water. If a large, warm thermometer is placed in a small test tube full of cool water, the heat from the thermometer will raise the temperature of the water. The thermometer then gives a reading of the new equilibrium temperature of the water. The attempt to measure the temperature of the water would be distorted by the heat of the instrument used. In a sense, the temperature of the thermometer, not the water, would be measured.

In the world of investments, there are usually multiple solutions to any investment situation. On a $1 million endowment, one can hire an investment manager to construct a portfolio of stocks and bonds, select mutual funds, or participate in a brokerage account wrap program. When asking what is best for the portfolio—when taking the investment temperature—one finds that the answer invariably depends to some extent on the chosen instrument. In other words, the answer depends on who is providing the solution.

Since the chosen instruments are human-made and therefore largely possessed of the same weaknesses, this instrumentation effect is unavoidable. It occurs in the most sophisticated of settings.[17] An understanding of how each potential advisor makes money helps an organization judge how much bias the advice contains.

DO NOT MUZZLE THE OXEN

It is inevitable that a substantial portion of any discussion about hiring investment help deals with the associated fees and expenses. Talk long enough, and soon it seems that the ultimate goal is to get fees and expenses as low as possible. This is particularly easy to do in a nonprofit setting where so much time and effort is spent either raising money or figuring out how to get by with what we have.

The ultimate goal in retaining investment help, however, is not to save money on fees and expenses. The ultimate goal is to maximize the organization's funds. There are many situations in which the least expensive help is not necessarily the best or the most appropriate for the organization. Consequently, even though many firms either reduce fees for charities or make contributions to the fund-raising efforts of their charitable clients, it is philo-

---

[17] A fascinating recent study found that securities analysts routinely inflated the values of stocks of those companies that the brokerage firms—the analysts' employers—were in the process of underwriting the shares (selling shares to the public for the first time). When the analysts' employers were the lead underwriters, the exaggeration was even worse. Are the analysts being deceitful? Not at all. They are merely human and enthusiastic. See "The Relation between Analysts' Long-Term Earnings Forecasts and Stock Price Performance Following Equity Offerings" by Patricia Dechow and Richard Sloan (Wharton School, University of Pennsylvania) and Amy Sweeney (Harvard Business School), September 1996.

sophically important that charities approach outside service providers with the expectation that they will pay them fairly for the services rendered. Such an approach moves the organization from asking for favors to expecting competent help.

Conclusion

At the end of the day, every organization with funds to invest needs help in all five of the areas discussed: custody, asset allocation, brokerage, investment selection, and performance reporting services. Each of these may be acquired separately, particularly as the amounts of money increase, or in various combinations. No single model is right for all situations. Exhibits 6.8 and 6.9, however, give rough guidance to the range of investment management options. Exhibit 6.9 provides an approximate idea of what those services might cost on a $10 million portfolio.

Collectively, all nine exhibits in this chapter are intended to serve as a pocket guide to the world of investment management services. That world is not as simple, of course, as the exhibits may suggest. But it is not as complicated as it first appears. Hold on to that thought as you begin looking for help.

EXHIBIT 6.8. Investment Management Options—Common Break Points Based on Dollars under Management

Service Options	Portfolio Size	Portfolio Characteristics	
		Common Allocations	Range of Fees
Single investment advisor with or without 3rd party reporting	Under $5,000,000	Single, balanced portfolio typically of U.S. equities	Investment fees of 1.25 to 1.5%
Two advisors with or without 3rd party reporting	$5,000,000 to $10,000,000	Two portfolios, different styles (e.g., value and growth) usually both balanced	Investment fees of 1.25% or less
Multiple advisors with 3rd party reporting	$10,000,000 to $25,000,000	Multiple portfolios with managers selected by investment style	Investment fees of 1.0% or less
Full consulting relationship (Note: The consulting relationship can be provided by contract with companies that act exclusively in that capacity or, in select cases, by registered representatives of major stock brokers. In the latter situations, the "consulting fees" may be charged directly or in the form of higher than institutional rate trading commissions.)	$25,000,000 or more	Mulitple portfolios with managers selected by asset class under sophisticated asset allocation models, regular rebalancing	Investment fees and expenses under 1.0%

**The information on this table represents an effort at describing complicated options in very general terms. Therefore, none of this information is likely to be completely accurate when applied to any one consultant, investment advisor, or stock broker. This page is designed to be used for general discussion purposes only.

EXHIBIT 6.9. Investment Management Options—Costs and Benefits of Direct Investment and Consultant Serviced Accounts

| Service Options | Analysis | | Cost estimates (based on $2,000,000 portfolio) |
	Advantages	Disadvantages	
Single investment advisor	Lowest cost. Simplest relationship	No independent performance review	Investment fees of 1.25 to 1.5% including expenses
Single advisor with 3rd party reporting	Single relationship 3rd party verification of performance	Slightly higher expenses	Investment fees plus $1,000 per quarter
Multiple advisors with 3rd party reporting	Potentially higher performance with 3rd party verification	Higher fees and expenses	Investment fees, plus $1,000 per quarter plus ½ of 1% increase in expenses
Full consulting relationship (Note: the consulting relationship can be provided by contract with companies that act exclusively in that capacity or, in select cases, by registered representatives of major stock brokers. In the latter situations, the "consulting fees" may be charged directly or in the form of higher than institutional rate trading commissions.)	Potentially higher performance with 3rd party verification Complete delegation of investment advisor oversight	Higher fees Potential loss of direct relationship with investment advisor Potential conflict of interest in certain brokerage relationships	Investment fees, plus ½ of 1% increase in expenses plus consulting fees (e.g., $10,000 per year vs. ½ of 1%)

**The information on this table represents an effort at describing complicated options in very general terms. Therefore, none of this information is likely to be completely accurate when applied to any one consultant, investment advisor or stock broker. This page is designed to be used for general discussion purposes only.

7 ▼ Investment Accounting and Performance Reporting

There are two critical components of any effort to manage financial issues: knowing the current situation and knowing its evolution. In the world of investments, knowing the current situation is a matter of appropriate accounting. Properly done, it describes current investments and their worth at particular points in time. Accounting, by itself, provides little information about the past and explains nothing at all about whether the current situation is appropriate. In the world of investments, the latter questions are answered by performance reporting.

The initial thought of most organizations is to set an income or return goal for their funds. Performance reporting simply states whether the goal was met. Consider the performance reporting meeting of the ACO's board.

At the ACO . . .

PERFORMANCE STANDARDS

"How do we know if they are doing a good job? We can't just give them the money and tell them to go manage. There has to be a standard."

The director advancing this argument is completely correct. There has to be a standard. "And there have to be regular reports on the portfolio's performance," said another.

"Well, we can tell how they're doing from the financial records. The CFO puts the value of our investments in the reports every month—so that's not an issue. The question is, what's the goal?"

"You're right," another responded. "What's the standard? What do we care about?"

"Well, for one thing, we want the portfolio to outpace inflation."

"Okay, so part one, the portfolio ought to achieve a rate of return that exceeds inflation by what, 5 percent?"

"That sounds great. That way we can spend 5 percent and still keep up with inflation."

"Good. Now what?"

"Well, if the managers are any good, they ought to be able to outperform the market. After all, they're pros. If they can't do better than the market, we should be using index funds."

"Agreed. So what's the standard?"

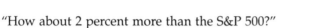

"How about 2 percent more than the S&P 500?"

"Sounds great, but what if they invest in a bunch of really risky stocks in order to beat the market? Aren't we setting ourselves up for more risk than we really want?"

"You're right. Let's put in something about risk."

"Okay, here is the performance standard: The manager is to achieve annually a return that exceeds the S&P 500 by 2 percent and that exceeds inflation by 5 percent. When investing to achieve these returns, the manager is not to take more than 80 percent of the risk of the S&P 500. Thus, in a down market, the portfolio should never be down more than 80 percent of what the market is down, less whatever dividends and interest are earned for that year."

There are many problems with the ACO's approach to performance. The most important problem is that setting a goal is not the same as measuring progress toward that goal. And setting a goal is not the same as determining whether the means to the goal is correct. To solve their problems, the ACO needs to do the following things: understand financial reports better, consider all its objectives and not just return goals, and understand which things can be measured on an absolute or relative basis. Let us see if we can offer some guidance.

The Role of Accounting-Based Financial Statements

The purpose of audited financial statements is to provide an accurate picture of the income and expenses of the organization for the period being measured and of its assets and liabilities at the conclusion of that period. Accounting statements are typically prepared internally by a financial officer and reviewed by external accountants from public accounting firms. A review conducted in accordance with the most stringent standards and resulting in a report attesting to the accuracy of those reports by the outside accountants is referred to as an audit. While it is possible to abuse the process, deceive the auditors, and thereby produce false reports, the focus of an audit is to present an accurate picture of the financial situation of an organization.

There are also several recent developments in accounting that bear directly on investment management. Marking to market, which means reporting the value of assets based on their current price in a public market, is among the more important. Before considering specific rules that apply to investment performance reporting, it is important to understand something of the basic requirements and limitations of accounting.

ACCOUNTING BASICS

A few years ago, I did a brief stint as a financial officer at a small company with annual revenues of about $1 million. While my title was chief financial officer, I was effectively a controller who also did internal accounting. The only way I could do the accounting was to carry a 3 × 5 card with notes on when to credit income, debit expenses, and the like.

Prior to that experience, I had heard of generally accepted accounting principles (GAAP) and naively believed that they were accounting rules. I discovered that although there are rules, an enormous amount of judgment is also involved, such that one person's expense can be another's investment. The goal of those setting the standards is to create a sufficient degree of uniformity so the public can rely on the information being presented.

Basic accounting standards are issued by the Financial Accounting Standards Board and are known as FASBs. In addition, the Association of Independent Certified Public Accountants (AICPA) issues commentaries on the FASBs, called pronouncements, along with its own publications on generally accepted accounting principles. While not laws, these accounting standards frequently have the same effect. Whenever one is required by a regulator, prospective lender, or voluntary regulatory organization to maintain audited financial records, those standards apply to the organization with the force of law. As a practical matter, to obtain a "clean" auditing letter, the standards must be met.

In the world of investments, the Securities and Exchange Commission (SEC) and the Internal Revenue Service (IRS) also dip their oars in these waters. While both refer often to generally accepted accounting principles as the reporting standard, there are also numerous situations in which these agencies specify the manner in which particular financial information must be reported. The SEC also plays a significant role in investment performance reporting. However, the intricacies of accounting for investment purposes are well beyond the scope of this book.[1]

MARKING TO MARKET

FASB 124, issued in November 1995, is applicable to financial years beginning after December 15, 1995, and requires that nonprofit organizations report the value of their financial investments based on current fair market value. This process, known as "marking to market," has not previously been the standard in accounting. Rather, investments have traditionally been reported at the lesser of their fair market value or cost. Under that standard, financial statements were almost no guide to the true value of investments.

For policy purposes, it is important to be aware of this new requirement. The sample policies require that investment managers provide market-based information to the organizational client on a monthly basis. Histori-

---

[1] For a good general guide to nonprofit accounting, see Melvin Gross, Richard F. Larkin, Roger Bruttomesso, and Macnully, *Financial and Accounting Guide for Not-for-Profit Organizations*, 5th ed., New York: John Wiley.

cally, this information was not necessarily available from the custodian. In addition, brokerage statements usually carried investments at market prices but did not show the cost basis of the assets. Consequently, it was not easy to obtain adequate accounting information from the participants in the investment management process.

Increasingly, that situation is changing with all of the participants (custodian, broker, and investment manager) now more likely to offer complete reports.[2] Nonetheless, there are still many investment managers, bank custodians, and brokers whose statements alone are inadequate for investment management accounting in accordance with FASB 124 standards. To be complete, such a report should show all pertinent information, including purchase price, purchase date, and present market value by tax lot.[3] A sample of such a report is included as Appendix E-1.

Accounting Is Not Enough

Traditional financial statements are inadequate as the reporting system that governs investment management, even with the improvements in financial accounting for investments mandated by recent FASBs. Why? First, accounting records are prepared on a point-in-time perspective. Audited financial statements received six weeks or more after the close of the fiscal year are considered timely by most accountants. From an investment perspective, six weeks can be an eternity, because an investment portfolio may be worth far less when you read the statement than it was worth during the period the statement reflects. Financial records are snapshots that are quickly dated.

Second, financial records contain little qualitative information about the assets they reflect. Consequently, when analyzing investment assets from financial statements, you will know the market value at the close of the period being reported and may find the cost basis in footnotes. Collectively, that will allow you to calculate the aggregate amount of unrealized gain or loss. But you have no idea of the source of the unrealized gain.

Consider the fund shown in Exhibit 7.1. It has a current market value of $1 million after having gained $100,000 in the previous year. In the three

---

[2] See Chapter 6 on hiring investment help for an explanation of the roles played by the different service providers. When investing exclusively in mutual funds or on smaller managed accounts that are maintained with a broker, the investment management, custody, and brokerage services might all be provided by the same company.

[3] A lot refers to the unit in which the securities were purchased. A holding of 1,000 shares of IBM, purchased at different times in increments of 600 and 400 shares respectively, represents two lots. If you know the lots and cost basis of each, you can sell shares from specific lots, and the realized capital gain will be based on the cost of those particular shares. In accounts with income tax ramifications, such as charitable remainder trusts, the ability to sell shares with a higher or lower basis according to tax concerns is an important investment nuance.

EXHIBIT 7.1. Portfolio Value in Thousands of Dollars

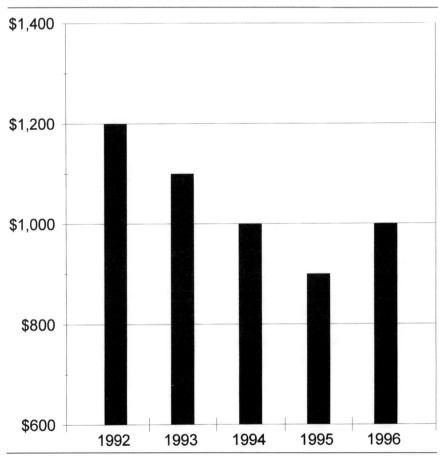

preceding years, however, the portfolio suffered successive $100,000 losses, following which the account was liquidated, and the proceeds were reinvested in a manner that generated the $100,000 gain.

The financial records would report the current value and in footnotes show that the basis of the assets was $100,000 less, suggesting a one-year 11.11 percent gain ($100,000/$900,000 = 11.11 percent). In truth, however, the portfolio has lost 16.67 percent of its value over four years. The annualized return over the last three years was actually negative. If those three years happened to be the last three years (when the market has been roaring), then the portfolio has underperformed the market by a double-digit number. Instead of being happy with 10 percent, the investment committee should be asking hard questions about why the portfolio is so far behind the market. The financial statements provide inadequate information about how the current situation developed.

Finally, and perhaps most troubling for those who have relied exclusively on financial records, the absence of qualitative information means that there is no risk analysis inherent in those records. You know what an asset is worth, but you have no idea how likely it is to retain that value. A properly diversified portfolio of U.S. stocks and bonds will be reported exactly the same way as a portfolio consisting of only a few positions all in the same sector but the risk inherent in each is vastly different.

Investment Management Performance Reporting

Investment management performance standards, as a practical matter, fall into two categories: absolute and relative. Absolute standards are those components of the investment advisor's performance (or of the fund's performance) that can be measured solely by reference to the investment policies. Relative standards are those performance characteristics that can be measured only in comparison to an external index. Both are important.

ABSOLUTE STANDARDS

Absolute standards might include:

1. Compliance with investment policies
2. Maintaining portfolios within established asset allocation parameters
3. Maintaining adequate liquidity
4. Meeting established absolute return goals.

Obeying the Rules
The first absolute performance standard is that of complying with the provisions of the investment policies. While this may seem obvious, there are a number of ways that managers can fail to comply with stated policies. At times, there are powerful incentives to do so.

The most common example of failing to comply with a policy in the case of larger, more sophisticated portfolios is when investment managers wander from their prescribed style and stated area of expertise in an effort to enhance a portfolio's performance. A number of U.S. equity managers in 1994 added substantial international stock positions. The temptation was based on strong international stock performance in the previous several years and weak U.S. equity performance in 1994. Managers who were being measured against the S&P 500 or another index of U.S. equities were hoping for performance enhancement from foreign securities.

There is nothing wrong with painting a room blue, unless the room was supposed to be painted white. Similarly, there is nothing wrong with investing in foreign securities, unless you were hired to do something else. It is extremely important that asset class managers maintain portfolios that are consistent with the style or asset class they were hired to manage. Failure to do so should be grounds for termination.

Asset Allocation Percentages

If the investment policy committee does its job properly and, with the advisor, establishes an acceptable range for each asset class, honoring those allocations becomes another absolute standard. Since different asset classes have disparate performances, which cause percentage changes over time, it is unrealistic to require that the equity allocation be a precise percentage. It is the advisor's duty to call the committee's attention to allocations that require rebalancing so that the portfolio may be maintained within targeted ranges (see "Rebalancing" in Chapter 3).

Liquidity

Assuming that the organization has clearly communicated its cash flow requirements, there is no reason for a portfolio to experience inadequate liquidity. If funds are not available when needed, something is wrong in the manager–chief financial officer relationship or elsewhere in the system.

Absolute Return Goals

Occasionally, a set of investment policies will establish absolute return goals. There are also times in the management of net income charitable remainder trust assets when the finance committee will attempt to satisfy the income beneficiary by earning a certain level of current return. Such absolute return goals should be implemented very cautiously.

It is fine to have an absolute return standard if it is within the ability of a manager to fulfill. In today's interest rate environment, a goal of 6 percent current income (net income trust) is certainly achievable. However, an 11 percent target would require extraordinary risk or the conversion of principal into income. If you are going to establish such standards, be aware of the risks that might be taken by managers in an effort to meet those standards.

Finally, board members who enthusiastically participate in establishing performance standards sometimes do not recognize these realities. After everyone has their say, the performance standard looks just like that adopted by the ACO.[4]

Here is a brief analysis of this standard. The "inflation plus" objective is

---

[4] "The manager is to achieve annually a return that exceeds the S&P 500 by 2 percent and that exceeds inflation by 5 percent. When investing to achieve these returns, the manager is not to take more than 80 percent of the risk of the S&P 500. Thus, in a down market, the portfolio should never be down more than 80 percent of what the market is down, less whatever dividends and interest are earned for that year."

an absolute standard, at least in comparison with the stock market. The manager is to achieve a certain rate of return relative to inflation even if the market, possibly as a result of very high inflation, is falling like a rock! Consequently, it will be only an accident of convenient circumstances and markets if the manager is able to achieve that goal while also attempting to achieve the relative performance goals.

Further, there is virtually no chance that the manager will be able to out-perform the markets over time while taking below-market risk. It is, from the board's perspective, a pipe dream standard. From the manager's perspective, it is a nightmare.

RELATIVE STANDARDS

Any investment performance standard can be unrealistic, as previously explained. Between the two, relative standards generally are the more helpful for two reasons. First, the overall goal is to participate in the financial markets and allow them to work for our benefit over time. From that perspective the principal concern is to choose the level of participation that best suits our growth objectives *and tolerance for risk.* Relative performance standards lend themselves to this effort.

Second, relative performance standards require results that are at least arguably within the managers' control. An organization can ask its manager to construct portfolios whose performance matches the market. But thinking back to the "inflation plus" standard, if the government decides to devalue the currency through either fiscal or monetary policies, there is little that any manager will be able to do—at least on a near-term basis—to "outperform" the resulting massive inflation. Many things are simply not within the manager's control.

Available Benchmarks

There are many readily available indexes and other benchmarks against which portfolio performance can be measured. Exhibit 7.2 is a list of investment funds from the Common Fund Annual Report which includes with each fund an appropriate published index for comparison purposes. The Common Fund's pools are in bold and the indexes are below that in regular type. The first six domestic equity funds are all measured against the S&P 500. This list shows both the index, the name of the company that publishes it (e.g., *Russell* 1000 Growth Index), and the segment of the market that is being measured. These indexes make it possible to know how the "market" is performing. In addition, the publishers make an effort to produce an index that is consistent over time.

How can these indexes be used to measure performance? There are two basic approaches. The first approach is for the do-it-yourself investment policy committee that actively supervises its investment managers without the help of an investment consultant. The second extends the self-help model

EXHIBIT 7.2. Common Fund Annual Report—Performance

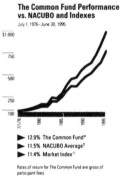

The Common Fund 1996 Annual Report

Investment Returns

The Common Fund Performance vs. NACUBO and Indexes

July 1, 1976 – June 30, 1995

$1,000
750
500
250
100

7/1/76 1980 1985 1990 1995

▶ 12.9% The Common Fund*
▶ 11.5% NACUBO Average†
▶ 11.4% Market Index◇

Rates of return for The Common Fund are gross of participant fees

* Annual actual asset allocation of participants in the NACUBO Survey, with The Common Fund Equity, Bond and Short Term Fund returns

† Average return for NACUBO participants

◇ Annual actual asset allocation of participants in the NACUBO Survey with S&P 500, Lehman Gov't /Corp. Bond Index and 3-Month T-Bill Index returns

Note: Returns in this report (except where noted) are gross of participant fees paid to The Common Fund, which are itemized on pages 72–73. Individual returns will be reduced by such fees. Information regarding performance net of fees is available upon request.

	1995-96 Fiscal Year Returns
Equity Fund	**23.9%**
Equity Allocation Pool	**23.2**
Domestic Equity Fund*	**19.2**
Core Equity Fund	**25.9**
Absolute Return (Equitized) Fund	**28.2**
Hedge Fund	**20.4**
S&P 500 Index	26.1
Russell 3000 Index	26.0
Growth Equity Fund	**28.1**
Russell 1000 Growth Index	27.8
Equity-Income Fund	**24.1**
Equity-Income Allocation Pool	**21.7**
Lipper Equity Income Fund Index†	20.9
Absolute Return Fund	**14.8**
3-Month Treasury Bill (Average Yield)	5.4
Small Cap Growth Fund	**25.7**
Russell 2000 Growth Index	26.5
Small Cap Value Fund	**27.1**
Russell 2000 Value Index	21.1
Global Equity Fund (Less Hedged)	**18.1%**
MSCI World Index	18.4
Global Equity Fund (More Hedged)	**21.6**
MSCI World Index (Hedged)	26.6
International Equity Fund (Less Hedged)	**16.3**
MSCI World ex-U.S. Index	13.3
International Equity Fund (More Hedged)	**23.1**
MSCI World ex-U.S. Index (Hedged)	28.1
Emerging Markets Fund	**13.1**
IFC Emerging Markets (Investable) Index	10.7
Bond Fund	**6.6%**
Bond Allocation Pool	**10.1**
High Quality Bond Fund	**6.8**
High Quality Bond Allocation Pool	**8.3**
Lehman Aggregate Bond Index	5.0
Global Bond Fund (Less Hedged)	**2.2%**
Salomon World Government Bond Index	0.4
Global Bond Fund (More Hedged)	**8.6**
Salomon World Government Bond Index (Hedged)	9.1
International Bond Fund (Less Hedged)	**0.6**
Salomon Non-U.S. Dollar World Government Bond Index	-1.7
International Bond Fund (More Hedged)	**10.8**
Salomon Non-U.S. Dollar World Government Bond Index (Hedged)	11.5
Intermediate Cash Fund	**5.8%**
Merrill Lynch 1–3 Year Treasury Index	5.5
Short Term Fund (Net Credited Rate)	**5.6**
3-Month Treasury Bill (Average Yield)	5.4

* Fund commenced operations September 1, 1995; return not annualized.
† Return reported net of expenses and exclusive of sales loads.

by including a consultant's technical expertise. Both approaches begin with asset allocation models.

Using Asset Allocation Models for Performance Measurement
Recall that investment policies include a recommended asset allocation model for each portfolio. Each model is, therefore, a collection of asset classes with a permitted range of investment percentages for each class. For each asset class, there is also at least one published index. Consequently, a very simple yet effective way to measure relative portfolio performance is to construct a model portfolio of the indexes and use it as the baseline against which to measure the portfolio's performance.

Exhibit 7.3 provides an example for a five-asset-class model. In the report, one can observe the asset class, the name of the manager or fund, the percentages that are applied, and the resulting weighted-average portfolio performance. The exhibit also shows the standard deviation of return for the model portfolio's performance over the periods in question. By applying the same percentage allocations to an appropriate index for each asset class it is possible to make an apples-to-apples comparison. This approach, which any investment policy committee could use, is a fair measure against which to compare a manager's performance. In addition, one can look a bit more deeply within each asset class by comparing the performance of the manager of that class against other managers on both a simple performance (Exhibit 7.4) or a risk-adjusted basis (Exhibit 7.5).

Frequency of Performance Measurement

How frequently should performance be measured? The standard in the institutional world is as follows.

On a monthly basis, organizations review an account statement to note transactions, verify that the assets on its books are reflected properly, and check the value of the account for a reasonable relationship to the previous month's value. The only reason for doing anything further is if this cursory review reveals something aberrational, such as unusual transactions, missing assets, or wild swings in value.

On a quarterly basis, organizations compare portfolio performance with the standard index discussed above. They also check to be sure that absolute standards and asset allocation parameters are being followed. Absent violation of those standards or the "red flags" already mentioned, nothing further is done.

In the annual review, organizations take a hard look at their relative performance and meet face-to-face with investment managers to discuss that performance. The annual review should include a study of investment performance and asset allocation and a determination of whether changes are needed. A typical policy would mandate rebalancing annually or whenever

EXHIBIT 7.3. Model Portfolio—Five Asset Classes

Performance Summary Sheet
V&H INCOME MODEL   AS OF Q2 1996

Allocations	Entity Name	Min %	Max %	Assigned %
	Van Deventer & Hoch - Eq - Value/Low P/E	0%	50%	5%
	Brandes Inv Partners - Intl Eq	0%	50%	10%
	MFS High-Income A	0%	50%	20%
	T-Bills	0%	15%	15%
	Payden & Rygel - Core Bond	0%	50%	50%

Summary Statistics

Total Quarters	50	# Up Quarters	42	# Down Quarters	8
Highest Quarter		11.20 %	Lowest Quarter		-2.41 %
Highest Year		25.29 %	Lowest Year		-1.50 %
Highest 4 Qtr Period		31.12 %	Lowest 4 Qtr Period		-1.50 %

Performance Statistics

	Annualized Return	Standard Deviation	Value Added	Sharpe's Ratio
Latest Quarter	1.48	.	.	.
Latest 6 Months	1.10	.	.	.
Latest 9 Months	4.96	.	.	.
Latest Year	7.88	.	.	.
Latest 18 Months	11.88	.	.	.
Latest 2 Years	9.60	.	.	.
Latest 3 Years	7.73	2.24	-1.72	.
Latest 4 Years	9.06	2.21	-0.49	.
Latest 5 Years	10.83	2.32	1.37	.
Latest 10 Years	9.98	2.37	3.23	.
Latest 15 Years	.	.	.	.
Latest 20 Years	.	.	.	.

Quarterly Returns

Year	Qtr 1	Qtr 2	Qtr 3	Qtr 4	Annual
1984	2.11	-2.03	6.17	3.96	10.41
1985	3.83	6.41	3.35	7.21	22.42
1986	11.20	1.00	0.20	2.96	15.87
1987	3.51	0.78	1.93	-2.41	3.77
1988	5.65	2.91	2.10	2.61	13.91
1989	2.37	6.18	1.82	1.86	12.73
1990	-1.05	2.47	-1.73	1.54	1.18
1991	7.60	3.49	6.73	5.42	25.29
1992	1.44	3.56	3.65	0.41	9.33
1993	5.51	3.04	4.02	3.11	16.61
1994	-2.05	-0.93	1.63	-0.12	-1.50
1995	4.31	5.17	2.78	3.82	17.05
1996	-0.37	1.48			

Produced by Capital Markets Research

allocations change by more than some amount, such as 10 percent, as a result of disparate investment performance between classes.[5] This is also the time

---

[5] Disparate performance by asset class is normal. Rebalancing the portfolio will also be a regular event and should not be viewed as punishment for the manager whose class is being reduced nor as a reward for a manager whose class is being increased. It is, in a sense, unrelated to their efforts.

EXHIBIT 7.4. Relative Performance Measurement—Third Quarter 1993 to Second Quarter 1996

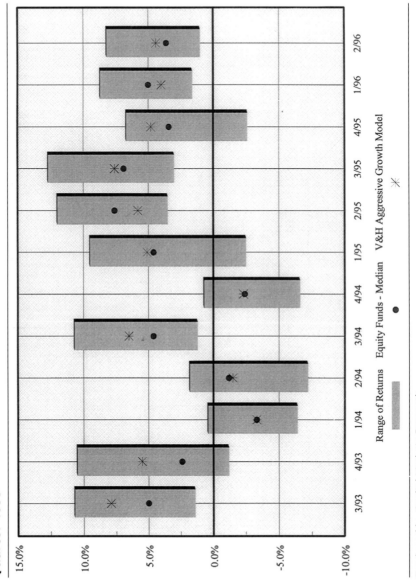

Range of Returns   Equity Funds - Median   V&H Aggressive Growth Model

Produced by Capital Markets Research

EXHIBIT 7.5. Return vs. Risk Analysis—Third Quarter 1991 to Second Quarter 1996

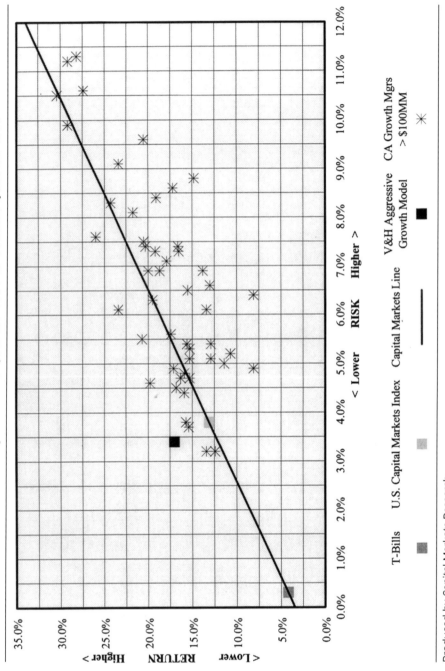

Produced by Capital Markets Research

to discuss with the manager the reasons for the portfolio's success or under-performance relative to the indexes.

Many institutions of varying sizes who employ investment consultants and outside managers meet with them for face-to-face meetings on a quarterly basis. For many established relationships (if the manager has been working for the organization for more than a year and there is a reasonable level of comfort), annual meetings are sufficient. This assumes that the investment policy committee receives appropriate quarterly reports and is capable of understanding them. This also assumes that there are not ongoing changes in the character of the funds being managed or other challenges that require more frequent meetings. Some portfolios have dramatic inflows and outflows of funds. Some portfolios represent pools with many interested parties to whom the board must report. In such situations quarterly meetings are in fact necessary.

When Should the Manager Be Fired?

This is a very tough question. Most organizations that employ multiple managers, each of whom is asset-class or style-specific, tend to be more performance-sensitive than they should be. The reason is that it is very difficult—and in fact it may be impossible—for managers actually to control their performance within a very tight range over short periods of time unless they are closet indexing.[6] The degree of precision necessary to perform within a narrow range on a quarterly or even an annual basis does not exist, at least not in the equity markets.

Consider once more Exhibit 7.5. It shows 5-year returns for all California value managers with more than $100 million under management. Notice the breadth of the range. The high end of the group is at 30 percent while the low end is at 7.5 percent. When risk is factored in the picture is cloudier still. More than one-half of those measured performed below the capital markets line.

As difficult as it may be, boards ought to take short-term underperformance with a grain of salt unless there are other reasons for concern. A manager who is providing good service, following the disciplines for which he or she was hired, and offering the capabilities of the firm should not be fired for merely one year of underperformance. The only exception might be for extreme underperformance, for example, for greater than one standard deviation from the average of comparable managers, as that suggests that something more fundamental may be wrong inside the manager's shop.

The best time to review manager performance that is not triggered by a

---

[6] That is, constructing portfolios intended to mimic "the market" as measured by a particular benchmark, such as the S&P 500, while professing to be pursuing a particular investment style, such as value or growth.

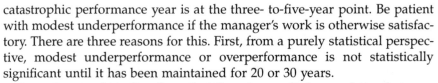
catastrophic performance year is at the three- to-five-year point. Be patient with modest underperformance if the manager's work is otherwise satisfactory. There are three reasons for this. First, from a purely statistical perspective, modest underperformance or overperformance is not statistically significant until it has been maintained for 20 or 30 years.

Second, several studies show that there is very little correlation between a manager's performance over a five-year period and over a succeeding five-year period. Clearly, however, if an organization terminates one manager for underperformance, it is unlikely to hire another underperforming manager. It will instead look for a star du jour with an upper-quartile five-year number. Based on the best evidence amassed to date, the likelihood of this star manager remaining in the top quartile five years hence is slim. The organization will essentially have gained nothing. Further, if a new manager is hired to change all or part of the portfolio, the manager will not review the holdings and say they look just fine. Doing so would be a tacit admission that the firm just fired was doing a good job. Rather, the new manager will sell the existing positions and buy other investments that put his or her firm's stamp on the portfolio. Therefore, the one sure result of any change is increased expenses due to "round-trip" transaction costs.

Consultant-Driven Performance Analysis

Increasingly, the consulting community has been able to raise the standards of performance analysis and reporting. The consultant community actively collects data from investment managers and uses it as a basis of comparison. With this information, the consultants rank managers by the investment styles they follow against all managers of that style. The consultants then group managers by style within quartiles, so that there is a top, second, third, and bottom quartile. They typically perform this analysis based on one-, three-, and five-year performance. When consultants talk about a first-quartile manager, they mean one whose performance over three or five years is in the top quarter of all managers of that style. If you hire a consultant, he or she will provide such an analysis of the current manager's performance.

PERFORMANCE REPORTS

Appendix E-2, cited earlier, contains a sample of a quarterly performance report provided by one consulting firm. It includes a tremendous amount of information on how the portfolio has performed in comparison to various indexes. Note that one difference between the high-end institutional world and do-it-yourselfers is that the consultants tend to produce their numbers quarterly on a trailing period basis. In other words, a consultant's five-year number as of June 1996 is based on the 20 quarters ending June 30, 1996, not the five years ending December 31, 1995.

Until recently, the type of information shown in the above-referenced report could *only* be obtained from consultants. They maintained the essential data on a proprietary basis. Increasingly Ibbotson, Nelson, Mobius and others sell reports in written and computer formats as well as entire databases updated quarterly, which make all the information available to anyone who owns those databases.

I still believe that a company such as Capital Markets Research (who produced the Appendix E-2 report) add value in both discipline and in deciding how to measure the managers, but the data for self-evaluation is now available. Morningstar produces similar information in printed and computer formats on thousands of mutual funds. The process of analyzing and comparing mutual funds is very similar to the process of analyzing and comparing investment managers as a mutual fund is, essentially, a vehicle for hiring investment management services. The service is less personal but also less expensive for very small dollar amounts.

PORTFOLIO ANALYSIS AND ATTRIBUTION TOOLS

Over the last few years, the increasing power of desktop computers and the amount of investment data gathering has led to yet another generation of performance analysis tools. Attribution analysis means examining the stocks, bonds, and other instruments in a portfolio and on the basis of those investments, determining the characteristics of the portfolio or by extension, the manager who created the portfolio.

Attribution analysis software is presently used exclusively by investment managers and investment management consultants. The managers use it to improve their performance. The software allows them to look at their holdings over a period of time and categorize them based on literally hundreds of statistics (everything from price/earnings ratios to the number and sentiment of the professional analysts following a particular stock). Their goal is to determine why some portfolios perform better than others.

Consultants use attribution software to work backward from a manager's known portfolios to determine whether the manager is following his or her stated investment style. It is also possible to determine how that style has changed over time and thereby get a sense of the manager's consistency in following a particular discipline. When linked to databases of market indexes, such software allows the consultants to analyze the managers' performance in ever finer ways.

Conclusion

Unlike the ACO board, the sample investment policies do not set any return or income goals for the portfolios. Rather, the policies reflect the need for performance reporting by requiring that the managers or consultants provide information on a monthly, quarterly and annual basis. The underlying assumption is that the organization has consciously established its asset allocation parameters in an effort to meet certain performance objectives while staying within acceptable risk parameters. If that translates into an absolute or a relative performance goal, well and good. But remember how you got there.

From that perspective, it is good performance reporting information that matters most. What is done with that information depends on the organization. In the early days, with relatively small funds and few asset classes, the organization can, with the help of a trustworthy broker or investment manager, do a very credible job independently. When the funds grow in size and complexity and involve multiple asset classes, the organization may need consulting help. In either case, the essential effort is the same, since it begins with asset allocation models, makes comparisons to outside indexes or performance of groups of managers, and watches for aberrational performance. The basics are what matter most. Thus, establish reporting procedures and let the details of becoming more sophisticated grow with the organization over time.

PART III

Unique Not-for-Profit Issues

8 Investment Policy as a Fund-Raising Tool / 173

9 Special Nonprofit Investment Problems / 205

10 Putting It All Together / 227

▼8▼ Investment Policy as a Fund-Raising Tool

Investment policy can be a powerful tool for increasing the overall effectiveness of nonprofit development programs. Appropriate investment policies not only will lead to higher returns on the various funds but, if widely disseminated and understood within the organization, may also lead to increased giving. When we consider the time and money organizations devote to seeking support, any set of decisions that might facilitate that effort ought to be carefully considered.

The relationship between investment policy and fund raising is complicated. The complexity stems largely from the intricacy of the potential gift instruments. To get a grasp of this subject, which is of central importance to considering investment policies, this chapter begins with an examination of endowments. The entire area of endowment creation and investment management is better understood than almost any other charitable area because of the long-standing commitment of the nation's colleges and universities to endowed funding. The original Ford Foundation studies, which helped launch changes in investment laws, were conducted for the benefit of the endowed funds of U.S. colleges and universities.

An understanding of endowments facilitates, in turn, an examination of the unique characteristics of planned gifts, particularly as those characteristics affect investment choices. As that discussion will reveal, from an investment management perspective, not all planned gifts are created equal. Rather, some planned gifts have greater potential for providing long-term funding from investment growth than do others. The chapter concludes with a review of policies designed to maximize the benefits of planned giving for both donors and charitable organizations.

At the ACO . . .

"NEVER EAT YOUR SEED CORN"

The board had heard a number of presentations on planned giving over the past several months from the development officer and various consultants. All had said more or less the same thing: "People over age 65 have all the money, and they're all going to die sooner or later, so if you want to get your share you'd better start a planned-giving program." So they did.

The development officer printed some new brochures on lifetime income from gift annuities and ways to avoid capital gains with charitable remainder trusts. The officer also got some attorneys and CPAs in town to agree to serve on a "planned-giving committee." One of the attorneys even spoke at a seminar on planned giving on a Wednesday night. But so far, they did not actually have any planned gifts.

One of the older board members decided that if they were going to have some planned gifts somebody had better start, so she told the development officer that she wanted to fund a charitable remainder trust. She owned a small apartment building, free and clear, which was increasingly more trouble than it was worth. But her cost basis was very low and she hated paying taxes, so the idea of donating it to a charitable remainder trust made sense.

When she met with the development officer the latter explained that she could use either a standard trust, which distributed a fixed percentage of the trust's net asset value each year, a net income trust, which distributed only the income earned, or a flip trust, which would probably be best.[1] Either way, they needed to decide on a payout rate. The development officer then spent considerable time explaining the characteristics and advantages of each type of trust.

Finally the director asked, "what are bonds paying these days?"

"Just over 7 percent" the development officer responded.

"Great," said the director, "make it a 7 percent net income trust."

"Why a net income trust?"

"Young man, you never eat your seed corn."

The foregoing story illustrates two very important points. First, at the end of the day *donors* choose what sort of trust or other planned-gift instruments they wish to use. Nothing that we are going to do with policy recommendations will (or should) change that. Thus, no matter how much "better" a standard CRT might be than a net income CRT for investment purposes, some donors believe passionately in "not eating their seed corn," meaning not invading principal. For such donors only a net income trust will do.

The other reality, however, is that development officers are frequently one of the donor's primary sources of information on planned gifts. Consequently, it is extremely important that development officers understand the investment management consequences that attach to the different types of gift instruments.

The entire purpose of this chapter is to explore and explain the investment management characteristics of planned gifts so that nonprofit boards, financial officers, and development officers can guide the organization and its donors down revenue-enhancing paths. Clearly such an effort cannot be divorced from the history of the organization and its fund raising, the character and desires of donors, the purposes for which funds are being raised,

---

[1] A flip trust is a trust that is initially a net income trust in order to hold an illiquid, non-income- or low-income-producing asset, typically real estate. When that asset is sold, the trust "flips," becoming a standard trust from that point forward.

or a hundred other factors, some of which will, from time to time, make investment concerns a distant second in importance. Nonetheless, there is power in understanding investment consequences—and in adding that understanding to the universe of advice given to donors.

The second significant point is that fixed-income investment management is an important part of the nonprofit world. Charitable organizations maintain both reserves and planned-gift assets which, frequently, must be managed to generate certain levels of income. Pooled-income funds and net income charitable remainder trusts, discussed below, fall into this category.

There has also been a historic tendency for nonprofit organizations to equate "yield" or income with that which is spendable. Just as our ACO director in the previous story felt, there is a certain comfort in the notion of spending only what you earn. To understand the problems with that approach, it is necessary to know a little bit about fixed-income investing and some of its unique risks.

The Yield Curve

Modern fixed-income investment management begins with a tool known as the yield curve.

Exhibit 8.1 is a picture of the "typical" yield curve for fixed-income instruments. The curve is typical in two respects. First, short-term rates are usually substantially lower than longer term interest rates. Secondly, the difference in rates is usually quite a bit greater as one moves from 30 days to 5 years than it is when one moves from 5 to 30 years. Collectively, these "typical" aspects of the debt markets give the yield curve the characteristic shape shown in the figure. While this might be thought of as a typical yield curve, the relationships expand and contract such that at times the curve is much flatter than at others. A flatter curve indicates that there is less difference between short- and long-term rates. Occasionally, in extremely unusual circumstances, the curve will actually reverse and short-term rates will be higher than long-term rates.

But working with the normal curve shown here, notice the difference in yield between 30-day treasury bills (the first dot on the curve) and 2- or 3-year treasury notes.[2] If all or a portion of an organization's funds are really

---

[2] Bills, notes, and bonds are not legally defined terms. The convention, however, is to refer to government instruments with a maturity of one year or less as "bills." These are typically sold at a discount from face value with the discount representing the interest you will receive. If a one-year bill is sold to yield 5 percent, then that means that you would pay $952.30 and in one year the government would pay you $1,000. The difference—$47.61—equals a 5 percent return on your $952.30 investment.

"Notes" are typically from 1 to 5 years in maturity and "bonds" are 5 years or longer. Both notes and bonds are sold in denominations of $1,000 or more and pay interest semiannually until maturity.

EXHIBIT 8.1. Yield Curve

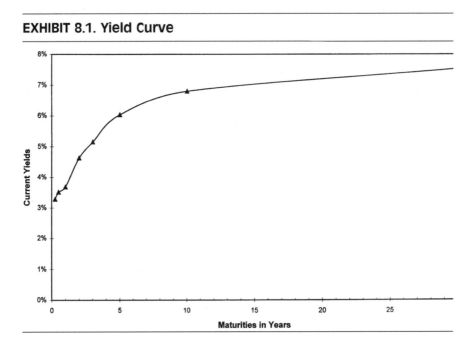

available for two or three years, there is an opportunity to purchase treasury notes of matching maturities and earn incremental yield. The treasury market is extremely liquid with billions of dollars worth of notes and bills traded daily. Consequently, even if one were to guess wrong about exactly when funds are needed, there is no particular risk of being caught without cash. Such a timing error would require that the organization sell a note or a bill in the secondary market as opposed to holding to maturity. The cost would be a modest commission and possibly a slight capital loss if rates had increased substantially and there was still a significant period of time before the scheduled maturity of the note. When dealing with one- to three-year treasury notes, these risks are modest.

The beginning of good short-term fixed-income management is a process of matching an organization's true cash flow requirements to the maturities in its reserves. Exhibit 8.2 shows a sample cash balance analysis for a large social service agency. Its original policy required that all funds be invested for a maximum of 36 months and that a substantial majority of funds be invested in notes with maturities of 12 months or less. What the cash flow analysis revealed was that while there were peaks when funds were flowing in and valleys when funds were flowing out, there was always at least $4 million in the account.

Such an analysis permits the creation of a tiered structure in which the longer-term funds may be extended out on the yield curve. Working against

EXHIBIT 8.2. American Charitable Organization—Operating Reserves—Month-End Account Balances

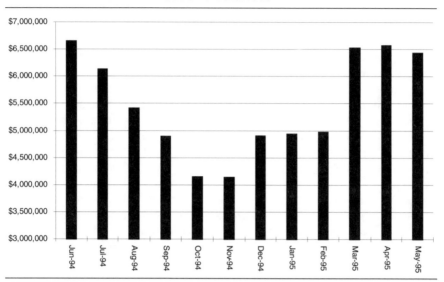

Produced by Capital Markets Research

a normal yield curve, the simple act of extending maturities in the zero to five-year portion of the curve greatly enhances returns. A simple way to execute this strategy is to "ladder" the maturities. Laddering maturities means buying obligations that mature in one, two, three, four, and five years—so that notes are always maturing as funds are due. This reduces expenses as there is no commission incurred when a note matures; one simply receives the money. The net effect of such a strategy is to extend the average maturity of the account to perhaps two and a half years, which typically results in higher returns than money market funds or rolling one-year CDs.

An understanding of the normal character of the yield curve and the true time characteristics of the funds that are being invested are the keys to achieving these incremental returns. What is wonderful about this particular step with *short-term funds* is that very little incremental investment risk is being taken. The incremental return is earned exclusively by matching the maturities of the portfolio to the true cash flow requirements of the organization.

LONGER-TERM FIXED-INCOME RISKS

While the strategy of extending maturities to increase returns usually works well for cash management and very short-term investments, the picture changes radically when longer-term investments are involved. Here it is as important to invest for total return as it is in equity investments. In addition, longer-term fixed-income investments in general and the pursuit of higher yields in particular bring with them a host of additional risks.

Consider again the "normal" yield curve picture in Exhibit 8.1. As we saw before, interest rates rise sharply for the first two or three years and then more slowly after that. Even though the increase in current yield is much slighter as one moves from the 5-year bonds to the 30-year treasury bonds, the increase can still be enough to motivate the yield-hungry investor to purchase long bonds. There are at least two problems with this approach.

First, the incremental total return for long bonds over intermediate bonds is not nearly so great as the incremental current yield might suggest. As Exhibit 8.3 illustrates, after 20 years a portfolio of intermediate-term bonds frequently produces nearly 95 percent of the total return that could have been earned on a long bond portfolio. Typically, total return does not increase nearly as much as the disparity between long bond interest rates and shorter-term fixed-income interest rates might lead us to believe.

Second, there is tremendously greater interest-rate risk in holding portfolios of long bonds than there is in portfolios of shorter-term fixed-income instruments. Exhibit 8.4 illustrates this risk by presenting the market price of a 20-year treasury note issued in 1973 with a stated interest rate of 6.75 percent. The bars show the market price of the bond at the close of each year during the 20-year period of time. By 1981 the market price of the bond was only $650. In other words, if forced to sell the $1,000 bond in 1981 for whatever reason, the seller would only receive $650. While a $350 loss may not sound too horrible, consider the fact that if an organization had invested its entire $1 million bond portfolio in 20-year treasuries in 1973, at the invest-

EXHIBIT 8.3. Total Return on 3- to 5-Year Treasuries—(Periods Ending April 30, 1994)

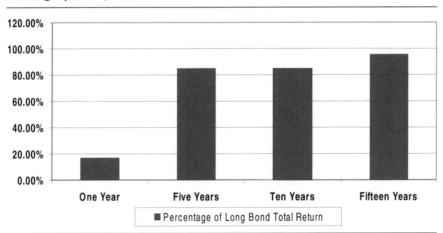

Produced by Capital Markets Research

EXHIBIT 8.4. Market Price of a 20-Year T-Note (6.75%)

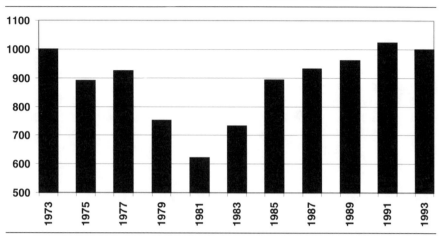

ment committee meetings in 1981 the chief financial officer would be trying to explain to the board why the bond portfolio had lost $350,000.

The bond does eventually regain its value as it approaches maturity. By 1993 when the bond is due, it is again worth $1,000. So if the organization were able to maintain its positions for the entire 20 years, it would not have had to realize any of the losses suffered through in the meantime.

The problem with the long bond is that, once issued, its value in the marketplace is tremendously sensitive to the general level of interest rates. The reason is that since the repayment of the principal obligation is so far away, 20 or 30 years, the discounted present value of that payment is very small.[3] Given the relatively small value of the future repayment, long bonds tend to trade on the value of the interest payment income streams.

What the $1,000 bond issued at 6.75 percent really represents is the government's agreement to repay the $1,000 in 20 years and to pay $67.50 in interest each year in the meantime. At a time when the general level of interest rates on 20-year obligations is just under 7 percent, that combination of interest income stream and future principal repayment is worth $1,000. But what if interest rates go to 10 percent? In that case, an investor purchasing a new 20-year obligation from the government can expect to receive the

---

[3] Discounted present value is essentially the amount that a person would be willing to pay for a future payment or stream of payments. Just a moment's reflection will show that $1,000 to be received 30 years from now is not worth $1,000. Paying someone $1,000 today in exchange for a $1,000 payment 30 years in the future means foregoing the use of that money for the entire 30 years. Consequently, there is some lesser sum that if invested at interest for 30 years and allowed to grow by retaining and reinvesting the interest income, would become $1,000 in 30 years. It is that lesser amount that is the discounted present value of the $1,000 payment. Obviously, it would be a fairly small number.

same $1,000 principal payment in 20 years, but a payment of $100 per year in the meantime. Clearly, therefore, no rational investor is going to pay $1,000 for a $67.50 per year payment (with $1,000 in 20 years) when he or she can get the same $1,000 in 20 years and a $100 per year payment. The older, lower coupon bond is now worth less. If the current yield were the only factor, the bond would be worth $675, since at that price the interest payment of $67.50 per year would also represent 10 percent.

This phenomenon is not confined to ancient history. Exhibit 8.5, below, shows the relative price performance of 5-year and 30-year treasury bonds in the market in early 1994 when the general level of interest rates was rising. While both bonds dropped in price, the long bond dropped to $850, representing a loss of 15 percent of its total value in only 13 weeks.

Most charitable organizations are probably better off avoiding long bonds (those with maturities in excess of 10 years) altogether. Much of the time the incremental yield and the potential for incremental total return simply do not justify the added risk. This may even be the case in professionally managed fixed-income portfolios in which analytic concepts such as duration (see Chapter 6, footnote 8) and convexity (a measure of price/yield relationships) are used to quantify and control interest-rate risks. There are of course some exceptions.

First, it is appropriate to use long-term bonds if they can be matched to long-term obligations. If there are amounts certain to be spent in 20 years

EXHIBIT 8.5. Comparative Price Performance—January through April, 1994

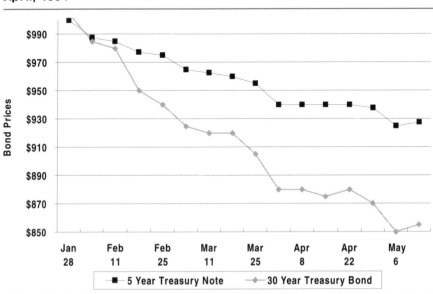

Produced by Capital Markets Research

and the organization wishes to set aside a sum that will grow to that amount in the meantime, then it makes sense to use 20-year obligations. In that event, so-called zero-coupon bonds are particularly helpful.

Second, there is certainly a reasonable temptation to want to tie up very high returns during periods of aberrantly high interest rates. Whenever long-bond interest rates approach historic average stock market returns of between 10 and 12 percent, then it is reasonable to invest more heavily in bonds. Realize, however, that most bonds issued today are callable. This means that the issuer of the bond has the right after just a few years to repay the bond early. Therefore, when corporations do borrow money during times of very high interest rates, once those interest rates decline, the corporations tend to "call," or repay the bonds, even if they simply turn around and sell new bonds at the lower rate then prevalent in the market. It is the corporate version of refinancing your home. This notion of early repayment is at the core of the next type of risk discussed.

EXTENSION AND REPAYMENT RISKS

A popular form of fixed-income investment due primarily to slightly higher yields is government-issued collateralized mortgage obligations (CMOs). These are also sometimes referred to as "Fannie Maes" or "Ginnie Maes," which are acronyms for the issuing agencies, the Federal National Mortgage Association and the Government National Mortgage Association, respectively. These are government-guaranteed obligations, so there is no more credit risk than with a traditional government bond; all the payments are guaranteed by the full faith and credit of the U.S. government. These collateralized mortgage obligations are debt instruments that the government issues in order to raise money to make loans. While not quite this simple in practice, the government is essentially borrowing money by selling the collateralized mortgage obligations and then making that money available to banks to use for home mortgage loans. The first security for the repayment obligations are pools of home mortgages. When the various homeowners make their principal and interest payments on their mortgages, those payments are collected on all of the mortgages in the pool and are used to make the interest payments on the government notes.

There are three problems with these instruments from an investor's standpoint. First, when interest rates rise, homeowners with fixed-rate mortgages keep their mortgages in place because they have a good deal. When interest rates drop, however, homeowners tend to prepay their existing mortgages and take out new mortgages in order to take advantage of the lower rates. Given that behavior, what happens to the pools that support the collateralized mortgage obligations? When rates are rising, the principal is repaid at the slowest possible rate. Therefore, the lender (which is the purchaser of these notes) made a bad deal by loaning money just before the interest rates went up. The lenders (the investors in the CMOs) experience what is called extension risk. The pace of repayment slows; therefore the effective term of the note, the time for which the money is actually invested extends.

Conversely, when interest rates decline, homeowners refinance their homes and pay off the old mortgages early. The effective note term shortens as the principal is repaid more quickly. Thus, just as when the corporations call their notes, the CMO investor receives principal back at a time when interest rates are not as high as they were when the note was purchased. The result is that the investor does not participate in the price appreciation that should result from holding a long-term bond during periods of declining interest rates.

The bottom line is that the collateralized mortgage obligations sacrifice total return in order to receive slightly higher current yields. The increased current yield comes at the price of both extension risk and prepayment risk, both of which collectively diminish total return. A final point on collateralized mortgage obligations is that they are a real headache from an accounting standpoint. Unlike traditional bonds, the payments on CMOs are a combination of interest and principal, just like a typical home mortgage, and tend to be made monthly as opposed to semiannual interest payments on traditional bonds. In order to keep track of the principal amount invested, one has to make a book entry in the accounting records *every month for every bond* to adjust the new principal basis of the investment.

CREDIT RISK

The final fixed-income risk we will consider is credit risk. Corporate debt is rated for credit worthiness by a number of agencies, including Standard & Poor's and Moody's. The rating scheme for each is slightly different, but essentially the highest category is AAA; the investment grade categories are AAA, AA, A, and BBB. When investors talk about junk bonds, they are referring to any bond rated lower than BBB. The ratings go all the way to D, which indicates that the company is actually in default on its bond, meaning it has missed one or more interest payments.

The lower the rating, the less creditworthy the issuing corporation is deemed to be. In other words, as the credit rating of the bond or the issuing company decreases, the amount of credit risk increases. Therein lies both the risk and the attraction of junk bonds.

The investor, choosing between lending money to the U.S. government by purchasing treasury bonds or lending money to the Disney Corporation, IBM, or McDonald's by purchasing their bonds, is relatively indifferent. There is not a great deal of additional risk of default (credit risk) in either case. The AAA companies named above are all highly likely to still be in existence and to still be paying their debts even 30 years from now.

But there is some incremental risk, as history shows. Even huge and tremendously successful corporations in the past have in fact gone out of business over long periods of time while the U.S. government continues. So, an investor willing to loan money to the government at 7 percent, might want 7.25 percent to loan it to a AAA company. Those 25 basis points represent incremental compensation for taking a small amount of credit risk.

When considering lending to companies in the junk bond category, some of which are very large and well known, the risk of default on their bonds is much greater. They are not as financially strong as the AAA credits. An investor purchasing their bonds at a time when government debt is paying 7 percent, might want to receive 8 or 9 percent or even more in order to consider it a fair investment. In this case, the incremental 200 or 300 basis points represents compensation for the much greater credit risk involved.

The attraction of junk bonds is twofold. First, for those not in default, the investor will receive a greater stream of income payments than for an issue of comparable maturity from a more creditworthy company. Second, consider what happens if the junk bond issuer improves its business and its balance sheet. In that case, its credit rating will eventually improve, and when it does the value of its bonds will increase so that the yield to maturity is comparable to the yield to maturity of other corporate bonds of the same higher credit rating. Consequently, the junk bond investor not only has the prospect of earning higher current yield, but also might see some appreciation in its bonds if the company can improve its financial condition.

The downside of course is that the company will not improve its financial condition and may even go broke. Many companies that are issuers of low-rated debt are in some way, shape, or form struggling in their businesses, and the potential for their failure is real. When such a company does fail, it would be a rare situation in which the incremental yield the investor had been receiving prior to default and ultimate bankruptcy was sufficiently great to compensate for the loss of principal. Junk bonds can, therefore, be very risky investments.

With the foregoing primer on fixed-income investing as background, we can now return to the relationship between investment policies and fund raising. The beginning point of such an inquiry is the world of endowments.

The Case for Endowment

The first thing one notices about endowments is that outside the educational setting, they are not particularly common. Indeed, in large segments of the nonprofit community, such as social service agencies and most pararreligious organizations, endowments are extremely rare. This is due in part to the relative youth of many of these organizations. American colleges and universities, by comparison, are the oldest entities in continuous existence in the nation. Some of them even predate the current forms of our state and federal governments. Part of the reason that Harvard University is the world's most heavily endowed institution is that it was formed in 1636.

There are other reasons for the scarcity of endowments. In the social service arena, it is difficult for those with daily involvement in the lives of desperately poor people to set aside funds for future use. The thought of not using all available resources to meet current needs seems appalling.

In certain segments of the religious community and among some conservative Christian groups in particular, there is a tendency to believe that organizational wealth and reserves would express a lack of faith. "If God wants us to do the particular work to which we are called," so the argument goes, "He will provide the resources we need. If He does not, perhaps we are not called to this task and should do something else." This is a powerful concern for those who adhere to it. There are, nevertheless, good reasons to consider endowments.

SAVING VS. HOARDING

First, there is a difference between managing and hoarding. Large sums of money capable of generating an income stream that is significant relative to the organization's budget represent assets that are uniquely capable of meeting certain funding requirements. Maintaining such an asset no more amounts to hoarding than does owning a building within which to conduct business. Many organizations without endowments have millions of dollars tied up in edifices. Owning a structure does not mean that they are not meeting the needs of their constituents. Everyone understands that the building is an asset required to facilitate their work. An endowment fund can also be an asset necessary to facilitate charitable work.

Part of that facilitation is a process of smoothing the income curve. Virtually all nonprofit organizations experience shifting cash flow as a result of donations coming in more heavily at year-end than at other times. But some organizations also have wildly varied cash flow for other reasons. To the extent that the flow of unrestricted funds from an endowment becomes a significant percentage of an operating budget, it represents a steady income stream and has a leveling effect on otherwise wildly fluctuating donations. The leveling of the income stream allows more graceful management, better planning, and more efficient utilization of resources. Less disruptive cash flow is a form of good stewardship.

DIFFICULT-TO-FUND PROGRAMS

There are also difficult-to-fund programs. Very little work done in the inner city, for example, is funded out of contributions raised there. To the extent that specific charitable endeavors can be identified, endowed funds can be raised and maintained for such purposes. In addition, many donors like to direct their gifts. When an organization identifies endowable causes, it can, to some extent, provide donors opportunities to direct gifts to places where they are really needed.

PROTECTING CURRENT INCOME

Raising endowment funds can also be a method for protecting the ability to spend money on a current basis. Many organizations have experienced the fact that a new building or campus brings with it a whole host of new, permanent expenses. Thus, one unintended consequence of a new facility can be an increase in operating expenses and a concomitant decrease in funds available for the core mission. When raising millions of dollars to construct the building, why not raise another million and use the flow of payments from that fund to maintain the building? This could be thought of as an endowment for maintenance and could be raised in conjunction with many capital campaigns.

GIFTS OF NET WORTH

Finally, and perhaps most important, there is a type of gift that many donors simply will not make to an operating budget. Many in the over-65 generation have enormous wealth (even if they do not think of themselves as wealthy) as a result of having lived and worked during the dramatic expansion and growth in the U.S. economy following World War II. Even inflation, which hurt some people, has tended to help this group, since they were already homeowners when inflation skyrocketed. Another common reason for their wealth is having lived frugally. This is also a generation that remembers the Great Depression. These frugal, wealthy donors will not donate any significant percentage of their life savings to an operating budget that will be spent in one year. These are not gifts of income, these are gifts of net worth.

The good news here is that in the minds of many donors, gifts of net worth are taken from a different "bucket" or pot of money than gifts of income. The final, compelling reason for forming endowments is that gifts to endowment funds do not compete with nor detract from gifts of current income. It is not an either/or situation, it is a "both/and." Donors, particularly major donors, who have been supporting an organization for years have a vested interest in its success. They will welcome the opportunity to leave bequests in their will or living trust and/or incorporate substantial planned gifts into their estate and financial planning. It is a way for them to perpetuate their giving.

Therefore, to position itself as a worthy recipient of major events of net worth, an organization must maintain an endowment so that donors' gifts of net worth can be preserved and used to generate funds that will support the organization for years to come. Though charitable trusts do not require an endowment, the fact that there is a place to maintain capital can even facilitate and encourage their formation. For all these reasons, many unendowed or under-endowed charitable organizations should consider forming and promoting such a permanent fund.

CANDOR AS AN ENDOWMENT FUND-RAISING TOOL

As there is no particular law of endowments, the term *endowment* includes both true and quasi-endowment funds.[4] This raises an important public relations issue. To the extent that a fund restricted only by board action is promoted to donors as a true endowment, there is a possibility of deception. Consequently, if the endowment fund is accessible to the board, the exact terms and conditions upon which the board can access the fund should be disclosed to every endowment donor at the time of the gift. If the endowment is other than a true endowment, it is also important to disclose its terms as part of all general marketing materials describing its existence. Such disclosure practices will substantially reduce the possibility of complaints from unhappy donors if the fund is ever invaded.

Establishing an Endowment

Appendix F contains two endowment forms. The first is an example of a board-created endowment, which might be considered a quasi-endowment. Both the form and the board resolution are rather simple. The second and longer form was developed by a national service organization. It is intended to be adopted by local chapters that wish to maintain endowed funds. This is a more formal example and involves the creation of a permanent trust for the benefit of maintaining these funds. In either case, as with all of the forms in this book, these are examples that are not intended to be used without review and modification by an attorney to satisfy the legal environment in which your organization operates.

Endowment Investment and Spending Policies

Endowments are usually thought of as permanent funds. Consequently, a normal investment management objective is to grow the fund by an amount that keeps pace with inflation after spending and expenses. The long-term goal is to maintain the purchasing power of the amount being distributed (spent) by the endowment. If that is achieved, whatever fund raising is done represents true increases to the size of the endowment.

The reason to discuss spending policy and investment policy jointly in

---

[4] A "true" endowment is one in which the organization cannot invade principal except to the extent of an annual distribution. In a true endowment the restrictions on such invasion are built into the governing instrument or imposed in some other manner by law. In a quasi-endowment the funds are beyond reach *only* by a vote of the governing body, which, clearly, can change its mind at some future date. Sometimes "quasi" funds are referred to as "board designated" while true endowments are referred to as "donor designated."

the context of an endowment is that the two are closely intertwined. An excellent article in *Managing Endowment and Foundation Funds* states, "Spending is the linchpin."[5] Spending policy is crucial because it is easy to spend more than a fund earns, particularly on an inflation-adjusted basis. Investment performance is not normally reported on an after-inflation basis. Additional assets are routinely being added to the fund. Consequently, it is easy to spend at a rate that far exceeds the actual investment growth of the funds. There are simply too many variables to monitor. The result is that over the years, a board may be unaware that the purchasing power of the distributed amount is decreasing.

There are three common spending models in the world of true and quasi-endowments:

1. Net income
2. A percentage of assets
3. A percentage of assets calculated on a rolling basis over some trailing period.

In the percentage of asset models, the typical percentage is between 4 and 6 percent, with 5 percent being the most common. For a variety of reasons, either of the percentage of asset models will invariably produce better results than the net-income model.

WHAT IS WRONG WITH AN INCOME SPENDING POLICY?

The fundamental problem with a spending policy based on income is that there is little or no correlation between the income a portfolio generates and its total return. Dividend and interest income is only a portion of total return, and in recent years has usually been less than the portion of total return contributed by capital gains. Even assuming that asset allocation is not influenced by the desire to generate current income, an income spending policy can still create unhelpful anomalies.

Consider Exhibit 8.6, which compares the portfolio yield and the portfolio return for a model portfolio invested 60 percent in the S&P 500 and 40 percent in government bonds for the two years 1994 and 1995. Notice that for 1995, despite a tremendous surge in the stock market, resulting in a very high level of total return (the S&P 500 was up 37.5 percent), the current distribution would be only 4 percent. Conversely, in 1994, while the market was suffering (the S&P 500 was down 3.1 percent), interest rates were quite high, leading to the incredible situation in which we are distributing nearly

---

[5] "Can Endowments and Foundations Meet Their Objectives?" by Ian Kennedy, Director of Research, Cambridge Associates, published in *Managing Endowment and Foundation Funds*, AIMR, March, 1996, page 8.

EXHIBIT 8.6. Portfolio Yield vs. Total Return—60% Stocks / 40% Bonds

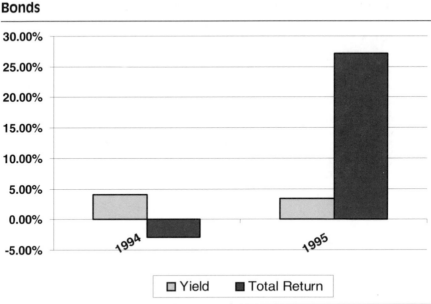

Produced by Capital Markets Research

50 percent at a time when our portfolio is actually losing money. These swings show that income will not follow increases or decreases in total portfolio value but will fluctuate instead with interest rates and other factors. So the first problem with an income-spending model is that any effort at a portfolio growth policy can lead to wild swings in distributions.

THE SIN OF REACHING FOR YIELD

In any situation in which the amount that can be spent is predicated on the amount of income earned from dividends and interest on a current basis ("yield"), there is a natural pressure and a natural tendency to try to manipulate the portfolio investments in order to increase yields. This might be thought of as the sin of reaching for yield. Typically, the results range from poor to disastrous. It turns out that reaching for yield is a high risk activity that typically involves distorting optimal asset allocations, creating excessive sector concentrations, and assuming one or more of the fixed-income investment risks described earlier. Each is usually a mistake.

Suboptimal Asset Allocation

When optimizing a portfolio across multiple asset classes, the factors that are considered are the anticipated returns by asset class, the investment time horizon, and the covariance relationships between the asset classes over similar time horizons in the past. Most important, anticipated asset class returns are all measured on a total return basis. Consequently, the current return or yield from an optimized portfolio is whatever it is.

When a current return requirement is added to the analysis, that requirement typically forces a skewing of the allocation away from the optimal points on the efficient frontier and toward some other result. That other result will, by definition, be less desirable as it will produce lower total returns for a given level of risk. There is really no mystery to this result. Fixed-income investments historically produce lower total returns, the overwhelming majority of which is in the current interest payment. Since 1958, interest payments on bonds have generally been higher than dividend yields on stocks. Thus in order to increase current return, we increase the allocation to bonds and decrease the allocation to equities. So in pursuing yield, the most likely result is lower total returns.

Excessive Sector Concentrations

Pursuing yield can lead to other portfolio distortions as well. One common example is excessive concentrations in one or two sectors of the market. I have, on a number of occasions, reviewed charitable portfolios in which more than 50 percent of the equity investments were in utility stocks. As previously discussed, the combination of an appearance of safety and a very high yield has led many charities to invest heavily in this area.

Almost all the incremental risks discussed in Chapter 3 are present when one concentrates a portfolio in a single economic sector. First, there is a sense in which you reintroduce specific risk to the portfolio at least in the form of the industry risk. If something happens in either a regulatory or an economic sense that badly affects the electric utilities, then they will all decline in price together, and the portfolio can suffer accordingly. Second, high yielding stocks such as utilities tend to be interest rate sensitive in the same manner as long bonds. So, concentrating the portfolio in utility stocks also increases interest rate risk. Third, it is highly unlikely that a portfolio concentrated in utility stocks would be the optimal portfolio that emerges from an asset allocation model based on total returns. Consequently, investing heavily in a single sector for the sake of high yields creates a suboptimal portfolio that will, in all likelihood, generate lower returns with increased risk.

SPENDING POLICY IMPLICATIONS OF REACHING FOR YIELD

As most of the techniques that increase portfolio income decrease total return, the best spending policy is one that spends a percentage of the value of the portfolio each year regardless of the amount of current income. There are two common ways to do this. The first is simply to spend a percentage, commonly 5 percent, of the value of the portfolio on the first day of the year divided into quarterly increments. That translates into a policy of spending

1.25 percent of the portfolio's asset value each quarter. If the distributions are made quarterly, it is possible to simply apply that 1.25 percent figure to the value of the portfolio on a certain day, such as the last business day of each quarter, to calculate the distribution amount.

With a spending policy predicated on a percentage of value, good investment experience leads to increases in spending over time, while poor investment experience decreases spending. Ignoring the increases due to additional contributions, a percentage of net asset value policy encourages the portfolio to be managed on a total return basis. All of the powerful tools available for maximizing total return and minimizing risk become available to the endowment when it is no longer slave to the need to generate current income.

The last refinement in the percentage of net asset value spending policy is to apply the percentage quarterly to a rolling historic period such as the preceding 36 months. The reason a number of institutions favor this rolling average approach is that it further smoothes the distribution curve and allows funds to be spent at a more even pace. The effect of very large increases or very large decreases in portfolio value are muted by the averaging. In addition, the use of trailing averages tends to slightly reduce the actual percentage being spent as a result of the historical long-term upward trend in the financial markets.

To illustrate the overwhelming importance of spending policy, consider Exhibit 8.7. The upper line represents the growth of a 60 percent equity, 40 percent bond portfolio, *net* of an annual 5 percent distribution on a trailing 12 quarters basis. The lower line represents the same portfolio distributing 6 percent on a current basis. The difference in value after 25 years is enormous. That difference is attributable entirely to spending policy.

Maximizing the Value of an Endowment

After adopting an appropriate spending policy, endowment funds should be the place where an organization takes the longest-term investment view since these are permanent funds. It is also a place where there are no competing interests to be served and therefore the limitations on risk are entirely a matter of the comfort level of the board. In light of these two factors, endowments and other permanent funds are the quintessential growth instruments.

There are three components of endowment investment strategy that can appropriately be addressed at the policy level:

1. Investment time horizons
2. Asset class selection
3. Volatility concerns.

EXHIBIT 8.7. Effect of Spending Policy—Compound Growth of $100

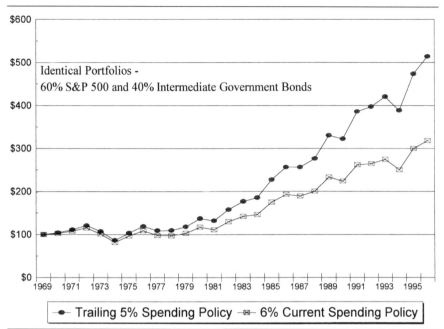

Identical Portfolios -
60% S&P 500 and 40% Intermediate Government Bonds

—●— Trailing 5% Spending Policy —☒— 6% Current Spending Policy

Exhibit 8.8 shows that the lowest asset allocation risk in our two-asset-class models shifts to a higher percentage of equities as we extend out time horizons. As a result, if we do nothing more than declare our endowment to be manageable on a 20-year basis and still opt for the lowest risk allocation, we increase our equity allocation from 30 percent to 50 percent and our anticipated annualized return from 8.38 percent to 9.23 percent.

The second graph, Exhibit 8.9, shows the benefits of adding additional asset classes, particularly those that are more risky on a standard deviation basis than are core U.S. equity holdings. As we add small capitalization U.S. stocks (which are largely not included in the S&P 500), international equities from both established and emerging markets, and perhaps even a small allocation to below-investment-grade debt, one can see that this new optimal portfolio (the "Aggressive Growth Model") would, on a historic basis, have significantly outperformed the portfolio that was limited to traditional U.S. stocks and bonds. If an organization is going to be more aggressive in pursuing incremental total return by including more volatile asset classes, this is the place. Recall, also, that a long-term perspective actually reduces investment risks (see Chapter 3, Exhibit 3.22 and related discussion). All the benefits of a long-term perspective come to bear here to reduce the true risks and to enhance the likelihood of success.

EXHIBIT 8.8. Efficient Frontier—Rolling Averages: 1945–1995

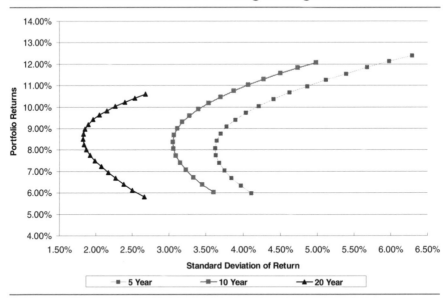

Produced by Capital Markets Research. (See Appendix E-2 for components.)

EXHIBIT 8.9. Return vs. Risk Analysis—First Quarter 1987 to Second Quarter 1996

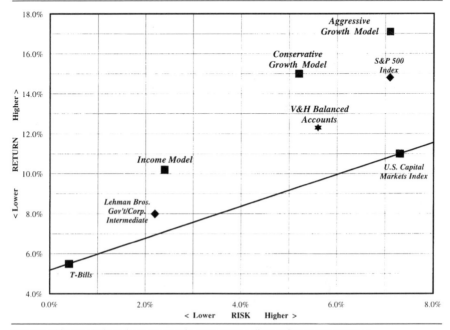

Produced by Capital Markets Research. (See Appendix E-2 for components.)

Planned Gifts

The lessons learned in the endowment context apply with equal force in the area of planned gifts. In searching for strategies to maximize the value of planned gifts the first goal is to identify and then favor in our fund-raising efforts those instruments that can be managed on a total return basis. Unfortunately, many planned gift programs have inadvertently taken exactly the opposite tack.

WHAT ARE PLANNED GIFTS?

The term *planned gift* is, like endowment, not a legally defined term. Rather, it is an appellation applied to a class of gifts that tend to share certain characteristics. The most common characteristic is the use of some form of legal instrument to control the asset to be gifted for some period of time. Typically, the term is measured by either the life or lives of the donor(s) or a stated number of years. For most planned gifts (not all) there is (1) deferred assignment of the funds to the charitable organization, and (2) some form of current income distribution to the donor. The most common planned gifts include the following:

1. Bequests
2. Charitable remainder trusts
3. Charitable lead trusts
4. Gift annuities
5. Pooled-income funds.

Let's take a brief look at each.

Bequests

A bequest is simply a gift made by will or by a will-substitute, such as a revocable living trust. This is the classic "deathbed gift" that we see in the old movies where the lawyer reads the will in the presence of the sobbing heirs, who sob all the more when he intones, "I leave all the rest and residue of my estate to the children's hospital and I hope that my own children learn to make their way in the world." Wills or bequests are generally thrown in with other planned gifts, as there is clearly a modicum of planning involved—the donor has to change his or her will to provide for the gift and receipt of the funds is deferred until the donor's death. Unlike the other planned-gift instruments we will examine, the donor retains complete ownership of the asset until death, at which time the gift becomes effective.

There is not much more to say about wills from an investment management standpoint, as there is really nothing for the nonprofit to manage; the donor retains complete control of the asset. Further, the experience of many charities nationally is that the overwhelming majority of these gifts were unknown to the organization before the check actually arrived. Supporters

EXHIBIT 8.10. Sample Charitable Remainder Trust

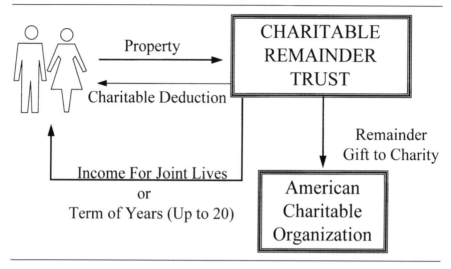

of the organization simply amended their wills and did not feel the need to tell anyone at the time. Because bequests are simple for donors to implement and carry no overhead with them for the charitable organization in the meantime, wills are a wonderful form of planned giving and ought to be encouraged first and foremost by those starting a planned giving program.

Charitable Remainder Trusts

Somehow, however, despite the economics, wills are not nearly as appealing as charitable remainder trusts, which have become the planned gift of choice for many an organization. Exhibit 8.10 illustrates the operation of such a trust. The donor contributes assets to the trust and receives in return both an income stream and an immediate income tax deduction. On the termination of the trust, either at the death of the last measuring life or after a term certain (the maximum period being 20 years), whatever is left in the trust, the remainder, passes to the designated charitable organization(s). Hence the name charitable remainder trust.

The value of the donor's income tax deduction is the value of the remainder interest that is passing to the charity calculated at the time that the trust is funded. Using tables provided by the IRS, the value of the remainder interest is calculated based on the trust payout, the likely duration of the trust (for life, two or more lives, or a term of years), and the rate of interest that the government uses for the calculation.[6] The higher the income distri-

---

[6] The rate is called the Applicable Federal Rate (AFR). It is roughly equal to mid-term government bonds. The calculation uses 120 percent of the AFR.

bution and the longer the term of the trust, the more the income stream is worth and, conversely, the less that can be expected to pass to the charity. Therefore, for a 50-year-old donor with an 8 percent remainder trust, the value of the remainder interest will be something less than the total, depending upon the AFR. Conversely, a 5 percent trust established for the benefit of an 80-year-old will have a remainder interest valued at 70 percent or more, again depending on the AFR. In each case, the results are intuitively correct. The total value of the income stream and the remainder interest cannot exceed the total amount transferred into the trust. So a large, long-term income stream would be a very high percentage of the total value whereas a low or very short-term income stream would be a very small percentage of the total value.[7]

There are a number of varieties of remainder trusts. They can be either annuity trusts or unitrusts. In an annuity trust, the income payment is a fixed percentage of the trust assets' initial fair market value; it never changes over the life of the trust. In a unitrust, the percentage to be distributed is applied to the net asset value of the trust, usually on the first business day of each year, although other, more frequent, valuation techniques are permitted. If the value of the assets inside the unitrust increases over time due to good investment performance, then the amount distributed increases over time as well. Conversely, if the unitrust corpus decreases in value, then the amount of the distribution decreases as well.

Finally, within the arena of unitrusts, there are so-called standard unitrusts and net income unitrusts. A standard unitrust is one in which the percentage distribution is applied to the assets and that is the amount distributed each year. A net income unitrust is one that distributes the *lesser* of the stated percentage or the net income the trust earns. That net income will be dividend and interest income and rents, as defined under every state's Uniform Principal and Income Act (or it can be defined differently in the trust instrument itself). As a final wrinkle in net income unitrusts, the trust can provide for a makeup of any amounts that were not distributed in prior years if, in subsequent years, the amount of income earned exceeds the stated percentage.[8] The minimum distribution amount for all remainder trusts is 5 percent, although net income trusts are allowed to distribute less than that if the net income is less than 5 percent.

---

[7] Shortly before publication of this book, the Taxpayer Relief Act of 1997 established that for a trust to qualify as a charitable remainder trust, no annual distribution may exceed 50 percent of the trust's full value and qualification will be denied if on the day of the trust's creation and funding, the charitable remainder is not valued at ten percent or more of its full value. The effect of the 10 percent requirement will be to require unitrusts to use lower distribution percentages, shorter trust terms, or a combination of the two, so that the value of the income stream (as calculated) does not exceed 90 percent of the total.

[8] Again, shortly before publication of this book, the IRS issued proposed Treasury regulations that would permit the use of a "flip" unitrust. A "flip" trust may be drafted so that it will be a net income trust initially and at some point thereafter convert to a standard unitrust.

Why Are Remainder Trusts So Popular?

The popularity of remainder trusts is due to their tremendous power and flexibility in both generating an income stream and reducing taxes. We have seen the basic operation in the previous description, but there is at least one other important characteristic: they are not themselves tax-paying entities. While the distributions from the trusts are taxable under a somewhat complicated scheme, the instrument itself does not pay income tax.[9] Most importantly, the instrument itself does not pay capital gains tax even if the property contributed is very low-basis.

In a typical situation, a 70-year-old donor in Southern California owns a small house at the beach that he bought in his beatnik days in the early 1950s for $7,500. That house today is worth $1.5 million, and he simply cannot stand the thought of paying $300,000 or more of capital gains tax by selling the property. The prospective donor also serves on the board of the local foundation for the advancement of jazz and other modern American music, having been nominated to the board when he donated a complete collection of 78 rpm Cole Porter records. He has decided that he would like to give the beach property to the jazz museum. He thought about gifting it outright and possibly endowing a Manard Kreps chair of music at some university, but decided that he really needed the income. Thus the obvious solution is a charitable remainder trust.

When the donor contributes the real estate to the remainder trust, that is not a capital gains generating taxable event. What he receives is an immediate income tax deduction, however, of more than $800,000 representing the value of the remainder interest.[10] The trustee of the trust, which could be either the donor himself, the charity, or an institutional trust company, then sells the real estate. When the trust sells the real estate, it again pays no tax as the trust is a tax-exempt entity. Therefore, the trust retains all $1.5 million of the sales proceeds, as no capital gain tax is due. Even with only a 5 percent trust, the donor will immediately begin receiving a $75,000 annual income stream. As there are a lot of assets with low basis or other bad tax attributes, some of which can be eliminated by contributing the assets to charitable remainder trusts, these trusts can be very powerful tools.

Charitable Lead Trusts

Charitable lead trusts are tremendously powerful instruments in the arsenal of planned-giving techniques. In operation, they are essentially the opposite

---

[9] Distributions to the income beneficiaries of a charitable remainder trust are taxed under the "tier system." That is, distributions are taxed first as ordinary income to the extent of the trust's ordinary income for the year and any undistributed ordinary income attributable to prior years; second, as capital gains to the extent of the trust's undistributed capital-gains income for the year and for prior years; third, as tax-exempt income to the extent of the trust's current and previously undistributed tax-exempt income; and finally, as tax-free return of principal.

[10] This assumes a 5 percent trust and an AFR of 7 percent or more.

of a remainder trust. Specifically, in a lead trust the income interest belongs to the charity for an initial term following which the remainder returns to the donor or passes to other individuals. Furthermore, lead trusts are not tax-exempt. Either the trust itself pays taxes on its income or the trust donor (the grantor) pays taxes on the trust income, depending upon how the trust is structured.

From an investment management standpoint, there is little that can be said about such trusts generically as each is typically established in unique circumstances. Some grantor lead trusts are funded with municipal bonds to minimize income taxes. Some lead trusts are funded with specific properties which the donor wishes to have his or her heirs receive at some point in the future. It is important to be aware of these instruments, but they will not feature in the subsequent discussion.

Before turning to how we maximize the value of our investments inside these instruments, let's take a quick look at the other commonly used planned-gift instruments.

POOLED GIFTS

The most commonly used pooled-gift instruments are the pooled-income fund and the charitable-gift annuity. In each case, the basic gift instrument is a very simple contract as opposed to a free-standing trust agreement. Consequently, the operational overhead associated with these instruments is much lower.

Unlike a charitable remainder trust, which requires extensive, ongoing accounting, as well as the annual filing of a 5227 tax return, the donor accounting associated with gift annuities is relatively modest. In addition, the income is reported to the donor with a simple Form 1099. In addition, for both gift annuities and pooled-income funds, the charitable organizations or sponsoring banks are able to pool the funds involved for investment purposes. As a result of these characteristics, pooled-income funds and charitable-gift annuities tend to be entry-level gift instruments, as they can be offered in very low dollar amounts. Many organizations permit the purchase of initial instruments in amounts as low as $5,000 and some as low as $1,000. These can be very useful tools for both donor development and fund raising from people who are not in a position to make the substantial gifts required for charitable remainder trusts.

Charitable-Gift Annuity

In its simplest form, an annuity contract is an agreement between the purchaser of the contract, or annuitant, and the issuer of the contract. Under such an agreement, the issuer agrees to make periodic payments to the annuitant for the annuitant's lifetime. The level of payment is primarily based on two factors: the age of the individual when he purchases the contract and the prevailing interest rate. The older the annuitant, the larger the payments, because his life expectancy is shorter. If the prevailing interest rate is high and the issuing company can therefore anticipate earning a greater return on the funds, it can offer a higher rate.

There are many variations on the basic annuity contract. The most common is a deferred annuity, a contract in which one pays today for an income stream that starts at some future date. The advantage of a deferred annuity is that from the purchase until the beginning of the payment stream, the contract amount is invested and grows, making the eventual payments significantly larger than those for an immediate annuity agreement. In the commercial world, there are also variable annuities, agreements in which the amount of the payment is dependent upon the investment experience of the underlying assets. In other words, if an individual invests $10,000 in a deferred variable annuity and the instrument in which the funds are invested compounds at a high annual rate, he will receive higher payments when the payments begin. On the other hand, if the investment performance of the $10,000 is poor, resulting in little growth or a loss, the payments will be much lower. Hence, the variability of the annuity contract.

In the charitable world, a so-called gift annuity, either immediate or deferred, is no different than a commercial annuity of the same type, except that the table from which the payments are calculated may be established at lower overall rates. The idea behind the gift annuity is that the donor enters into a contract with the charity by donating a certain amount. In exchange for his donation, the donor receives annual payments for his lifetime, beginning when the contract is formed in an immediate gift annuity or at some later date in a deferred gift annuity. Since the payment obligation ends on the annuitant's death, the charity retains the balance of the contract amount as its gift. The most commonly used tables anticipate that half the initial capital will be left at the death of the annuitant.

When a person purchases a gift annuity, he receives a tax deduction for a portion of the contract amount—essentially the present value of the amount anticipated to be remaining at his death. The payments he receives during his lifetime consist of an interest or income component and a return of capital component. This last feature explains the popularity of these instruments among donors, particularly during periods of low interest rates.

A 75-year-old donor can buy a one- or even a five-year bank certificate of deposit and use the regular interest stream to supplement his retirement income. He can also purchase a gift annuity agreement from his favorite charity. For older people, the payment stream from the gift annuity is invariably larger than what they can earn from interest-bearing instruments, because the gift annuity's payment stream includes a partial return of capital. One key difference between a gift annuity and a certificate of deposit is accessibility. The donor can withdraw his money from the CD, but a gift annuity represents an irrevocable agreement with the charity.

Pooled-Income Funds

A pooled-income fund is a pool of money held in trust, usually by a bank or a trust company, in which a donor may purchase units or shares[11]. The money inside the pool is then invested and whatever amount is earned as dividend and interest income is distributed to the holders of the units of the fund on a pro rata basis. It is functionally similar to an income-only mutual fund. On the death of the pooled-income fund investor, the principal amount attributable to that investor's shares is distributed to the designated charitable organization. The donor to a pooled-income fund receives an income stream and a charitable contribution for the value of the remainder interest. That again is calculated at the time the gift is made on an actuarial basis.

Not All Planned Gifts Are Created Equal

There are a great many details on the exact use of the charitable instruments described above that are tremendously important for those implementing a planned-giving program. Those differences are not, necessarily, significant for investment management purposes. The factors that matter for our purposes are the following:

1. Are the distributions based on "income," or are they calculated on some other basis?
2. How long will the funds be available to invest?
3. Are there any restrictions on permitted investments?
4. Are there tax consequences that may be affected by the investment decisions?

Exhibit 8.11 presents the answers to those questions, in summary form, for each of the various instruments thus far described, excepting charitable lead trusts.

This table is a good place to begin understanding that not all planned gifts are created equal from an investment management perspective. Specifically, some gifts by nature of their distribution provisions force the organization to attempt to generate current income with the problems discussed above under the sin of reaching for yield. Conversely, some of these instruments are ideal total return vehicles.

---

[11] Technically, a pooled-income fund must be owned or controlled by a charity. Thus, the charity must either trustee the trust or retain the right to remove the institutional trustee.

EXHIBIT 8.11. Characteristics of Planned-Gift Instruments

	Distribution Requirements	Term	Investment Tax Consequences	Investment Restrictions
Endowments	Depends on endowment spending policy	Perpetual	Irrelevant	Board level restrictions
Standard charitable remainder unitrusts	Percentage of net asset value	Live(s) of donors or a term of years	Multi-tier distribution system	Board, donor, or original property
Net income charitable remainder unitrusts	Lesser of income or a percentage of net asset value	Live(s) of donors or a term of years	Multi-tier distribution system	Income driven
Charitable remainder annuity trust	Percentage of initial net asset value	Live(s) of donors or a term of years	Multi-tier distribution system	Board, donor, or original property
Charitable gift annuities	Fixed contractual amount (immediate or deferred)	Effectively perpetual*	Irrelevant	Possible state regulation
Pooled-income funds	All income	Effectively perpetual*	Irrelevant	Income driven

*Depending on effectiveness of on-going fund raising

THE GOOD INSTRUMENTS

The good planned-gift instruments are those that can be managed on a total return basis. Unfortunately, applying the total return standard to planned-gift instruments is not quite so straightforward as one might hope.

Remainder Trusts

In the area of remainder trusts, both standard unitrusts and annuity trusts are total return instruments. In each case, the required annual distributions are based on a net asset value and are unaffected by income. Therefore, in each case the assets may be managed for total return.

Consider, therefore, the following policy suggestion for the use of charitable remainder trusts:

It is the policy of American Charitable Organization (ACO) to encourage the use of planned gifts which can be managed on a total return basis and to minimize the use of those which cannot. In that regard, our gift-acceptance policies are modified as follows:

> CHARITABLE REMAINDER TRUSTS
> The preferred forms of CRT shall be a standard 5 percent unitrust or an annuity trust up to 10 percent, depending upon the age of the donor. The use of net income unitrusts shall be limited as set forth below. These trusts shall be accepted in the amounts and for the ages shown on the attached pages, but only to the extent permitted under the then current Internal Revenue Code and IRS regulations.
>
> *Net Income Remainder Trusts*
> Net income charitable remainder trusts shall only be used in the following circumstances:
> A. Retirement planning for younger donors with initial amounts of at least $500,000 or a plan which anticipates regular annual contributions.
> B. Real estate or other non-income producing property where it is not feasible for the donor to use a flip trust or to contribute operating expenses (including initial trust distributions) prior to sale.
> C. Donors who are at least 80 years of age.
> D. For sophisticated donors who are using such trusts in order to have a variable income stream.

One may quarrel with the numbers: 80 may be too old, 10 percent may be too little, and so on. In addition, as noted earlier in this chapter, there are donors who want only net income trusts. Thus, this may be unworkable as a hard and fast policy. But do not miss the point: The foregoing restrictions would result in far more low-payout total return instruments. The result of that change would be enormously greater investment growth for the ultimate benefit of the charitable organization.

The better course with remainder trusts is to use the standard unitrust for those donors who have sufficient life expectancy that they are likely to benefit from increases in the value of the trust assets. For older donors who are most concerned with receiving a certain payout at a high rate, the annuity trust can be used to achieve precisely that result. In both cases, you are left with an instrument that can be managed on a total return basis, which, ultimately, is in the best interest of both parties. The interest of the charity is served in potentially increasing or at least minimizing the decrease in the value of the trust assets over time. The interest of the donor is served in either increasing their payment over time, if the instrument is a unitrust, or in maximizing the earnings in the annuity trust and thereby reducing the risk that the annuity trust might run out of funds during the income beneficiary's lifetime. The confluence of interest between the donor and the charitable organization is a powerful reason to incorporate a modicum of investment sophistication into our gift acceptance policies.

Gift Annuities and Pooled-Income Funds

With these pooled instruments, the thinking and analysis is really very similar. The pools of funds that are generated by gift annuities are, in the absence of state regulation to the contrary, an ideal total return instrument. If the organization has an active program of raising funds through the sale of gift annuities so that there is a steady flow of funds into the pool, then the pool can be managed on a total return basis and can be effectively very long-term as well. In that circumstance, the gift annuity pool can be managed exactly like an endowment, discussed above, with the levels of risk and the use of multiple-asset classes being determined by the comfort level of the board and not by other factors.

On the other hand, since a traditional pooled-income fund invests exclusively in fixed-income instruments and pays out interest income, it has no potential for growth. Given that fact, the ideal policy for such instruments from an investment perspective might read as follows:

> GIFT ANNUITIES AND POOLED-INCOME FUNDS
> To the extent that state law permits ACO to invest gift annuity reserves on a total return basis, we shall encourage the use of gift annuities in accordance with our other gift-acceptance policies. Our offering of pooled-income funds will be limited to those which can be administered by major banks or other institutions on a net to ACO basis (meaning that all costs of administration are borne by the pools) or, if self-administered, can be positioned as "growth" vehicles for younger donors and managed on a total return basis.

The thinking here is to (1) favor growth instruments and (2) avoid expending organizational energy otherwise.

Gift Annuity Regulation

Unfortunately, there are a number of states, most visibly California and New York, that regulate the issuance of gift annuities by charities to the residents of those states. The rules are generally authorized by statute and issued or enforced by the insurance commissioners of those states. Insurance commissioners are involved because gift annuities are contractual obligations similar to commercial annuities, which are universally issued by insurance companies.

Under most state laws, a charity that issues gift annuities is entering into simple contracts with annuitants. Consequently, the organization's entire net worth—all its assets—stands behind its obligation to make payments under the annuity contract. In spite of that fact, in states where the insurance commissioner regulates the issuance of gift annuities, a charitable organization is required to reserve and sometimes segregate an actuarially determined amount of their obligation to annuitants. Depending upon the ages of the donors in the gift annuity program, that reserve amount can range from 60 percent to 90 percent or more of the face amount of the annuity contracts.

We have already seen the national trend toward incorporating modern portfolio theory in various versions of the Prudent Investor Rule. Unfortunately, one of the last bastions of the Prudent Man Rule is the various state insurance regulations that apply to the investment of gift annuity reserves. Thus, in California and New York, the maximum amount of the gift annuity reserve that may be invested in equities is 10 percent. As a result, many charitable organizations are required to maintain 90 percent or more of their gift annuity reserves in U.S. government bonds.

Compliance with these regulations makes it virtually impossible for charitable organizations to earn enough on their funds to make the annuity payments without invading and thereby diminishing the principal amount used to purchase those agreements. The great irony is that charitable-gift annuities are an ideal total return instrument. The payment is fixed by contract the day the contract is signed and is completely independent of the type of income generated from the underlying assets. In other words, it does not matter whether the pooled gift annuity reserve funds generate dividend and interest income or only capital gains. The payments are not dependent on either the character or the amount of the underlying income.

When insurance commissioners enforce their rules, they eliminate that valuable characteristic by forcing charitable organizations to invest exclusively in fixed-income instruments. As the investment community wrestled with these issues over the last quarter-century, the conclusion is that such restrictions increase risk, not just for portfolio reasons but also as a result of a constantly diminishing return. As the fund is unable to earn enough on a current basis to make the payments and begins invading capital, the amount of the fund diminishes so that, over time, it is less capable of earning the amount necessary to make the annuity payments.

What happens if the charity gets caught in a combination of long lifetimes and low interest rates? The long-lifetime issue, while undocumented, is nonetheless a legitimate concern. A common joke in the development community is that if a donor wants to live five or ten years longer than his projected life expectancy, he should buy a gift annuity.

The final area of concern regarding the investment of gift annuity reserves is that several states are aggressively asserting their jurisdiction over the issuance of these contracts. If an issuer in California has to comply with the California rules, must that issuer comply with California rules when entering into a contract with a New York resident? All the states are in agreement in such a case, but must the California charity also comply with New York's requirements? This subject, which lawyers call conflict of laws, has been a headache since ten minutes after the adoption of the Constitution, and in the absence of some sort of uniform charitable-gift annuity act adopted by multiple states, it will likely continue to be a headache.

Conclusion

Charitable organizations have a tremendous opportunity to enhance the value of their fund raising programs by incorporating investment awareness into such work. All planned gifts are truly not created equal, particularly from an investment perspective. By favoring those that can be managed on a total return basis, to the extent consistent with the interests of the donors, the organization should earn a tremendously greater return on its planned-gift assets for years to come.

9 ▼ Special Nonprofit Investment Problems

As I have at least alluded in prior chapters, nonprofits have a seemingly limitless ability to make poor investment decisions. I used to think this applied only to relatively small and clearly unsophisticated charities. But events of the last several years have shown that the vulnerability of nonprofits to make embarrassingly bad decisions and participate in outright scams is not limited to the small or inexperienced. Among those involved in the *New Era for Philanthropy Fund* was a former secretary of the treasury. Anyone can make a bad investment or a really stupid decision.[1]

At the ACO . . .

TURNED DOWN

Despite the now-obvious weaknesses of the ACO board, they were one of the few organizations in their city that did not get taken in by the *New Era for Philanthropy Fund*. They heard about the program, of course, and had their development officer investigate. The officer discovered that a number of well-known organizations in their community were already participating. Several to whom he spoke had already received a double-your-money matching grant. All gave glowing reports of the program in general and of Jack Bennett, its founder, in particular. So the ACO completed all the paperwork needed to apply for a grant and sent it in to the Foundation.

Fortunately for them, Jack Bennett turned them down![2]

---

[1] Concerning the bad decisions referred to here, I will discuss the New Era for Philanthropy scam later in this chapter.

As far as my own experience is concerned, at one time I helped form a real estate limited partnership in which I was also a general partner. We bought 50 gorgeous, flat developable acres at the corner of Highway 90A and the future freeway in Houston, Texas. Seven years of Texas oil and banking disasters later, the freeway still wasn't built and we ended up deeding the property back to the bank. My partners and I lost $1 million. I personally try not to do business with people who haven't previously lost money, because they just don't know how easy it is to do.

[2] As whimsical as this scenario may seem, a number of organizations were in fact turned down. No one really knows why. The other large category of nonprofits that were not in New Era were those not well enough connected in fund-raising circles to have learned of the program.

Cultural Vulnerabilities

Before examining the particular problems and issues in the materials that follow, consideration must be given to why nonprofits have these vulnerabilities. The most obvious observation is that many of these problems grow out of the charitable organization's dependency on fund raising. Some grow out of their dependency on volunteers. All are intimately tied to their character. These character issues are the cultural vulnerabilities of charitable organizations.

GENTLENESS

The first component of the cultural vulnerability of most charities is gentleness. In my experience, the nonprofit world is kinder and less demanding than the world of business. Almost everyone employed by or associated with nonprofit organizations is aware of the organization's continuing need for fund raising and so adopts an open and inviting manner in dealing with the public. With such openness and gentleness often goes a certain vulnerability to the hustler. Voltaire said, "The beginning of wisdom is doubt." That type of cynicism is frequently lacking in charitable organizations.

THE DESIRE TO PLEASE

Some of the unique problems of nonprofit organizations grow out of a desire to please. Organizations are sensitive to their constituents generally and to the constituency of donors in particular. That sensitivity leads them to do things or to accept responsibilities that, in the harsh light of self-interest, they might otherwise reject. Social or morally based investments, serving as trustee, and accepting troubled properties as gifts are all examples of accepting responsibilities to please others. The overwhelming majority of organizations have struggled at one time or another with all of these issues.

THE WILLINGNESS TO TRUST

Another source of peculiarly charitable problems are those that arise from trusting others. Trust, as we all know, is a wonderful thing. It is an essential component of all important relationships and friendships. But for those very reasons, excessive or misplaced trust is a dangerous and abiding problem. Within the world of charitable investing, conflicts of interest, in particular with volunteers, the failure to supervise, and outright scams can all result from misplaced trust.

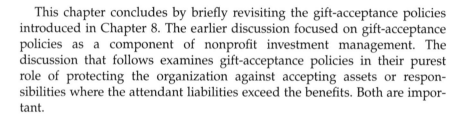

This chapter concludes by briefly revisiting the gift-acceptance policies introduced in Chapter 8. The earlier discussion focused on gift-acceptance policies as a component of nonprofit investment management. The discussion that follows examines gift-acceptance policies in their purest role of protecting the organization against accepting assets or responsibilities where the attendant liabilities exceed the benefits. Both are important.

Socially Responsible Investing

Many organizations want their investments to be consistent with organizational beliefs. The various manifestations of the Prudent Investor Rule allow nonprofit organizations to take account of social and moral concerns when investing. To eschew a particular investment because it is offensive to the goals and character of a particular organization is neither improper nor imprudent.

Social and moral investment concerns can, however, lead to problems or become problems in and of themselves. It is easy, for example, to be excessively concerned with these issues to the detriment of the greater responsibility to invest prudently. It is also possible to pursue a moral or social objective as a primary investment goal and thereby make a truly poor investment decision. An understanding of the proper place and weight for such concerns can eliminate the problems.

THE PROBLEM OF PURITY

Among the more common restrictions on investments in nonprofit portfolios are bans on tobacco, alcohol, gambling, and nuclear power stocks. In the many policies that I have reviewed, however, I have yet to see a ban on U.S. government bonds. Indeed, such bonds are usually the foundation of the fixed-income portion of the portfolio. This is hugely inconsistent. Any close inspection finds that the federal government is either a sponsor or beneficiary of each of these precluded activities. It is the government that has developed nuclear power and weapons; it is the government that has authorized the native American gambling casinos that are now exploding across the country; and it is the government that receives billions of dollars in tax revenues from the sale of tobacco and alcohol. How can a charity exclude direct investments in those activities and yet blithely invest in their principal sponsor, protector, and client?

But organizations do. Why? Because it is virtually impossible not to. Organizations need the ultimate stability and safety of government bonds. Therefore, they compromise and begin socially responsible investing with

an exception that dwarfs the rule. The reality of investing is that there are simply too many interlocking relationships between companies, their pension plans, their subsidiaries, and their other investments to isolate a portfolio completely from a particular activity. Purity is literally impossible.

Further, this same complexity will make it difficult to identify the consequences of an organization's actions in this arena. It is extremely difficult to identify exactly who is being helped and who is being hurt. Consider the issue of tobacco. One economic result of the recent boom in cigars has been a tremendous increase in income for Latin American tobacco producers, many of whom are relatively poor, indigenous people. Is it the goal of a no-tobacco investment policy to further impoverish these people? Clearly not. But that, arguably, is one of the likely results.

So what to do? Abandon the effort and buy the same things that everyone else does? No. The answer is to recognize that the true goal of social or moral investment restrictions is to make a statement. The organization wants its constituents to know what it believes and to see it acting in a way that is as consistent with those beliefs as possible. Thus an inner-city mission that fights alcoholism and its consequences would clearly not invest in distillers of whiskey. It might, however, invest in a glass manufacturer even if the glass company profits from the sale of beer bottles. Why? Investing in the distiller could be viewed as an endorsement of alcohol consumption, while owning the glass company's stock is unlikely to have that effect. Here, it is perception that matters.

It is also important for the board to realize that investment restrictions based on moral or social concerns may lower portfolio performance. Several studies found a reduction in annual return of one-half of 1 percent in portfolios prohibiting tobacco, alcohol, and gambling stocks.[3] While such restrictions are permitted by the Prudent Investor Rule, the board should be aware of the cost associated with them.

SOCIAL CONSCIENCE AS A DOMINANT OBJECTIVE

The final area concerns when organizations occasionally invest in an activity *just because it is a socially or morally important activity.* These investments will usually not be financial or portfolio investments at all but are more likely to be direct investments in small companies or loans to local entities or individuals. Most denominations, for example, loan local churches money with which to build sanctuaries. Some social service agencies have small business

---

[3] See Christopher Luck and Kathy Word, "The CFA Digest," The Association for Investment Management and Research, Fall, 1993:45–47.

programs. Many organizations make educational loans for college students and others.

These are all arguably investments, but they are also all clearly motivated primarily by social or ministry concerns and not by investment management concerns. Where do such activities fit in the investment management program? They do not, but that is okay.

Unusual investment opportunities are inappropriate for nonprofit organizations. Too often it seems as if the proponents of such opportunities rely on their close personal friendships with the promoter, developer, or owner of the opportunity. Their enthusiasm usually includes statements to the effect that the project "won't cost us anything," because of the return on the investment. Enthusiasm for the underlying social objective blinds the organization to the true risks of the investment.

The better way is to recognize that projects intended to help people are wonderful but are not financial investments. Investors do not buy stock in Microsoft to help Bill Gates make *another* billion dollars. They buy Microsoft stock expecting that Gates will make money for them. And that makes it a financial investment with risk and reward characteristics that can be dispassionately analyzed and measured.

Special projects—low income housing, start-up loans, educational loans, building loans to affiliates, equity investments in the inner city—and similar activities should be analyzed as part of the mission of the organization. To do that, simply assume that from an investment standpoint the project is a loser, on which the organization will never recover a nickel. It will, in fact, cost even more money on down the road when it fails and the organization, as the only entity with any reserve, will have to step in and clean it up. On those assumptions, is the organization still interested in taking that risk for the sake of the mission possibilities? If so, then the only other question is whether the organization can afford to spend this money *from its operating budget or some other fund established to take such risks, since it is clearly NOT a prudent investment?*

Do you see the pattern? It is fine to take wild and extravagant risks. For many of the downtrodden in the world, someone with money taking wild and extravagant risks is their best hope for a better life. Such risk-taking is laudable, but not with the pension plan money or any other fund where the *primary duty* is to invest it prudently *for the benefit of some other constituency.*

If an organization wishes to make these sorts of investments as part of its mission, then it should create its own "Wild and Extravagant Investment Fund." Even here, label the community investments "grants" for internal purposes in order to remember the true objectives, and then never cross the line by pretending that a grant is an investment. If the organization actually makes some money, throw a big party and then go take some more wild and extravagant risks with the proceeds.

Serving as Trustee

Many charitable organizations serve as trustee on charitable remainder trusts, charitable lead trusts, and revocable trusts. Even though the practice is widespread, serving as trustee may still be a mistake because of the risks and responsibilities that an organization assumes when it serves as trustee. To appreciate all the reasons *not* to be trustee, and to understand what it means to avoid these liabilities, one first has to understand the legitimate reasons why organizations have served as trustee in the past and will continue to do so in the future. The balance of this section consists of a discussion of the reasons to serve as trustee, then the reasons not to serve as trustee, and finally a strategy for serving donors without being served up as trustee.

THE PRESSURE TO SERVE AS TRUSTEE

There is enormous pressure on charitable organizations to serve as trustee. The pressure stems largely from the established practice of many large organizations, such as the nation's universities, of serving as trustee on these instruments "without charge." Planned gift officers fear that if they do not mimic other local organizations that serve as trustee for free, they will not get the gift. This is a valid concern. There are, in fact, some donors who will choose the free university trusteeship over any structure that imposes trustee fees on their trust. So we need to be cautious in our advice and clear in stating our understanding that those organizations that choose *not* to serve as trustee are, to some extent, swimming upstream.

REASONS TO SERVE AS TRUSTEE

There are a number of reasons to serve as trustee. First, institutional trust companies have historically done a poor job of investing and managing charitable trusts. Until very recently, the approach of the banking industry to fiduciary investing has been extremely conservative both as a matter of law and a matter of habit. In addition, since the most capable investment managers could make far more money on Wall Street, it has been difficult for banks to retain high-end investment talent. Consequently, many bank-managed common trust funds, which have been the primary investment vehicle for institutional trustees, have had poor performance records.

Second, many banks still charge more than charitable trusts can bear. Most banks (the term includes nonbank institutional trust companies) commonly look for a minimum trust size of at least $250,000, for which they charge 1.5 percent or more. In the nonprofit world, there are many trusts under $250,000. If, by way of example, a $3,750 minimum annual fee is applied to a $50,000 trust, the whole thing quickly falls apart, since no trust can sustain a 7.5 percent annual fee.

Third, trust officers in banks are not usually well-versed in the charitable world. Rather, they are accustomed to dealing with individual trusts. Out of a portfolio of 200 relationships or more per trust officer, they may each be aware of only one or two charitable trusts, which they tend therefore to view as something unusual and difficult to handle.

Such a view does not help with customer service. The typical private trust with a bank as trustee is more often than not funded at the trustor's death or became irrevocable due to a death or incompetency. On most of these trusts, the beneficiaries can change trustees only by going to court. This is not an atmosphere that promotes a great deal of customer service mentality—a fair number of the original clients are dead.

That is clearly not the case with most charitable trusts. For these trusts, the donor/trustor has an ongoing interest as either the income beneficiary (of a CRT) or the transferor of an inheritance to a family with a charitable lead trust. Consequently, many of these trustors care a great deal about how their funds are invested. Many have retained the right to change trustee, and all need to be "handled" in a high-end customer service manner. That has not been the long suit of many trust companies.

What's more, the current generation of charitable trusts is quite recent, as they were first authorized by Congress in 1969. These trusts have been formed in large numbers just in the last few years. Consequently, it is only in the last few years that trust officers have had any real contact or experience with charitable trusts. In many cases to this day, the large university trust operation with a substantial in-house staff has vastly more expertise and experience in the charitable arena than does the local (or national) bank trust department.

Finally, there is a sense in which both the desire of a donor to entrust funds to an organization and the organization's desire to maintain direct contact with the donor are better served when the organization serves as trustee. This remains an issue when an organization retains an institutional trustee and is a powerful argument in favor of serving as trustee. Donors rarely give all they intend to give at one time. Therefore, good fund raising requires steady, long-term contact even after a donor has funded a trust. If an organization loses contact by substituting a third-party institution as trustee, its fund-raising efforts may suffer significantly.

REASONS NOT TO SERVE AS TRUSTEE

The reasons not to serve as trustee can be summarized as follows: expense, liability, and diversion. Take a look at each.

It Is Not Your Mission

Serving as trustee represents a diversion of time and attention. If the organization is large enough to have one or two full-time people on its accounting staff, it can undoubtedly handle the incremental accounting and check writing of a few trusts. But let the program have any success and grow to dozens of trusts and the organization will soon be hiring staff, buying additional software, and otherwise diverting organizational resources away from the primary mission.

This is not speculation. This diversion of attention and resources happens repeatedly in charitable organizations of all sizes. There are now some major organizations with trust departments larger than their local bank's. Yet none of those organizations advertises its mission as providing free trust services to wealthy donors. *The irony of in-house trust programs that provide free services is that the charity ends up using current funds to provide a commercially available benefit to its wealthiest donors.*

Serving as Trustee Is Fraught with Liability

If the true liabilities associated with serving as trustee were known, reduced to a dollar amount and reflected on the balance sheet of the nation's nonprofit organizations, many seemingly prosperous organizations would be bankrupt. Here is why.

A trustee is a fiduciary responsible for multiple duties, including the following (first listed in Chapter 2):

- A duty of loyalty to trust beneficiaries
- A duty to keep records
- A duty to furnish information
- A duty to exercise reasonable care
- A duty to take and keep control of trust property
- A duty to protect property of the trust
- A duty to enforce claims of the trust
- A duty to defend the trust against claims
- A duty to pay income beneficiaries
- A duty to deal impartially with beneficiaries

Loyal Yet Impartial. One of the most important of these duties, that of loyalty, means the trustee must put the interests of the beneficiaries ahead of its own interests. That is closely followed by a duty of impartiality between beneficiaries. A trustee cannot, in other words, favor one beneficiary over another. Taken together, these two duties can place the charity-trustee on the horns of a dilemma.

For the overwhelming majority of the trusts on which nonprofits serve as trustee, the organization is also either an income or a remainder beneficiary. It is not, however, the only beneficiary. Rather, the donor or the donor's relative is a beneficiary as well. Consequently, when a beneficiary becomes sufficiently unhappy with the trust's performance or with another aspect of the trust's administration to file a lawsuit, he does so as a member of a favored class. He is a beneficiary to whom the charity, as trustee, owes a fiduciary duty. When the organization is also a beneficiary, how can it ever hope to prove both that it was impartial regarding its own interest and those of the other beneficiaries *and* that it put the beneficiary's interests ahead of its own? The short answer is that doing so is a daunting task even in a favorable factual situation.

Duties to the Next Generation. Because charitable trusts are fairly new instruments, as noted earlier, most organizations have not yet experienced very many donor deaths with the subsequent distribution of the funds to the organization. As that begins to occur, we will see disgruntled heirs who thought that they would inherit substantial sums from their parents only to find that those sums were in a remainder trust and are now going to charity. Some of those heirs are going to march into their attorney's office and ask if anything can be done. If an organization is serving as trustee of such a trust, it has greatly increased the difficulty of its defense. Of perhaps greater importance, the odds of a suit being filed have also increased. When an organization is not serving as trustee, there is a good chance that the attorney says to his potential client, "I really don't see a claim here. The charity is merely another beneficiary like you. Even if they encouraged the original gift, the bank served as an independent trustee for all these years so you really have no claim against the charity." When, on the other hand, the charity serves as trustee, the attorney now says, "Since the university served as trustee, they had a duty to you through your parents to manage these assets in your parents' best interest. Let's see if they did that." And he heads on down the road to rattle your cage and cause constant annoyance.

Once the attorney starts down that path, a host of other duties emerge to haunt the organization serving as trustee. As shown above, the organization has a duty to maintain good records, even if the trust lasted for 30 or 40 years. The organization also has a duty to make that information available to beneficiaries who are, of course, questioning its integrity. If the organization fails to give them the information they seek (even though everyone knows they will use that information as the basis of subsequent allegations in their lawsuit), the organization is violating another duty, and the plaintiff beneficiaries can get relief for that reason. **The basic rule for fiduciaries in disputes with beneficiaries is simple: the fiduciary loses.**

Trusts That Revert to the Donors. These issues are bad enough on remainder trusts. They are horrible on lead and revocable trusts. In lead trusts, the income goes to the charity and the remainder to beneficiaries who are typically descendents of the donor. In this case, the donors are getting what is left after the nonprofit has used the property for a number of years. In almost every instance, these donors will take a hard look at everything the organization has done to see whether it protected and preserved the property for the donors' benefit. Because of the number of decisions that could be made over a period of many years, even in a trust with only investment assets (stocks and bonds), there are many opportunities for the nonprofit to make what will, in hindsight, look like an improper decision.

Assume, for example, that the organization maintained only 30 percent equities in a lead trust portfolio over a 20-year period. Perhaps they saw my chart, determined that 30 percent equities is the lowest risk allocation, and decided not to take any greater risk. Their motives were as pure as the driven snow.

But the heirs come along and claim that the organization selected an allocation designed to maximize current income. To support their claim, they compare the compound performance of their trust with a 30 percent equity allocation to the compound performance of the organization's endowment funds (which are not managed by the development office), which happens to have a 60 percent equity allocation. The organization's allocation, though innocent, increased its income and significantly decreased the value of the heirs' remainder interest. The bad news is that the organization is going to lose the lawsuit and will potentially be liable for the difference in return between a 30 percent equity portfolio and a 60 percent equity portfolio, with interest, penalties, and attorney's fees. It will not be a pretty sight.

Success Can Lead to Further Regulation

Charities have authority to serve as trustee, typically, when doing so is "incidental to the principal objects of the corporation."[4] As the trust administration department of a successful planned giving operation grows, it begins to look an awful lot like the trust department of a bank. In that case, there are banking and trust laws that regulate companies that provide banking and trust services. California's statute is typical in defining regulated providers as those companies "which are in the business of providing trust services."[5] A great many regulatory statutes begin with such circular and therefore all encompassing definitions. As a result, state regulators are in a position to assert their jurisdiction very broadly should they choose to do so.

This is particularly true with revocable trusts in which the organization has no presently vested interest. In a revocable trust, the donor has merely

---

[4] California Corporations Code, §5140 (K).

[5] California Financial Code, §100 et saq.

expressed an intention to make a gift. Under most such trusts, *if* the trust is still in existence *and* funded when the donor dies, then the proceeds are to be distributed to the charity. The organization is, in essence, "selling" services in exchange for a future gift. While there has not been much activity in this area, we may yet see the day when state banking and trust regulators attempt to impose their rules on the "trust departments" of larger charitable organizations. If they do, they will undoubtedly find numerous violations of state laws as such organizations have not been making any effort to comply with those laws on the theory that they are not "in the business" of providing trust services.

Institutional Trustees Have Improved

The final reason not to serve as trustee is that institutional trustees are rapidly improving. Many institutional trustees, particularly among independent trust companies, now utilize both mutual funds and outside investment managers either in place of or in addition to common trust funds. Indeed, some of the larger U.S. trust companies view their ability to provide trust services primarily as a tool for gathering investment assets for the benefit of their more important investment management business. While that mind-set clearly brings with it concerns of its own, it nonetheless points to the fact that top-quality investment management is no longer absent from the world of the institutional trustee.

With the growth of the charitable trust business, institutional trust services have also become more affordable. The incremental cost of hiring a trustee versus the cost of investment management services alone might now be as little as one-half of 1 percent per year on a single trust and even less when the charitable organization is retaining an institutional trustee for its entire portfolio of trusts. If one begins comparing those costs, even if paid directly by the organization, to the cost of staffing an in-house trust department, the outside services may actually be quite attractive. And remember, that price comparison does not include the incomparable value of reducing the organization's long-term liabilities.

WHERE TO GO FROM HERE?

There are three possible reactions to this analysis: Ignore these concerns and maintain business as usual, get out of the trust business, or form a trust company subsidiary. For the very small organizations with only one or two trusts, serving as trustee is clearly an accommodation to their donors. And just as clearly, such organizations are not in the business of providing trust services. For the very largest organizations, forming a trust company for the sake of serving as trustee might be a viable option. For those organizations in the middle, the prospect of state regulation of trust services, while remote, is nonetheless one more reason to consider getting out of the trust business.

There is a world of difference, however, between concluding that the organization really does not want to serve as trustee and getting out of that business. Nine times out of ten the nonprofit is not writing on a blank page. Instead, it has a whole host of existing relationships and commitments that, as a practical matter, it cannot just drop even if it wanted to. Consequently, an organization must find a way to move gracefully from the current strategy—doing it all themselves—to a strategy that relies more heavily on third-party service providers. Consider some of the options in that regard.

Remember—Donors Want to Support Your Cause

A good place to begin is by remembering that donors really want to help. To be technical, most gifts are motivated by donative intent. Wealthy donors want to express their support of *your* organization by establishing a remainder trust for its benefit. Therefore, the fact that a different charity will provide free trust services is frequently irrelevant.

Second, the service is not free. The university is paying for trust services with its remainder interest and to that extent diminishing the value of donors' gifts. That same result can be achieved in a remainder trust either by allocating fees in the trust instrument to principal or by having the institution pay those fees directly. The services still cost what the services cost; the organization is merely choosing to pay for them.

Third, when an organization chooses not to serve as trustee it can legitimately promote its prudence and good judgement to donors. It has intentionally chosen not to assume substantial, long-term obligations. It has chosen not to serve as trustee because it is not the organization's mission and it can hire others who can do the job better for a reasonable fee. The organization has chosen not to serve as trustee because it wants to spend donors' money on its mission, not on administrative expenses. The nonprofit may still lose the occasional gift, but in the end, "time's glory is to calm contending kings, to unmask falsehood, and bring truth to light."[6]

Get Help Even If You Cannot Get Out

Not serving as trustee, particularly if it results in poor service or loss of direct contact with donors, can also be a mistake. In addition, it will frequently be difficult, if not impossible, to substitute out as trustee on existing trusts. Some trust instruments will not permit substitution of trustees. More commonly, older trustor-donors who rely on the organization would be

---

[6] William Shakespeare, *The Rape of Lucrece,* line 939.

so powerfully upset if the charity substituted out as trustee that doing so would be counterproductive. Therefore, we must consider a number of options that may be used, singly or in combination, to reduce trustee-related work and liabilities while retaining essential donor relationships.

Hire a Trust Company as Trust Administrator. There are a great many services that need to be performed by the trustee on behalf of a trust. Those include maintaining trust accounting records, making income distributions, preparing tax returns, and investing the funds. There is nothing in the law that prevents a trustee from hiring help. When that help is an institutional trust company there is a de facto reduction in liability. Even in those areas where the organization remains fully liable, as a matter of law, for the actions of its agent, the institutional trust company will, in turn, be liable to the organization. Most of the time, if the institutional trust company makes a mistake, it will bear the cost of that error.

Such arrangements are also fairly easy to establish. Since the organization is not changing trustees, it generally does not need to amend the trust or even have the beneficiaries' permission to take this action. Its authority as trustee is sufficient to hire help.

Delegate Investment Responsibilities. In the area of investment management, "hiring help" is an even better solution than it is for other trust services. As discussed in Chapter 2, the Uniform Prudent Investor Act (see Appendix B-2) now permits trustees to delegate investment responsibility. Therefore, when properly done, the trustee is relieved of liability for investment performance not just as a practical matter but as a matter of law. Even in those situations where an organization needs to continue serving as trustee, it does not need to retain liability for trust investments. Rather, if the state in which it resides has adopted a version of the Uniform Prudent Investor Act that permits delegation to outside managers, the organization may rid itself of these liabilities.

Changes in Future Trusts: Using Cotrustees. Even if the board feels compelled to continue serving as trustee on new trusts, an organization can still improve both the work and liability picture by taking the idea of hiring a trust administrator a step further. Specifically, it can create trust instruments in which the organization serves as cotrustee with an institutional trust company. When a cotrustee relationship is created by the trust instrument, the instrument can actually allocate specific responsibilities between trustees. Thus, the organization's responsibilities might be limited to hiring, supervising, and firing the institutional cotrustee. In that model, the organization maintains all the donor contact and relationship that it wishes, but it really has eliminated all of the work and much of the liability.

Do Not Forget Other Gift Options. It is helpful to remember that there are other gift options such as gift annuity contracts and pooled-income funds, that can frequently be used in place of a charitable remainder trust. While these instruments are more commonly used for smaller gifts, there is nothing inherent in the instrument that disallows a $1 million gift annuity. A little awareness of the utility of other instruments can reduce the number of times the organization is tempted to serve as trustee.

Serving as Trustee—Make a Decision and Stand Firm

Once the organization determines the best course, it should adopt a policy. Remember, development officers cannot be expected to turn down serving as trustee merely because the board has expressed concern about potential liabilities. Rather, the organization must implement a board-level decision in its gift-acceptance policies that declares the circumstances under which the organization will and will not serve as trustee. The sample gift-acceptance policies in Appendix C-1 in fact anticipate that the charity will serve as trustee.

It is also important to publish the policy with an explanation that allows everyone to understand the organization's position. In writing the explanation, always appeal to the donor's sense of the organization's mission. Once the donor understands that the organization has taken an informed position to do the best job of carrying out its mission, much of the opposition will disappear.

Do Not Overlook New Marketing Opportunities

In a community where most charitable organizations serve as their own trustee, a nonprofit has a unique opportunity to build alliances with institutional trust companies. Once the trust companies understand the nonprofit's policy of not serving as trustee—which means that it will be hiring them to manage trusts—when the trust companies have influence with prospective donors, those gifts are far more likely to be directed to such an organization than to those that serve as their own trustee and thereby "take" business from the trust companies. Obviously, the significance of these relationships will vary, but there is clearly some opportunity to enhance fund raising by working with third-party service providers.

Avoiding Bad Gifts—The Primary Role of Gift-Acceptance Policies

The principal idea behind gift-acceptance policies is to establish policies that protect the organization against "bad gifts." As noted in Chapter 8, since the advent of environmental laws requiring cleanup of polluted prop-erties, there are many landowners who would gladly give away their prop-erty if they could. In many cases, the potential liabilities associated with owning the property exceed the value of the property itself. Clearly, it would not be in the best interest of an organization to accept property containing a toxic-waste dump as a gift. It is a small step from that obvious conclusion to the understanding that even things as formally innocent as the corner gas station may be a gift an organization does not want. It only takes a little leakage from subterranean tanks to ruin one's whole day.

Polluted real estate is not the only "bad gift." Virtually anything other than cash and marketable securities can fall into that category. Many wealthy individuals have extensive art collections, wine cellars, and garages full of classic cars. All of these things are marketable, but none of them are easily marketable. Therefore, the organization could spend an enormous amount of time trying to realize value from these gifts.

If the donors are still living and wish to fund a trust with such assets, the situation is even worse. They will have an interest in and strong opinions concerning the values that they expect to receive. They may volunteer to provide their own appraisals. All of these things can get the organization into trouble.

So be careful. The IRS has detailed appraisal requirements for deductions based on non-readily-marketable gifts. IRS regulations also impose penal-ties in certain instances if the ultimate sale price is substantially less than the appraised value. The penalty provisions include penalties for aiding and abetting, which can be imposed directly on the charitable organization. At least one IRS publication urges IRS examiners to consider the applicability of such penalties when reviewing a charitable organization's books and rec-ords.[7]

Willingness to Trust

Charitable organizations tend to be more trusting than for-profit businesses. An overly trusting character affects nonprofit investment management in areas such as conflicts of interest, failure to supervise, and vulnerability to outright fraud or scams. All of these areas deserve books in their own right, some of which have been written. We will nonetheless consider two of these areas from the perspective of nonprofit investment policies.

---

[7] The publication is section X of the "Exempt Organizations Charitable Solicitations Com-pliance Improvement Program Study Check Sheet" (form 9215). For a good discussion of char-itable organizations' tax concerns, see Bruce R. Hopkins, *The Tax Law of Charitable Giving* (New York: John Wiley and Sons, 1993).

CONFLICTS OF INTEREST

There is a continual need to address potential conflicts of interest within the nonprofit community. Directors sell properties to the charities on whose boards they serve, participate with the charity in joint ventures, loan money, borrow money, provide services, hire relatives, and direct gifts to other organizations or individuals. For the most part, the laws concerning conflicts of interest are intended to provide a corporate governance structure for dealing with, and in a sense therefore allowing, such conflicts.[8]

As important as such rules are, when it comes to serving on the investment or finance committee of the board while participating in the management of the organization's funds, there is a simple rule. Do not do it. Do not try to sit on both sides of the table. If you are on the investment committee, do not allow your company to participate in the management of the organization's funds, *even if you are providing services without charge*. If you want to bid on the business and be a paid service provider, resign from the committee. Do not just "excuse" yourself from the voting, as many laws dealing with conflict of interest allow, or allow someone else in your firm to manage the account. It just complicates everyone's life.

The reason is that no one can objectively supervise himself. If, as discussed in Chapter 5, the investment policy committee of the board is to be the primary supervisory group, how can they really do that if one of their members is performing the underlying service? They cannot. People want to be loved, hate criticism, and are at least somewhat afraid of conflict. Add it all up, and the presence of someone on the committee whose work the committee is supposed to supervise ultimately means that the supervision will be weak, muted, and inadequate.

To the potential service providers themselves the same advice applies. There are hundreds of thousands of charities in the United States. A person does not have the time to be a really first-rate director for more than one or two. By agreeing to serve as a director such a person is excluding only one or two organizations from the universe of potential clients. He or she ought to be able to afford that sacrifice. If not, the person should wait a few years before serving as a director until his or her business has matured to the point that the person can afford to be a true volunteer.[9]

---

[8] For a good, short discussion of the law of conflicts of interest as it pertains to charities, see *How to Manage Conflicts of Interest* by Daniel L. Kurtz in *Nonprofit Organizations, Overview and Update* (1995) Practicing Law Institute.

[9] When a board has an investment policy committee to which it has delegated investment authority, then it is probably acceptable for an investment manager to remain on the board if not serving on that committee. In theory, at least, someone else is supervising his work. Even here, my preference is for service providers to not serve on the board whenever it is feasible for them to avoid doing so.

On the other side of the coin, there is no shame and frequently no loss of influence in declining to serve as a director. Most of my clients in the past have known that I would not serve as a director while my company was retained as investment advisor. In many of those situations, I nonetheless had access to the charity that allowed me to be something of a de facto director, primarily through close working relationships with the staff. The only real loss is that I did not usually get to know the other directors as well as if I were on the board.

To sum, the best, simplest, and least burdensome rule with regard to investment management and conflicts of interest is simply to avoid them. Choose a position, be a service provider or be a director, but do not try to do both. Everyone will be relieved of many actual and potential problems with this approach.

OUTRIGHT SCAMS: THE NEW ERA FOR PHILANTHROPY FUND

The New Era for Philanthropy Fund[10] was an outright scam. Here again, however, the dominant failure of the participants was at the board level. As easy as it is to get caught in such schemes, this scam was avoidable, as a few very cautious organizations demonstrated.

John G. Bennett, Jr., a former administrator of a drug and alcohol abuse program, director of several nonprofit groups, and an active leader of Christian prayer breakfasts, formed the "Foundation for a New Era in Philanthropy" in 1989. The foundation promised to double the money of nonprofit institutions, telling participants that their money would be matched by anonymous, "extremely wealthy" philanthropists who did not have time to find worthy causes and trusted New Era to do it for them.

An organization that wished to receive a double-your-money back grant had to deposit the money for six months with New Era in a brokerage account, which New Era described as a "quasi-escrow" account and from which New Era kept the interest. At the end of the six-month period, the organization would receive double its money back. The ostensible purposes of the "quasi-escrow" account were (1) to demonstrate that the participating charity was not desperate but had the ability to raise such funds on its own and (2) to provide a source of income for New Era in the form of interest earned on the deposits.

The program, called the "New Concepts in Philanthropy Fund," had as many as 180 participants during its six years in existence. It grew quickly,

---

[10] The factual information on the New Era for Philanthropy is taken from the articles cited in the bibliography under that title.

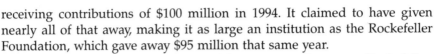

receiving contributions of $100 million in 1994. It claimed to have given nearly all of that away, making it as large an institution as the Rockefeller Foundation, which gave away $95 million that same year.

Among the more prominent participants were Lawrence Rockefeller, United Way of Southeastern Pennsylvania, the University of Pennsylvania, and William Simon, former Secretary of the Treasury. The majority of the participating organizations were Christian ministries, churches, and colleges.

The program appeared to work remarkably well until it was discovered to be a Ponzi scheme for which there had never been any anonymous donors. Bennett had merely taken the money of subsequent participants to make the promised double payment to earlier participants. Eventually, of course, those organizations that entered the scheme late in the game were left without their promised payoffs and without their principal, as it had been used to pay off earlier participants. This fiasco landed in the bankruptcy courts.[11]

Scam Proofing

Many careful and conservative ministries were deceived by the promoters of New Era. The magnitude of the deception is mind-boggling. Jack Bennett deceived the officers, directors, and advisors of hundreds of ministries and public charities. How was it possible for so many well-intentioned people—there is no suggestion of self-dealing or other improprieties on the part of those deceived—to make such bad decisions?

Gift or Investment: The Importance of Semantics. For the participants in New Era it was semantics that proved deadly. Having once mislabeled the "deposit" as something other than an investment, they dropped their guard and were vulnerable from that point on.

One prominent nonprofit leader, when discussing his ministry's participation in New Era wrote, "It [the deposit] wasn't an investment at all. . . . It was a temporary deposit for a matching grant program." If New Era has revealed a single, consistent structural flaw in many organizations, it is on this point. *The deposit required for the matching grant program was not analyzed as an investment.* Rather, it was thought of as something else and either exempted from the organization's normal investment policies or not subjected to the scrutiny of those policies at all. Picture the board or finance committee meeting at which the CFO announces, "Great news. I've found an invest-

---

[11] A remarkable and uplifting outcome of the New Era scandal was the voluntary return of funds by many of the ministries involved so that those who were defrauded could be repaid. This effort, known as United Response, was led by the Evangelical Council for Financial Accountability in Washington, DC.

ment that will yield a 100 percent return in just six months." It would never have been approved. Thus, for most of the New Era victims, semantics proved deadly.

Expense, Investment, or Mistake. If an organization is receiving money, it is a gift. If an organization is expending money, that is, writing a check (of any amount, for any reason, to anyone, at any time), it is either an expense, an investment, or a mistake.

The first part is easy. If the money is coming in the door, it is a gift; if it is going out, it is not. Even in such areas as planned giving, the difference between the costs incurred to develop and service the gifts and the amount eventually realized is clear. Those upfront expenditures are clearly expenses.

If, on the other hand, money is spent, is it an investment or an expense? The accounting profession has a number of somewhat complicated ways to answer that question. For some purposes, an easier test will suffice: Do you expect to get the money back? If so, it is an investment. If not, it is an expense.

There are few expenditures which will not fit into one category or the other. Consider, for example, legal fees for the drafting of a major donor's trust. It is an expense. It may be worth it, it may be a good expense, but you do not expect to get that money back, so it is not an investment.

What about deposits made to qualify for a matching grant program? If the organization expects to receive those funds back, it is an investment. To make the point painfully clear, the New Era deposits were investments because the organizations anticipated the return of and a return on their funds. If the program had been analyzed as such, even under a bare-bones set of investment policies such as those found in Appendix G-1, it would never have been approved. The reason is that the promise to repay is not a permitted form of investment. It was neither a publicly traded security nor a deposit with a federally insured institution. It was a mere promise from another charitable organization. Viewed strictly as an investment, most organizations would not have approved the transaction.

Defeating the Psychology of a Hustle

A number of years ago as a young attorney, I was negotiating an agreement by which my clients were buying into a new business. The "gentlemen" on the other side of the table, the sellers, were very aggressive, and while I could not point to anything in particular, I did not trust them.

On the night of the first face-to-face meeting with clients and counsel, the sellers' spokesperson said, "We've been working on this deal for weeks and we can't wait on you. We either make a deal tonight or the deal is off."

I had a sick feeling in the pit of my stomach. I knew that my clients should not do business with such people. But I did not have sufficient control to kill the deal, and I was too young and inexperienced to just close my briefcase and walk away. That is what I should have done.

The best way to deal with scams and to protect an organization is to have all of the policies, procedures, and organizational structures in place that are described throughout this book. But clearly, that alone will not always be enough. What else should be done?

Cultivate a Culture of Patience

The principal tool of all hustlers is a sense of urgency. We see it every day in junk mail. "One-time offer" is perhaps the most oft-repeated phrase in American advertising. Thus the most important protection against hustlers is to cultivate a culture of patience in an organization. To begin with, the idea of a "one-time offer" is a lie—there is always another deal. Believing that, or at least acting as you think you would act if you believed it, is step one. If you believe that there is always another deal, then you can walk away from this one.

In that same vein, be patient with the dissenters on the staff or on the board. Some people are against everything; this principle does not concern those folks. If they are against everything, then by extension they are never for anything. But there are also people on the board or on the staff who, like you, try to make good decisions. If one of them—*just one*—is opposed to an investment, then slow down and be very careful before overriding that person's opposition with a vote.

I have worked with a great many Christian ministries. When speaking to them on this point, I remind them that there is never any voting in the Bible and that invariably the majority is wrong. In the biblical world, it is the lone voice of the prophet through whom God tries to warn his people.

According to many people involved in New Era, in a number of cases the financial officers inside participating organizations, the outside CPAs, or even an occasional director tried to warn the board that something was rotten in Denmark. In nearly every case, however, the dissenters were derided by others and told, "This is fund raising, not accounting, so don't worry about it."

It is hard to be patient. It is hard to listen to peers when you disagree with what they say. When it comes to resisting hustlers, however, patient listening to more cautious peers is one of the few real protections.

Conclusion

A willingness to trust and a desire to please both lead those in the nonprofit world to assume responsibilities and to take risks not necessarily in their best interests. Here, as elsewhere, policy matters. By attempting to deal with such issues on a case-by-case basis, one will end up serving as trustee for healthy 45-year-old couples, owning gas stations, "investing" in halfway houses as rental properties, and participating in the Newer Era for Philanthropy. To avoid that, investment policies, gift-acceptance policies, and structures, such as those recommended throughout this book are required. Add to that a dedicated board and a modicum of patience and your organization will avoid many potentially disastrous problems.

10 ▼ Putting It All Together

In the world of nonprofit investment management, "Where to begin?" can be an intimidating question. Many organizations in fact get stymied at the very beginning. Part of the problem is that implementing investment policies is a multi-task endeavor. There are many steps in the process, each of which must be taken at some point. Indecision and hesitancy are natural reactions to such situations. Fortunately, there are relatively easy ways to resolve multi-task problems. Before examining one approach, let's make a final visit to an ACO board meeting.

At the ACO . . .

"WE CAN ALWAYS STAY IN CDs"

In each chapter, the ACO board members have struggled with their investments. If there was a way to get into trouble, these hapless but well-intentioned directors found it. But now they are filled with a great desire to do a better job. One of the directors, an accountant, attended a seminar on charitable investment policies at the AICPA's National Nonprofit Conference. She was so inspired by the speaker that she marched right out and purchased 20 copies of the speaker's excellent booklet on investment policies. Having each read the guide, the board members now want to adopt and implement such policies. They want to do a better job with the organization's funds, but the prospect of getting started leads to an argument.

>   "Let's have Joe, our current broker, just follow the policies in Fry's booklet," one argues. "Isn't that good enough?"
>   "Well, it may be," answers another, "but how do we know that Joe's good enough?"
>   "That's what performance reporting is for," says a third, in a tone that implies "you meathead."
>   "So we need to hire a consultant to review Joe's work," the meathead responds.
>   "Joe's not going to like that," continues the first board member.
>   "I'm tired of the whole thing," complains another, clearly expressing the dominant emotion in the room.
>   "Well," chimes in a third, "we can always stay in CDs."

Closing the Loop

Any complicated problem, any operation that involves multiple steps, multiple partners, or both can be daunting. Implementing investment policies is clearly such an operation as the steps that must be taken include:

- Adopting policies
- Creating or empowering a finance committee of the board to supervise the policies
- Identifying existing investment service providers
- Identifying manageable funds
- Examining fees and expenses of the current system
- Incorporating finance goals into investment objectives
- Incorporating development goals into investment objectives
- Preparing Requests for Proposals (RFPs) for new or additional service providers
- Retaining and empowering service providers
- Reviewing portfolios for policy compliance
- Reviewing investment performance
- Reviewing and revising policies

One approach to handling multi-task problems is to "close the loop." Consider the diagram in Exhibit 10.1. On it, most of the major investment policy implementation steps are shown as circles. It is a simple picture of what needs to be done.[1]

The good news is that you can start almost anywhere: Point A, Adopt Policies; Point B, Create an Investment Committee; or Point C, Hire Help. *It really doesn't matter.* The organization has to take all of these steps eventually, but within very wide limits it does not matter in what order they are taken. *So to get started, pick whatever task is easiest and do that one first.*

ADOPTING A POLICY

Adopting a policy is an easy place to start. It is something that can be done in a single board meeting, on a first reading, with very little discussion. Adopt a policy. Adopt any policy. Adopt a wrong policy. It really doesn't matter—the point is to get started.

The charitable organization with money under management, but with no investment policies protecting it, can begin by simply adopting the sample policies at the back of this book.[2] The important point about getting started in this manner is that the board adopt a policy on an interim basis. Doing so provides a framework within which to make the decisions and achieve the ultimate refinements to which the organization aspires in managing its funds.

If the organization has existing policies, the board should review them,

---

[1] This particular picture was actually drawn on a computer . . . by my son, Jonathan, age 11.

[2] See Appendix C-1. Let me be very clear about what I am *not* saying. I am not saying that the sample policies are adequate or appropriate for your particular organization or wisely adopted without review of counsel. *I am saying that almost any beginning is better than worry-induced paralysis.*

EXHIBIT 10.1. Implementing an Investment Policy

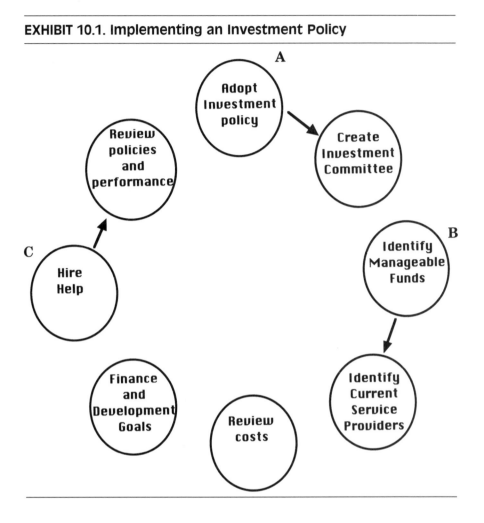

make any obvious changes and readopt them, again on an interim basis. The resolution should declare that the board has undertaken to review its asset management and the possible revision of its investment policies is part of that review. When adopting new policies or readopting existing policies, the board resolution should also authorize the organization's officers to take such further action as may be necessary to complete the review. Ultimately, these actions will lead to the adoption of a final set of investment policies.

CREATING AN INVESTMENT COMMITTEE

Recall from Chapter 4 the importance of the investment committee. If an organization does not have one, it should create one if it can. If the board is resistant (as some boards are) then there is a need to educate the board on the liabilities and responsibilities that attach to directors that retain investment authority. Most directors eventually decide that they do not want to be involved in every step. Scheduling weekly board meetings to interview investment managers can help them reach that conclusion.

IDENTIFYING CURRENT ADVISORS

The Internal Self-Guided Investment Management Assessment Form discussed in Chapter 5 (and contained in Appendix D) is a potentially useful tool for several steps on the loop, including identifying current advisors. It is important to consciously identify those currently being relied upon for advice. The form asks the question at several points. When listing the current advisors, quantify their usefulness based on the length of the relationship, the manner of payment, the fund or funds for which the advisor has been responsible, the level of satisfaction with the services rendered, and at least an estimate of the advisor's proficiency within his or her area of expertise. In making this list, look for obvious gaps. If, for example, a fund is about to be invested in equities for the first time, the organization probably has a gap in not having an equity investment manager. The entire discussion of existing service providers is one of the few that may really be worth spending several hours on at a board meeting.

A SPECIAL WORD ON ATTORNEYS AND CPAs

Attorneys and accountants can be important players in this process even though they will rarely, if ever, be the individuals primarily responsible for managing the funds. Matters within their areas of expertise will frequently bear directly on the manner in which the organization's funds may be invested. Therefore, get their input early in the policy formulation or policy review process.

Many businesspeople do not use attorneys and accountants wisely. To avoid incurring fees, clients tend to wait until the last possible moment to give a document to the attorney for review and tend not to deal with the accountant until he or she is preparing the tax returns or conducting the annual audit. Frequently, if matters have been handled improperly, it is too late for professionals to make a difference.

This approach is a mistake because advice received in advance is frequently the best deal in town. Assume, for example, that your attorney charges $250 an hour. It will take her no more than an hour to review the sample policies. If she then spends an hour thinking about it, an hour dictating her comments, and a final hour correcting her secretary's transcription errors, the total cost for the advice will be only $1,000. That will almost always be money well spent. Out of the one hour of "thinking time," a good attorney will identify areas of concern (which alone would be well worth the cost) and, frequently, will also provide the benefit of wisdom acquired over the years.

IDENTIFYING MANAGEABLE FUNDS

The next task is to identify existing funds noting those that can be managed. Some funds, such as an existing endowment fund, are obvious and are usually being managed already. Others, such as operating reserves, are not at all obvious and yet can involve substantial amounts of money. All are important. Once again, the self-assessment form contained in Appendix D and described in Chapter 5 can be a useful tool.

REVIEWING COSTS

The whole area of cost analysis and control is a difficult one when applied to the management of financial assets. The tendency of many organizations is to be overly concerned about external costs and fees, inadequately concerned about internal expenses, and, frequently, unaware of various soft costs such as the use of a volunteer or board member's time. Here's why.

External Expenses

As was discussed at length in Chapter 6, there are many sources of external costs and fees. Although assessing them for purposes of a review is not easy, it is possible. There is almost always a formal disclosure of such fees somewhere. Even indirect charges such as the internal management fees on mutual funds are therefore accessible.

Internal Expenses

The analysis can be more difficult for internal expenses. While every organization will know the salary and direct expenses of the financial officers and accounting staff, the portion of such expenses attributable to management of the organization's funds is rarely tracked. Consequently, it is functionally an unknown expense. It is the quality of being unknown that leads to it being underestimated or underemphasized in comparison with external fees.

Soft Expenses

Soft costs, such as the use of volunteer time, are even more difficult to track. In some small- to mid-size charitable organizations, the directors spend an enormous portion of the time they have available to the organization engaged in managing its funds. If asked the cost of this endeavor, such organizations invariably reply there is no cost at all because the participants are volunteers. The objectionable part of that equation is the notion that the time of the volunteer board members is free.

After speaking to hundreds of development officers around the country,

I can count on one hand the number of such officers who believe that his or her board does an outstanding job at fund raising. On the contrary, most development officers and executive directors readily admit that their board members do not spend enough time raising money from among their friends and colleagues. Clearly, as we discussed in Chapter 4, picking stocks is fun and asking friends for money is not. Consequently, many boards cling to their investment management role for as long as possible. This is part of the "soft cost" of having board-managed funds. When board members busy themselves with any task for which help could be hired, to the detriment of their fund-raising responsibilities, their "free assistance" may ultimately be the most expensive help the organization receives.

INCORPORATING FINANCIAL GOALS

There is a purpose for each fund the organization maintains. The fulfillment of that purpose expresses itself in part in financial goals. The purpose of operating reserves, for example, is to provide adequate liquidity to meet the organization's cash flow requirements during periods when income is less than expenses. Similarly, the purpose of an organization's endowment funds is to provide a growing source of revenue with which to support the organization's charitable purposes. Those objectives can be expressed in concrete terms such as minimum balances for reserves or distributions of a stated dollar amount from the endowment.

Those financial goals of the organization cannot be derived from the investments themselves nor be recommended by investment advisors. Rather, they have to be identified or deduced from the operating experience of the organization in each of those areas. A moment's reflection might suggest that this process could be part of the annual budgeting process; it clearly could. But most of the time, a budgeting process that is uninformed by the need to create financial goals for the benefit of establishing appropriate investment policies would not produce adequate information.

The chief financial officer might review last year's income contribution from the endowment, for example, and simply budget for that amount again, with or without some escalating factor. The mere fact that the CFO has depended on that income stream by incorporating it into the budget is information that needs to be communicated in a timely manner to those who are managing the organization's funds. A thousand different factors could have contributed to the level of last year's income, some of which might change. Something as simple as the current yield on the fixed-income portion of a fund can vary enormously from one year to the next. Thus the organizational expectations need to be communicated through investment policies to those managing the funds.

This process is reiterative. The chief financial officer communicates to the fund managers that he is planning on the same level of income he received last year. The fund managers advise him that he is crazy because there were extraordinary items in last year's income or that he is budgeting too low because they are shifting more funds into fixed income. The CFO now plans on a different level of income. The manager, advised of the plan that now reflects investment reality, proceeds to invest the funds. And so it continues. Again, the *process* is everything since neither the budgeting decisions nor the investment management decisions can be effectively made in a vacuum.

INCORPORATING DEVELOPMENT GOALS AND OBJECTIVES

Just as there are financial objectives that have an impact on the implementation of investment policies, so are there development or fund-raising objectives that have a similar impact. To the extent, for example, that the organization manages funds resulting from different types of gifts, it needs a process by which to apply its investment policies to such funds. The various forms of planned-gift instruments, discussed in Chapter 8, have particular investment characteristics that usually result in different asset allocation models for each class of gift instrument and sometimes for particular trusts or agreements within a class as well.

Consequently, before the organization can implement its investment policies, the senior development officer must identify and characterize the gifts currently being administered as well as the instruments and types of gifts that are currently being solicited. Once again, the *process* is important and reiterative. The development officer identifies specific gifts that have been received and describes their history and the expectations of the donors. The investment manager develops strategies appropriate for the gifts. Each informs the other. In the process, the development officer acquires information about how such gifts are being managed in general, which helps in future fund raising. The development officer's input has now become an appropriately important part of the overall investment management process.

Hiring the Necessary Help
In closing the loop, the organization has now drafted investment policies, identified current investments, analyzed its costs and expenses, and described financial and development goals. It is now ready to hire help. A subject only touched on in Chapter 6 is the use of requests for proposals (RFPs). Most investment advisors have mixed feelings about RFPs. On the one hand, it is encouraging to be asked to bid on business, particularly if the RFP has been given by invitation to a limited group. On the other hand, responding to RFPs can be a grueling task. It is rarely a manager's first choice for how he or she would like to be hired because an RFP, by its very nature, belies any existing relationship. It is a bidding process similar to that which the construction industry uses in granting contracts.

There is, nonetheless, a place for RFPs and there are ways to use them more effectively. The good part about the RFP is that it forces the charitable organization to articulate clearly its goals and objectives and the services it requires. Such clarity is helpful, whether the organization ends up formally issuing the RFP or not. A sample of the questions an RFP might contain is included in Exhibit 6.7.

The only caution on using an RFP is that it can in fact be a relationship-dampening device. The goal should not be to hire by the numbers but to find investment advisors who will have a good relationship with you, who will care about your organization, who will provide excellent service, and who will be valued accordingly. This must begin with your first contact and the steps you take to hire them. Treat them like a mere provider of a fungible service that is going to the lowest bidder and they will likely respond in kind. Treat them like peers who will become trusted colleagues and you will be amazed at their willingness to help and at the candor and integrity they will bring to the table.

REVIEWING EXISTING INVESTMENT MANAGEMENT OPERATIONS

The final step in getting started is to review the existing investment management operation for compliance with the new policies. Here, both the self-assessment form and the assistance of those whom you have now hired is important. If the management team includes a board level investment committee and an investment consultant, then there are now people in a position to review both the organization's operations (the investment committee) and the internal composition of the portfolios (the consultant.) Collectively, the process will provide a complete picture.

Compliance at the Organizational Level
A great many issues and items of concern might emerge from the overall review of the organization's investment operation. One might discover, for example, that historically all of the assets have been under the unsupervised control of a very few people. Many organizations pay less attention to who is authorized to order disbursements from the brokerage accounts than to who has access to the corporate checking account. Ironically, the brokerage account frequently contains dramatically greater sums of money and invariably receives less regular scrutiny, making it the ideal embezzlement account. If the same degree of control that one would normally apply to the operating cash of an organization is not in place on the organization's brokerage and other long-term accounts, that is a critical hole to plug immediately.

In a similar vein, the process of marking to market discussed in Chapters 7 and 9 is of critical importance. Implementing that process requires that the organization know the current fair market value of its holdings and the cost of those investments.

Sometimes, it can take significant work to identify the cost basis of existing investments. Unfortunately, if the organization is to have proper performance reporting and receive regular reports such as those illustrated in Appendix E, then the basis of the organization's investment assets is an essential piece of information. If the organization is not currently receiving such a statement on its investment funds, then that, too, is an omission that should be addressed quickly.

Portfolio Compliance
Inside the portfolios, the approach is similar. Some investment sins are worse than others. A portfolio that is overweighted in the utility sector would not represent the same degree of risk nor call for the same immediacy of correction as a portfolio that is grossly undiversified as a result of being invested in a single, highly volatile stock. In the latter case, if market conditions permit, it would be wise to take corrective action immediately. When the organization's managers review the portfolio for compliance with the new or revised investment policies, they should also identify critical changes that need to be made.

Conclusion

There is a lot to do to manage a nonprofit organization's funds. Many people are needed, many steps are involved, and, by definition, the work is never done. But it is great and rewarding work to do. A final word of encouragement is this—do not be intimidated by the information or the process. Managing an organization's funds is an important and challenging task, but it is one that any nonprofit organization can do well. Once you decide to be in charge, which is what having an investment policy really means, the decisions are relatively few and straightforward. And since making decisions can become habit-forming, it gets easier with experience. There are also many smart, committed, and honest people who are more than willing to help.

So take charge by creating and implementing investment policies that are appropriate for your organization. And if you run into any board members from the ACO, give them my apologies.

Appendixes

A   Glossary / 239

B-1 Uniform Management of Institutional Funds Act / 242

B-2 Uniform Prudent Investor Act (1994) / 246

C   Sample Gift-Acceptance Policies / 250

D   Internal Self-Guided Investment Management Assessment Form / 257

E-1 Sample Monthly Report / 271

E-2 Sample Quarterly Report / 275

F-1 Sample Endowment Resolution / 280

F-2 Sample Endowment Trust Agreement / 282

G-1 Sample Investment Policies—General / 287

G-2 Sample Investment Policies for Operating Reserves / 290

Glossary

asset allocation The process of allocating investment funds to different asset classes. This is usually done as part of the process of creating a portfolio with certain expected risk and return characteristics.

asset class Any of a number of categories of assets. The broadest categories for investment purposes include cash, equities (stocks), bonds, real estate, and commodities.

capital gain The excess by which proceeds from the sale of a capital asset exceed the cost basis.

certificate of deposit (CD) A receipt for a deposit of funds in a financial institution that permits the holder to receive interest plus the deposit at maturity.

commercial paper A short-term unsecured promissory note issued by a finance company or a relatively large industrial firm. The notes ($25,000 minimum) are generally sold at a discount from face value with maturities ranging from 30 to 270 days.

commodity A generic, largely unprocessed, good that can be processed and resold. Commodities traded in the financial markets for immediate or future delivery include grains, metals, and minerals.

common stock A class of capital stock that has no preference to dividends or any distribution of assets. Common stock normally conveys voting rights and is often termed capital stock if it is the only class of stock that a firm has outstanding. Common stockholders are the residual owners of a corporation in that they have a claim to what remains after every other party has been paid. The value of their interest depends on the success of the firm.

convertible security A security that, at the option of the holder, may be exchanged for another asset, generally a fixed number of shares of common stock. Convertible issues frequently are fixed-income securities such as debentures and preferred stock. Their prices are influenced by both changes in interest rates and the values of the asset into which they may be exchanged.

corporate bond A bond issued by a corporation as opposed to a bond issued by the U.S. Treasury or a municipality.

debt instruments Securities representing borrowed funds that must be repaid. Examples of debt securities include bonds, certificates of deposit, commercial paper, and debentures.

derivative instrument A financial instrument whose value is based on, and determined by, another security or benchmark, such as a stock, bond, futures contract, or commodity. One common example is the separation of the interest payment of a mortgage-backed bond from its principal obligation.

diversification The process of reducing the risk associated with any one investment by acquiring a group of unrelated investment assets. Effective diversification requires assets on which returns, over time, are not directly related to any other asset in the total investment portfolio. A diversified securities portfolio generally includes 18 to 20 issues of firms that are not similarly affected by the same outside economic events.

dividend A share of a company's net profits distributed by the company to a class of its stockholders. The dividend is paid in a fixed amount for each share of stock held.

equity Stock, both common and preferred.

fiduciary A person or an organization that is entrusted with the property of another party, in whose best interests the fiduciary is expected to act when holding, investing, or otherwise utilizing that party's property.

fixed-income security A security, such as a bond or preferred stock, that pays a constant income each period. Price changes in a fixed-income security are caused primarily by changes in long-term interest rates.

inflation A general increase in the price level of goods and services that reduces the purchasing power of the affected currency.

investment grade A designation applied to a bond or other fixed-income investment indicating its suitability for purchase by institutions. Investment grade designations are made by various rating agencies such as Moody's and Standard & Poor's (S&P), based on the credit worthiness and financial strength of the company issuing the debt. S&P investment grade ratings are AAA, AA, A, and BBB.

junk bond A high-risk, high-yield debt security that, if rated at all, is graded less than BBB. These securities are most appropriate for risk-oriented investors.

leverage Use of fixed costs (typically borrowed funds) in an attempt to increase the rate of return from an investment by allowing the purchase of larger positions. While leverage can operate to increase rates of return, it also increases the amount of risk inherent in an investment.

liquidity A position in cash or in assets easily convertible to cash.

margin account A brokerage account that permits an investor to purchase securities on credit and to borrow on securities already in the account. Interest is charged on any borrowed funds, but only for the period of time that the loan is outstanding.

market value The price at which a security currently can be sold.

Moody's® A trademark for one of the companies that issues ratings, denoting the relative investment quality of corporate and municipal bonds.

portfolio theory The theory of selecting an optimal combination of assets such that the investor secures the highest possible return for a given level of risk or the least possible risk for a given level of return. Using portfolio theory, an investor assembles a group of assets on the basis of how the individual assets interact with one another. Thus, a security would be purchased not on the basis of how that security is expected to perform in isolation but rather on the basis of how that security can be expected to influence the risk and return of the investor's entire portfolio.

preferred stock A security that shows ownership in a corporation and gives the holder a claim prior to the claim of common stockholders on earnings and also generally on assets, in the event of liquidation. Most preferred stock issues pay a fixed dividend set at the time of issuance.

principal Capital funds, such as the amount contributed to a trust, the repayment obligation (as opposed to the interest obligation) on a bond, or the amount initially invested in securities by an investor.

return on investment A measure of the total return an investor is able to earn (income plus capital appreciation) expressed as a percentage of the amount of his investment. Return on investment is calculated by dividing total assets into net profits and may be calculated on either a before tax or after tax basis.

risk   Within the investment community, risk usually means the variability of returns from an investment. The greater the variability (i.e., of dividend fluctuation or of security price), the greater the risk. Since investors are generally averse to risk, investments with greater inherent risk must promise higher than expected returns. In more common parlance, risk is the chance of a result that is less than you had expected.

risk-free asset   A risk-free asset is an asset that has, theoretically, no risk or volatility. Such assets might include treasury bills, money market instruments, and certificates of deposit (under $100,000).

risk-free rate of return   The risk-free rate of return is either a rate at which you could lend money to a risk-free asset such as a treasury bill, or a rate at which you can actually borrow money. The most common measure of so-called risk free return is the 30-day U.S. Treasury bill.

sector   A group of securities that share certain common characteristics based, generally, on the type of products or services they provide. One common division allocates companies into the following sectors: Basic Materials, Consumer Cyclical, Consumer Non-Cyclical, Energy, Financial Services, Industrial, Technology, and Utilities.

short selling   Selling a security that must be borrowed to make delivery. Short selling normally entails the sale of securities that are not owned by the seller in anticipation of profiting from a decline in the price of the securities.

speculation   The taking of above-average risks to achieve above-average returns, generally during a relatively short period of time.

Standard & Poor's Corporation   An investment advisory service that publishes financial data. A subsidiary of McGraw-Hill, the company also rates debt securities and distributes a series of widely followed stock indices.

Standard & Poor's 500 Stock Index (S&P 500)   An inclusive index made up of 500 stock prices including 400 industrials, 40 utilities, 20 transportation, and 40 financial issues. The index is constructed using market weights (stock price times shares outstanding) to provide a broad indicator of stock price movements.

time horizon   The time interval over which an investment program is to be completed. An investor's time horizon is very important in determining the types of investments that should be selected.

total return   Dividend or interest income plus any capital gain less capital losses and expenses. Total return is generally considered a better measure of an investment's return than dividends or interest alone.

U.S. government securities   All bonds issued by the U.S. Treasury or other agencies of the U.S. government.

unrealized gain   The increased market value of an asset that is still being held, compared with the asset's cost of acquisition.

unrealized loss   The reduction in value of an asset that is being held compared with the original cost.

yield   The percentage return on an investment from dividends or interest.

▼ B-1 Uniform Management of Institutional Funds Act

An Act to establish guidelines for the management and use of investments held by eleemosynary institutions and funds.

Section
1. Definitions
2. Appropriation of Appreciation
3. Rule of Construction
4. Investment Authority
5. Delegation of Investment Management
6. Standard of Conduct
7. Release of Restrictions on Use or Investment
8. Severability
9. Uniformity of Application and Construction
10. Short Title
11. Repeal

Be it enacted . . . .

§ 1. Definitions

In this Act:

(1) "institution" means an incorporated or unincorporated organization organized and operated exclusively for educational, religious, charitable, or other eleemosynary purposes, or a governmental organization to the extent that it holds funds exclusively for any of these purposes;

(2) "institutional fund" means a fund held by an institution for its exclusive use, benefit, or purposes, but does not include (i) a fund held for an institution by a trustee that is not an institution or (ii) a fund in which a beneficiary that is not an institution has an interest, other than possible rights that could arise upon violation or failure of the purposes of the fund;

(3) "endowment fund" means an institutional fund, or any part thereof, not wholly expendable by the institution on a current basis under the terms of the applicable gift instrument;

(4) "governing board" means the body responsible for the management of an institution or of an institutional fund;

(5) "historic dollar value" means the aggregate fair value in dollars of (i) an endowment fund at the time it became an endowment fund, (ii) each subsequent donation to the fund at the time it is made, and (iii) each accumulation made pursuant to a direction in the applicable gift instrument at the time the accumulation is added to the fund. The determination of historic dollar value made in good faith by the institution is conclusive.

(6) "gift instrument" means a will, deed, grant, conveyance, agreement, memorandum, writing, or other governing document (including the terms of any institutional solicitations from which an institutional fund resulted) under which property is transferred to or held by an institution as an institutional fund.

§ 2. Appropriation of Appreciation

The governing board may appropriate for expenditure for the uses and purposes for which an endowment fund is established so much of the net appreciation, realized and unrealized, in the fair value of the assets of an endowment fund over the historic dollar value of the fund as is prudent under the standard established by Section 6. This Section does not limit the authority of the governing board to expend funds as permitted under other law, the terms of the applicable gift instrument, or the charter of the institution.

§ 3. Rule of Construction

Section 2 does not apply if the applicable gift instrument indicates the donor's intention that net appreciation shall not be expended. A restriction upon the expenditure of net appreciation may not be implied from a designation of a gift as an endowment, or from a direction or authorization in the applicable gift instrument to use only "income," "interest," "dividends," or "rents, issues or profits," or "to preserve the principal intact," or a direction which contains other words of similar import. This rule of construction applies to gift instruments executed or in effect before or after the effective date of this Act.

§ 4. Investment Authority

In addition to an investment otherwise authorized by law or by the applicable gift instrument, and without restriction to investments a fiduciary may make, the governing board, subject to any specific limitations set forth in the applicable gift instrument or in the applicable law other than law relating to investments by fiduciary, may:

(1) invest and reinvest an institutional fund in any real or personal property deemed advisable by the governing board, whether or not it produces a current return, including mortgages, stocks, bonds, debentures, and other securities of profit or nonprofit corporations, shares in or obligations of associations, partnerships, or individuals, and obligations of any government or subdivision or instrumentality thereof;

(2) retain property contributed by a donor to an institutional fund for as long as the governing board deems advisable;

(3) include all or any part of an institutional fund in any pooled or common fund maintained by the institution; and

(4) invest all or any part of an institutional fund in any other pooled or common fund available for investment, including shares or interests in regulated investment companies, mutual funds, common trust funds, investment partnerships, real estate investment trusts, or similar organizations in which funds are commingled and investment determinations are made by persons other than the governing board.

§ 5. Delegation of Investment Management

Except as otherwise provided by the applicable gift instrument or by applicable law relating to governmental institutions or funds, the governing board may (1) delegate to its committees, officers or employees of the institution or the fund, or agents, including investment counsel, the authority to act in place of the board in investment and reinvestment of institutional funds, (2) contract with independent investment advisors, investment counsel or managers, banks, or trust companies, so to act and (3) authorize the payment of compensation for investment advisory or management services.

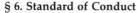

§ 6. Standard of Conduct

In the administration of the powers to appropriate appreciation, to make and retain investments, and to delegate investment management of institutional funds, members of a governing board shall exercise ordinary business care and prudence under the facts and circumstances prevailing at the time of the action or decision. In so doing they shall consider long and short term needs of the institution in carrying out its educational, religious, charitable, or other eleemosynary purposes, its present and anticipated financial requirements, expected total return on its investments, price level trends, and general economic conditions.

§ 7. Release of Restrictions on Use or Investment

(a) With the written consent of the donor, the governing board may release, in whole or in part, a restriction imposed by the applicable gift instrument on the use or investment of an institutional fund.

(b) If written consent of the donor cannot be obtained by reason of his death, disability, unavailability, or impossibility of identification, the governing board may apply in the name of the institution to the [appropriate] court for release of a restriction imposed by the applicable gift instrument on the use or investment of an institutional fund. The [Attorney General] shall be notified of the application and shall be given an opportunity to be heard. If the court finds that the restriction is obsolete, inappropriate, or impracticable, it may by order release the restriction in whole or in part. A release under this subsection may not change an endowment fund to a fund that is not an endowment fund.

(c) A release under this section may not allow a fund to be used for purposes other than the educational, religious, charitable, or eleemosynary purposes of the institution affected.

(d) This section does not limit the application of the doctrine of *cy pres*.

§ 8. Severability

If any provision of this Act or the application thereof to any person or circumstances is held invalid, the invalidity shall not affect other provisions or applications of the Act which can be given effect without the invalid provision or application, and to this end the provisions of this Act are declared serverable.

§ 9. Uniformity of Application and Construction

This Act shall be so applied and construed as to effectuate its general purpose to make uniform the law with respect to the subject of this Act among those states which enact it.

§ 10. Short Title

This Act may be cited as the "Uniform Management of Institutional Funds Act."

UNIFORM MANAGEMENT OF INSTITUTIONAL FUNDS ACT
TABLE OF ADOPTING JURISDICTIONS

Jurisdiction	Statutory Citation
Arkansas	A.C.A. §§ 20A-69-601 to 20A-69-611
California	West's Cal.Probate Code, §§ 18500 to 8509
Colorado	West's C.R.S.A. §§ 15-1-1101 to 15-1-1109
Connecticut	C.G.S.A. §§ 45a-526 to 45a-534

Jurisdiction	Statutory Citation
Delaware	12 Del.C. §§ 4701 to 4708
District of Columbia	D.C. Code 1981, §§ 32-401 to 32-409
Florida	West's F.S.A. § 237.41
Georgia	O.C.G.A. §§ 44-15-1 to 44-15-9
Hawaii	HRS §§ 517D-1 to 517D-11
Illinois	S.H.A. 760 ILCS 50/1 to 10
Indiana	West's A.I.C. 30-2-12-1 to 30-2-12-13
Iowa	I.C.A. §§ 540A.1 to 540A.9
Kansas	K.S.A. 58-3601 to 58-3610
Kentucky	KRS 273.510 to 273.590
Louisiana	LSA-R.S. 9:2337.1 to 9:2337.8
Maine	13 M.R.S.A. §§ 4100 to 4109
Maryland	Code, Estates, Trusts, §§ 15-401 to 15-409
Massachusetts	M.G.L.A. c. 180A, §§ 1 to 11
Michigan	M.C.L.A. §§ 451.1201 to 451.1210
Minnesota	M.S.A. §§ 309.62 to 309.71
Missouri	V.A.M.S. §§ 402.010 to 402.055
Montana	MCA 72-30-101 to 72-30-207
Nebraska	R.R.S. 1943, §§ 58-601 to 58-609
New Hampshire	RSA 292-B:1 to 292-B:9
New Jersey	N.J.S.A. 15:18-15 to 15:18-24
New York	McKinney's N-PCL §§ 102, 512, 514, 522
North Carolina	G.S. §§ 36B-1 to 36B-10
North Dakota	NDCC 15-67-01 to 15-67-09
Ohio	R.C. §§ 1715.51 to 1715.59
Oklahoma	Okl.St.Ann. §§ 300.1 to 300.10
Oregon	ORS 128.310 to 128.355
Rhode Island	Gen. Laws 1956, §§ 18-12-1 to 18-12-9
South Carolina	Code 1976, §§ 34-6-10 to 34-6-80
Tennessee	T.C.A. §§ 35-10-101 to 35-10-109
Texas	V.T.C.A., Prop. Code §§ 163.001 to 163.009
Vermont	14 V.S.A. §§ 3401 to 3407
Virginia	Code 1950, §§ 55-268.1 to 55-268.10
Washington	West's RCWA 24.44.010 to 24.44.900
West Virginia	Code 44-6A-1 to 44-6A-8
Wisconsin	W.S.A. 112.10
Wyoming	W.S. 1977, §§ 17-7-201 to 17-7-205

Uniform Prudent Investor Act (1994)

§ 1. Prudent Investor Rule.

(a) Except as otherwise provided in subsection (b), a trustee who invests and manages trust assets owes a duty to the beneficiaries of the trust to comply with the prudent investor rule set forth in the [Act].

(b) The prudent investor rule, a default rule, may be expanded, restricted, eliminated or otherwise altered by the provisions of a trust. A trustee is not liable to a beneficiary to the extent that the trustee acted in reasonable reliance on the provisions of the trust.

§ 2. Standard of Care; Portfolio Strategy; Risk and Return Objectives.

(a) A trustee shall invest and manage trust assets as a prudent investor would, by considering the purposes, terms, distribution requirements, and other circumstances of the trust. In satisfying this standard, the trustee shall exercise reasonable care, skill and caution.

(b) A trustee's investment and management decisions respecting individual assets must be evaluated not in isolation but in the context of the trust portfolio as a whole and as a part of an overall investment strategy having risk and return objectives reasonably suited to the trust.

(c) Among circumstances that a trustee shall consider in investing and managing trust assets are such of the following as are relevant to the trust or its beneficiaries:

(1) general economic conditions;

(2) the possible effect of inflation or deflation;

(3) the expected tax consequences of investment decisions or strategies;

(4) the role that each investment or course of action plays within the overall trust portfolio, which may include financial assets, interests in closely held enterprises, tangible and intangible personal property, and real property;

(5) the expected total return from income and the appreciation of capital;

(6) other resources of the beneficiaries;

(7) need for liquidity, regularity of income, and preservation of appreciation of capital; and

(8) an asset's special relationship or special value, if any, to the purposes of the trust or to one or more of the beneficiaries.

(d) A trustee shall make a reasonable effort to verify facts relevant to the investment and management of trust assets.

(e) A trustee may invest in any kind of property or type of investment consistent with the standards of this [Act].

(f) A trustee who has special skills or expertise, or is named trustee in reliance upon the trustee's reputation that the trustee has special skill or expertise, has a duty to use those special skills or expertise.

246

§ 3. Diversification.

A trustee shall diversify the investments of the trust unless the trustee reasonably determines that, because of special circumstances, the purposes of the trust are better served without diversifying.

§ 4. Duties at Inception of Trusteeship.

Within a reasonable time after accepting a trusteeship or receiving trust assets, a trustee shall review the trust assets and make and implement decisions concerning the retention and disposition of assets, in order to bring the trust portfolio into compliance with the purposes, terms, distribution requirements, and other circumstances of the trust, and with the requirements of this [Act].

§ 5. Loyalty.

A trustee shall invest and manage the trust assets solely in the interest of the beneficiaries.

§ 6. Impartiality.

If a trust has two or more beneficiaries, the trustee shall act impartially in investing and managing the trust assets, taking into account any differing interests of the beneficiaries.

§ 7. Investment Costs.

In investing and managing trust assets, a trustee may only incur costs that are appropriate and reasonable in relation to the assets, the purposes of the trust, and the skills of the trustee.

§ 8. Reviewing Compliance.

Compliance with the prudent investor rule is determined in light of the facts and circumstances existing at the time of a trustee's decision or action and not by hindsight.

§ 9. Delegation of Investment and Management Functions.

(a) A trustee may delegate investment and management functions that a prudent trustee of comparable skills could properly delegate under the circumstances. The trustee shall exercise reasonable care, skill, and caution in:
  (1) selecting an agent;
  (2) establishing the scope and terms of the delegation, consistent with the purposes and terms of the trust; and
  (3) periodically reviewing the agent's actions in order to monitor the agent's performance and compliance with the terms of delegation.
(b) In performing a delegated function, an agent owes a duty to the trust to exercise reasonable care to comply with the terms of the delegation.
(c) A trustee who complies with the requirements of subsection (a) is not liable to the beneficiaries or to the trust for the decisions or actions of the agent to whom the function was delegated.
(d) By accepting the delegation of a trust function from the trustee of a trust

that is subject to the law of this State, an agent submits to the jurisdiction of the courts of this State.

§ 10. Language Invoking Standard of [Act].

The following terms or comparable language in the provisions of a trust, unless otherwise limited or modified, authorizes any investment or strategy permitted under this [Act]: "investments permissible by law for investment of trust funds," "legal investments," "authorized investments," "using the judgment and care under the circumstances then prevailing that persons of prudence, discretion, and intelligence exercise in the management of their own affairs, not in regard to speculation but in regard to the permanent disposition of their funds, considering the probable income as well as the probable safety of their capital," "prudent man rule," "prudent trustee rule," "prudent person rule," and "prudent investor rule."

§ 11. Application to Existing Trusts.

This [Act] applies to trusts existing on and created after its effective date. As applied to trusts existing on its effective date, the [Act] governs only decisions or actions occurring after that date.

§ 12. Uniformity of Application and Construction.

This [Act] shall be applied and construed to effectuate its general purpose to make uniform the law with respect to the subject of the [Act] among the States enacting it.

§ 13. Short Title.

This [Act] may be cited as the "[Name of Enacting State] Uniform Prudent Investor Act."

§ 14. Severability.

If any provision of this [Act] or its application to any person or circumstance is held invalid, the invalidity does not affect other provisions or applications of the [Act] which can be given effect without the invalid provision or application, and to this end the provisions of this [Act] are severable.

§ 15. Effective Date.

This [Act] takes effect . . . .

§ 16. Repeals.

The following acts and parts of acts are repealed:

(1)
(2)
(3)

TABLE OF JURISDICTION WHEREIN ACT HAS BEEN ADOPTED

Jurisdiction	Statutory Citation
Arizona	A.R.S. §§ 14-7601 to 14-7611
Arkansas	A.C.A. §§ 24-3-417 to 24-3-426
California	West's Ann.Cal.Probate Code, §§ 16045 to 16054

Jurisdiction	Statutory Citation
Colorado	West's C.R.S.A. §§ 15-1.1-101 to 15-1.1-115
Florida	West's F.S.A. §§ 518.11, 518.112
Idaho	I.C. §§ 68-501 to 68-514
Illinois	S.H.A. 760 ILCS 5/5, 5/5.1
Maine	18-AM.R.S.A. §§ 7-302, 7-302, note
Minnesota	M.S.A. §§ 518.11 to 518.112
New Jersey	N.J.S.A. 3B:20-11.1 to 38:20-11.2
New Mexico	NMSA 1978, §§ 45-7-601 to 45-7-612
New York	McKinney's EPTL 11-2.3
Oklahoma	60 Okl. St.Ann. §§ 175.60 to 175.72
Oregon	ORS 128.192 to 128.218
Rhode Island	Gen. Laws 1956, §§ 18-15-1 to 18-15-13
Utah	UCA 1953, 75-7-302
Virginia	Code 1950, § 26-45.1
Washington	West's RCWA 11.100.010 et seq.
West Virginia	Code, 44-6B-1 to 44-6B-15

Sample Gift-Acceptance Policies[1]

The Board of Directors of AMERICAN CHARITABLE ORGANIZATION (ACO), with an understanding of its mission and responsibilities to those it serves, has established the following Gift-Acceptance Policy Guidelines.

I. Effective Date
A. These Policy Guidelines shall become effective on _____.

II. Amendments and Review
A. Responsibility for review of and recommended amendments shall be that of the Gift-Acceptance Committee (GAC). These Guidelines shall be reviewed at least annually and whenever they become inconsistent with IRS regulations or other applicable state or federal laws.

B. To amend these Guidelines, a written amendment shall be prepared by the GAC and submitted to the Board of Directors to be placed on the agenda of the next Board meeting.

III. Management Committees
A. The Gift-Acceptance Committee shall consist of the Director of Development, _____, and _____. The GAC shall exercise the oversight and responsibilities specified in these Guidelines. The GAC, or a member of the committee, shall report to the Board of Directors quarterly.

B. The GAC may, at its discretion, create a Development Committee to assist both the GAC and such other of ACO's officers as are involved in fund raising. Since the Development Committee's role shall be advisory, this Committee may be composed of such a mix of officers, outside agents and other professionals as the Director of Development finds helpful.

IV. Authorization for Negotiations
A. The members of the Gift-Acceptance Committee (GAC) are each authorized to negotiate and accept gift agreements with prospective donors in accordance with these Guidelines and the format of the approved specimen agreements without further Board action or approval. The current approved specimen agreements will be prepared and maintained by the GAC and incorporated into these Guidelines by reference.

B. All agreements that do not follow the format of the specimen agreements or otherwise meet the requirements of the following Guidelines may be executed only with the approval of the Director of Development and the President (Executive Director) or the Chief Financial Officer. The GAC shall include a description of any approved exceptions in their periodic reporting to the Board of Directors.

---

[1] This form is for illustration purposes only and should not be used by any organization unless reviewed, modified, and approved by that organization's legal counsel.

C. The President, Executive Vice President or Chief Financial Officer shall have the authority to sign agreements on behalf of ACO.

V. Governing Property Received

A. General Rule. ACO may accept gifts of cash, cash equivalents, fully paid life insurance, listed securities and over-the-counter securities without prior GAC approval. For all other assets, the approval of the GAC shall be required. Such approval shall be granted based on the conditions stated below.

B. General Restriction on Liabilities and Expenses. Unless a specific exception is granted by the GAC for good cause, ACO will not accept any gift if its ownership (1) is likely to expose ACO to litigation or other liabilities, (2) requires the payment of maintenance costs or other expenses (e.g., debt service) for which no specific provision has been made, or (3) is likely to generate unrelated business taxable income (UBTI).

C. Specific Rules for Various Classes of Assets

1. Real Estate. ACO may accept gifts of real property if it receives (1) a preliminary title report clear of unacceptable encumbrances, performed by a reputable title insurance company, (2) an independent appraisal by a qualified appraiser, and (3) a phase one environmental audit indicating that ownership will not expose ACO to environmental liabilities. The GAC may waive the phase one requirement for non-farm residential properties.

2. Gifts of Personal Property and Special Assets. ACO may accept gifts of personal property, unlisted or assessable securities, partnership interests, closely held business interests and other illiquid financial assets subject to the general conditions set forth above, whenever the intended gift asset is marketable or the GAC finds that the gift may be appropriately retained and used by ACO.

3. Gifts of Real Property with Retained Life Estate. ACO may accept gifts of real property with a retained life estate subject to both the general conditions and the guidelines for acceptance of outright gifts of real property as set forth above. In addition, the agreement creating the life interest must provide that the donor and/or life tenant shall remain responsible for the payment of mortgages, taxes, insurance, utilities and other costs associated with the property, unless other specific provisions are made for the payment of these expenses.

D. Marketability and the GAC's Discretion

In accepting any of the assets to which these provisions apply, the GAC may consider the intended holding period and the probability of sale in determining the adequacy of the provision that has been made for the payment of mortgages, taxes, insurance, utilities and other costs associated with the maintenance of the property. In no event, however, will ACO accept encumbered or other UBTI-producing property as gifts to charitable remainder trusts or other instruments for which such income causes a loss of tax-exempt status nor will ACO serve as trustee of charitable trusts that contain such assets.

VI. Acknowledgment, Valuation and Other Procedures

A. Minimum Values. The GAC shall establish minimum gift amounts for each category of asset and planned-gift instrument. The current minimum gift amounts are attached to these Guidelines as Exhibit A.

B. Valuation. All valuations of gifts of partial interests shall be made in accordance with the IRS valuation guidelines in effect as of the time of the gift. For gifts of

EXHIBIT A. Minimum Dollar Amount and Age Requirements

Planned-Gift Instrument	Minimum Dollar Amount	Minimum Age of Youngest Beneficiary
Charitable remainder trusts	$100,000	45
Pooled-income funds	5,000	No minimum
Charitable-gift annuities—current	5,000	Lowest age in American Council on Gift Annuities table
Charitable gift annuities—deferred	5,000	Lowest age in ACGA table

Other Valuation Provisions

Minimum value—outright gifts of real estate	50,000	No minimum

Guidelines approved by the ACO Gift-Acceptance Committee

_____

Date

property with a stated value in excess of $5,000.00, other than cash or marketable securities, ACO will require that the donor provide it with a qualified appraisal (as required by IRS Regulations issued under IRS Section 170(a)(1)) before issuing an acknowledgment which values any such gift.

C. Acknowledgment. ACO will acknowledge the receipt of all gifts in writing and in a manner which satisfies the IRS substantiation requirements for the deduction of charitable gifts by individual donors currently found in IRS Section 170(f).

D. Investment Disclosure for Pooled Funds. The GAC will prepare and/or approve a standard set of disclosures that describe the material aspects of any pooled funds maintained as part of the fund-raising effort. The purpose of this provision is to require compliance with the Philanthropy Protection Act of 1995 and other such laws as may require disclosures.

E. Compliance with Tax Laws. Should the IRS change its requirements with regard to valuation or substantiation, ACO will comply with such additional requirements.

F. Procedures. The GAC shall establish such staff procedures as it determines to be necessary and helpful in carrying out these Gift-Acceptance Policies.

G. Claims and Litigation. The GAC may authorize staff to submit normal claims to probate proceedings and otherwise cooperate in the collection of bequests. ACO may not, however, initiate or voluntarily participate in contested claims or other litigation to collect putative gifts without the approval of the Board of Directors.

VII. Governing Planned Gifts in General

A. Available Instruments. ACO offers its donors a variety of vehicles with which to make planned or deferred gifts. The current vehicles are:

  1. Charitable Remainder Trusts (both unitrust and annuity trusts)
  2. Pooled-Income Funds
  3. Charitable-Gift Annuities (both current and deferred)

B. Unmanaged Gifts and Bequests. In addition, ACO gratefully acknowledges that it has been named a beneficiary under wills and revocable living trusts of many of its supporters and may, from time to time, also be the beneficiary under other instruments such as charitable lead trusts. The primary purpose of the policies dealing with all of these instruments is to specify the circumstances under which ACO will assume responsibility for the management of the funds involved or of the gift instrument itself or both. In placing restrictions on the services ACO is willing to provide, it is in no way declining to accept beneficial interests in trusts, estates or other instruments managed or administered by others.

C. Administrative Tithe. It is the policy of ACO to request that the donor designate 10% of the income portion of each planned gift as an unrestricted gift to ACO. The purpose of this donation is to provide current support for the administrative and donor services of ACO. Gift annuities are excluded because ACO is able to utilize a portion of such gifts on a current basis.

VIII. Governing Trusts of Which ACO is Trustee

A. ACO is willing to serve as trustee or cotrustee for charitable remainder unitrusts and annuity trusts whenever the conditions of this Section are met. ACO will not serve as trustee on revocable trusts (including *inter vivos* or living trusts) or on charitable lead trusts. ACO is willing to serve as trustee whenever the following specific conditions are met:

1. ACO is irrevocably designated as beneficiary of at least 50 percent of the trust distribution at termination,

2. The minimum dollar amounts and age requirements specified in Exhibit A are met,

3. The value of the charitable interest, as computed using the applicable IRS tables, is at least $10,000.00 and

4. There are no more than two income beneficiaries for trusts established for the lives of the income beneficiaries. For trusts established for a term of years, any reasonable number of beneficiaries is acceptable.

B. The trusts may be either unitrusts or annuity trusts established for either lives in being or for a term of years or a combination thereof to the extent permitted by the Internal Revenue Service Code and IRS regulations. For the unitrusts, they may be either standard, net income, net income with makeup, or flip trusts, all as provided by applicable Internal Revenue Code and IRS regulations.

C. ACO will not act as trustee on a charitable remainder annuity trust unless there is at least a 10 percent probability of a charitable remainder interest, as computed using government tables.

D. Donors who establish charitable remainder unitrusts may make additional capital contributions to such trusts from time to time. As the Internal Revenue Code does not permit donors to make additional contributions to charitable remainder annuity trusts, ACO will not accept additional contributions to annuity trusts.

IX. Administrative Provisions for Remainder Trusts

A. The following general rules and provisions shall govern the administration of all charitable remainder trusts for which ACO serves as trustee.

1. The annual percentage distribution to the income beneficiaries shall comply with the Internal Revenue Code provisions and interpretive IRS regulations which currently require a minimum payout of 5 percent.

2. No property will be accepted in a trust that violates any section of the Tax Code pertaining to charitable remainder unitrusts.

B. ACO, as trustee, will only accept a trust with non-income producing property or with property which produces less income than that required for the annual distributions, if the following conditions are met:

1. The property consists of readily marketable securities or other liquid assets which can be sold as needed to produce sufficient cash flow or

2. The trust is a net income trust and there is either (a) sufficient liquidity in the trust or (b) other provision has been made to cover trustee fees, real estate taxes and all other out-of-pocket expenses required to maintain the property and administer the trust.

C. ACO, as trustee, is responsible as a matter of law for the tax accounting and income tax returns of the trust. The GAC is expressly authorized to retain an independent accountant or qualified trust management company as needed to perform these tasks.

X. General Provisions Governing Commingled Planned-Gift Instruments

A. Available Instruments. ACO currently offers its donors the following planned-gift instruments in which funds are commingled for investment purposes:

1. Pooled-Income Funds

2. Charitable-Gift Annuities (both current and deferred)

B. Minimums. The current minimum dollar amounts and age requirements as established by the GAC are set forth in Exhibit A.

C. Acceptable Assets. Participations in commingled funds shall be issued only for cash, cash equivalents and marketable securities with a readily determinable value. In the case of pooled-income funds, the donor must have held the securities for at least one year. Any contribution of other assets requires the approval of the GAC and, in the case of a pooled-income fund, must be consistent with the policies of the corporate fiduciary.

D. Valuation Dates. When accepting nonliquid assets, the date the gift is mailed shall be the date of the issue. The value of marketable securities with a readily determined value shall be the mean of the high price and the low price on the date of mailing. When accepting property other than nonliquid assets, the date of transfer shall be the date of issue.

E. Payment Dates. Payments on commingled gift instruments shall be made at the direction of the donor on a quarterly, semiannual or annual basis, but in no event shall the amount of such payments be less than $50.00, except for annual payments. Payment dates will be limited to a stated business day following January 1, April 1, July 1, or October 1, in each calendar quarter.

F. Two Lives. No commingled gift instrument will be issued for more than two lives and there shall be no exceptions to this provision.

XI. Particular Provisions Governing Pooled-Income Funds

A. Management of Pooled-Income Funds. ACO may operate and maintain one or more pooled-income funds under appropriate trust agreements prepared by its counsel or it may use a corporate fiduciary that regularly provides pooled-income fund administration and management services for the benefit of ACO as determined to be in the best interest of ACO by the GAC.

B. Administrative Donation. The pooled-income funds into which ACO accepts additional donations after the effective date of this agreement shall provide that 10 percent of the income otherwise distributable to the donor be payable to ACO.

XII. Particular Provisions Governing Charitable-Gift Annuities

A. Gift Annuity Reserves. ACO recognizes that its obligation under charitable-gift annuities is a general obligation of the organization and that the donor is not protected by a security interest in any particular assets of the organization. Nonetheless, as a matter of investment prudence, ACO will establish and maintain a reserve for the payment of gift annuity amounts as follows:

1. Initial Reserved Amount. ACO will retain in its gift annuity reserve fund an amount equal to 85 percent of the amount contributed under each gift annuity agreement. The remaining 15 percent shall be made available to support the administrative costs of the planned giving of ACO.

2. Limitation of Ongoing Reserves. Whenever as a result of investment performance, the total amount of the gift annuity reserves exceeds 100 percent of the face amount of the then outstanding gift annuity agreements, the Chief Financial Officer may transfer the excess to the general operating fund to be used for ACO purposes.

3. Annual Review of Reserve Policy. The GAC shall review the reserve policy at least biannually, to determine if it would be prudent and advantageous to (a) reduce the reserve requirement to an actuarially determined amount, (b) replace the maintenance of reserves with the purchase of commercial annuity contracts, or (c) otherwise modify the methods for managing reserve funds.

B. Gift Annuity Rates. Charitable-gift annuity rates shall be those established by the GAC which shall use rates suggested by the American Council on Gift Annuities or such other appropriate agency as the GAC determines to be reasonable and prudent.

C. Minimum Gift Amount. No annuity agreement shall be issued unless the charitable gift as computed using government tables exceeds 10 percent of the value transferred for the annuity.

D. State Law. ACO charitable-gift annuities shall be issued under the laws of the state of _____ but may be issued to donors residing in any state unless ACO is prohibited from issuing annuities by the laws of that state.

E. Deferred Gift Annuities. Deferred gift annuities shall be issued on all of the same terms and conditions as regular gift annuities, but subject to the additional restriction that the period of deferral between the transfer for the deferred payment gift annuity and the date annuity payments commence shall be not more than twenty years.

XIII. Governing Use of Legal Counsel

A. All specimen agreements of ACO shall be reviewed by legal counsel upon adoption of these Gift-Acceptance Policy Guidelines and ACO shall seek legal counsel for any agreement or transaction that does not fall within the scope of these Guidelines. The decision regarding which agreements do not fall within the scope of these Guidelines shall be the responsibility of the GAC.

B. Prospective donors shall be urged to seek their own counsel in matters pertaining to planned-gift agreements, tax or estate planning issues.

XIV. Governing Legal Instruments

A. ACO is not engaged in the practice of law, and therefore will not draft any legal instruments pertaining to any one individual's estate plan. In all cases, an individual will be advised to seek private counsel.

B. Where desired, ACO will recommend legal counsel for the drafting of instruments, and will provide sample documents for the donor's legal counsel, with an accompanying letter stating that such instruments are for counsel's review.

C. No legal fee shall be paid by ACO when it pertains to the drafting of wills or other trust instruments not qualified as unitrust or annuity trust agreements.

XV. Governing the Reporting of Planned Gifts

A. Preservation of Agreements. ACO recognizes its position of trust with respect to donors. Therefore, all governing instruments will be stored in a locked, fireproof facility.

B. Confidentiality. ACO will maintain the utmost confidentiality of all documents in its care. Files and agreements shall be made accessible to appropriate individuals only with the GAC's approval. All reports shall be made by number.

C. Valuation. The GAC shall develop a consistent procedure for the reporting of planned gifts which, in its opinion, fairly states the values of the gift interests received.

XVI. Governing Designated Proceeds

A. All designated proceeds at time of death will be used in accordance with the requested designation, with the exception that 15 percent of the gift will be available to the general fund to help underwrite the planned-giving program.

B. All undesignated bequests and matured deferred gifts will be used for general operating obligations as determined by the Board of Directors.

XVII. Existing Agreements

A. All existing agreements will continue under the Guidelines in place at the time the agreement was implemented.

Internal Self-Guided Investment Management Assessment Form

Part I: General Information

(This portion is to be completed by the Executive Director)

1. **Institution:** _____

2. **Senior Staff:**   **Name**   **Phone**

Executive Director _____ _____

Senior Devel. Off. _____ _____

CFO   _____ _____

Board Chairman   _____ _____

Invest. Comm. Ch. _____ _____

3. **Type of Institution:**   School or College   Retirement Home
                            Hospital   Church
                            Pension Plan   Other Religious Organization
                            Public Foundation   Social Service Agency
                            Private Foundation   Other Public Charity

4. **Business Structure:**   Unincorporated Nonprofit Association

                           Nonprofit Corporation (Type) _____

                           Limited Liability Company (Type) _____

                           Other _____

5. **Mission Statement:**   (Attach copy or brief narrative description)

6. **Approximate Annual Budget: $**_____
(For reference purposes, please attach a copy of your most recent financial statements)

7. **Origins:**   Founded By: _____ Date: _____

Founded in (City, State & Country) _____

8. **Incorporation:**   State: _____ Date: _____

9. **Address of Corporate Headquarters:** _____

_____

_____

10. **Geographic Service Area:** (Describe and also list states in which you have at least one full-time employee and a physical location) _____

_____

_____

_____   _____

This Page Completed By (Name)   Date Completed

Part II: Development (Fund-Raising) Information
(This portion is to be completed by the Senior Development Officer)

1. Current staffing of development program:

Full-Time Development Staff	Number of Professionals	Number of Support Staff
Other Staff (Names) who spend some time in Development	**Regular Position**	**% of Time Spent in Development**

2. What percentage of your organization's total income comes from donations (gifts as opposed to fees for services, sales of products, etc.)? _____

3. When did you start a full-time fund-raising program? _____

4. When did you start soliciting and/or accepting planned gifts? _____

5. Please indicate the composition of gift income by category over the last 3 years.

	Average Annual %, past 3 years	Highest Annual % in last 3 years	Lowest Annual % in last 3 years
Individual Contributions			
Corporate Gifts			
Grants			
Bequests			
Lifetime Planned Gifts			
Special Events			
Gifts in kind; sponsorships			
Other			

6. Of the categories listed in the above table, which do you believe are most likely to increase or decrease as a percentage of total annual gift income over the next 3 years?

Most likely to increase   _____   _____   _____

Most likely to decrease   _____   _____   _____

7. Please rank each of the following areas to indicate your fund-raising priorities in terms of the allocation of development staff time for the coming year.

Fund-Raising Categories	Rank (1st–5th)	Allocable % of Staff Time
Current Annual Giving		
Planned (Deferred) Giving		
Capital Campaign		
Events; Sponsorships		
Corp./Foundation Grants		

8. What are the types, ages, and minimum dollar amounts of the deferred gifts and trusts which your organization accepts?

	Accepted (Y/N)	Minimum Age	Minimum $ Amount
Gift Annuities			
Charitable Remainder Trusts			
Charitable Lead Trusts			
Pooled-Income Fund			
Donor-Advised Fund			
Life Interest Agreements in Real Property			
Life Insurance			
Other			

9. Please briefly describe the additional staff support, funding, administrative support, or other assistance, if any, that you believe would permit you to more effectively raise funds for your organization over the next 3 years.

_____

_____

_____

_____

_____

_____

10. Which of the following outside service providers do you currently use in development?

	Organization	Key Contact	First Service (Date)	Address (City, State)	Phone
Fund-Raising Consultants					
Collateral Material Services					
Securities Broker/ Consultant					
Bank or Trust Company					
Investment Advisor					
CPA					
Attorney					
Insurance Agent or CFP					
Other					

This Page Completed By (Name)　　　　　　Date Completed
Internal Self-Guided Investment Management Assessment　　Page 4 of 14

Part III: Investment Accounting, Gift Administration and Reporting
(This portion is to be completed by the Chief Financial Officer.)

1. What planned gifts, endowments, or other funds does your organization currently have?

Type	No. of gifts	Total Dollar	Median Size	Oldest Donor	Youngest Donor	Largest Gift—$	Smallest Gift—$
Gift Annuities							
Pooled-Income Funds							
Remainder Trusts							
Revocable Trusts							
Operating Reserves							
Endowments							
Retirement Plans							
Capital Campaign Funds							
Other							

2. How much do you spend administering planned gifts, endowments, or other reserves in each of the following categories: Accounting, Tax Returns, and Investment Management?

	$ Cost	Inside or Out	Service Provider or System Used
Gift Annuities			
Pooled-Income Funds			
Remainder Trusts			
Revocable Trusts			
Operating Reserves			
Endowments			
Retirement Plans			
Capital Campaign Funds			
Other			

---

3. How do you allocate administrative expenses for each of the following investment instruments (express on a percentage basis)?

	Operating Budget	Charged to Trust or Fund	Comments
Gift Annuities			
Pooled-Income Funds			
Remainder Trusts			
Revocable Trusts			
Operating Reserves			
Endowments			
Retirement Plans			
Capital Campaign Funds			
Other			

4. For each of the following instruments, how frequently do you make income distributions and send reports? Who serves as trustee on the trusts and what information do you provide when reporting?

Key: Frequency: Q = quarterly, M = Monthly, A = Annual;
Reports: 1099, K-1, IP (Investment Performance)

	Trustee	Income Distributions Frequency	Reports—Frequency & Content
Gift Annuities			
Pooled-Income Funds			
Remainder Trusts			
Revocable Trusts			
Operating Reserves			
Endowments			
Retirement Plans			
Capital Campaign Funds			
Other			

5. Do you have established investment policies for your managed funds? (Y/N) _____

Who sets the policies? _____

Are the policies disclosed to your donors? (Y/N) _____

This Page Completed By (Name)   Date Completed

6. Which outside service providers do you currently use in administering your planned-gift and investment management assets?

	Organization	Key Contact	First Service (Date)	Address (City, State)	Phone
A) Securities Broker/Consultant					
B) Bank or Trust Company					
C) Investment Advisor					
D) CPA					
E) Attorney					
F) Insurance Agent or CFP					
G) Other					
H) Other					
Other					

This Page Completed By (Name)   Date Completed

7. Who in your organization is responsible for supervising each of the following areas?

	Name	**Phone**
Trust Administration	_____	_____
Investment Management	_____	_____
Donor Reporting	_____	_____
Financial Accounting	_____	_____
Regulatory Compliance	_____	_____
Tax Compliance	_____	_____

8. Please indicate which of the service providers, if any, listed in question 6, above, assist you in the following areas. Write the letter for each provider (see #6) in the space provided.

Communicating investment options to prospective donors? _____

Establishing investment objectives and policies? _____

Constructing planned-giving presentations for major donors? _____

Matching return expectations to spending needs and obligations? _____

Reporting investment results to donors and management? _____

Providing information for trustee decisions on risk/return relationships, asset allocation, and other similar issues? _____

Analyzing investment performance for the benefit of donors and management? _____

Segregating charitable remainder trust funds for independent management based on category of trust (e.g., Income Only, Income Only with Makeup, 5%, 8%, etc.)? _____

9. Do you accept gifts of illiquid assets, such as real estate and collectibles? _____

10. Who helps with the management and/or liquidation of such assets?

_____

11. What are the most pressing problems that you face in the areas of trust administration, investment management, or planned-gift administration?

_____

_____

Part IV: Investment Philosophy and Objectives

(To be answered by the Investment Committee of the Board or by the full Board if there is no committee. For those organizations that maintain multiple funds, these questions should be answered with regard to the endowment or other perpetual or long-term funds.)

Goals and Objectives

1. How would you categorize your overall investment objectives? Choose one.

_____ Growth—maximum growth of capital with little or no income consideration

_____ Growth with income—primarily capital growth with some focus on income

_____ Balanced—equal emphasis on capital growth and income

_____ Income oriented—primary emphasis on income

_____ Capital preservation—preserve original value regardless of income or growth

2. What average annual "absolute" rate of return, if any (as opposed to a return "relative" to a market index) do you consider appropriate for long-term investments?

_____ % per year   _____ % per year above inflation (CPI)

_____ Prefer a relative standard

3. Relative to popular stock market indexes (such as the S&P 500), rank your preferences for portfolio performance; 1 is your strongest preference and 5 is what you least prefer.

_____ Outperform the market in UP market years

_____ Decline less than the market in DOWN market years

_____ Outperform the market on average over an extended period, without regard to individual years

_____ Match market performance over an extended period

_____ Ignore relative performance and focus solely on the absolute return goal(s) identified in question 2, above.

4. Please rank your preference for the following investment performance reporting options from 1 to 5, with 1 being your strongest preference.

_____ Measuring current return or yield relative to required distributions

_____ Comparing account returns to an "absolute" percent return target

_____ "Relative" comparison (comparing the account returns to various market indexes)

_____ Comparing to a "real" return (i.e., exceeds the inflation factor by X%)

_____ Using "absolute" and "relative" total return measures without regard to yield.

5. Please describe any specific return requirements or performance-reporting concerns that have not been addressed by the preceding questions.

_____

_____

_____

_____

Risk Questions

6. Please rank the following risks in the order of greatest concern (1 being the highest concern, then 2, etc.).

_____ The failure to generate enough current income to cover required distributions

_____ The possibility of not achieving an intended rate of return

_____ Decreasing purchasing power due to inflation

_____ Wide swings in the value of our investments over 3 to 5 years

_____ A large drop in the value of any one or more investments, wholly apart from overall portfolio performance

_____ Other (Please specify) _____

7. What is the maximum loss you could tolerate in your most aggressively invested portfolio over the following time frames?

_____ % per quarter   _____ % in any two-year period

_____ % per year   _____ Other (Please describe) _____

8. Compared to a broad stock market index such as the S&P 500, how much fluctuation can you tolerate in the equity portion of your portfolio in any given year?

_____ Much more fluctuation than the market

_____ Slightly more fluctuation than the market

_____ Approximately the same fluctuation as the market

_____ Slightly less fluctuation than the market

_____ Much less fluctuation than the market

9. Please describe any risk concerns that the preceding questions have not addressed.

_____

_____

_____

Investment Advisor Questions

10. Which statement best reflects your opinion as to how managers should implement your investment goals?

_____ We should establish overall objectives for the plan and allow the manager complete discretion regarding implementation.

_____ We should establish asset allocation parameters with the investment manager and then allow the manager discretion in selecting investments within those parameters.

_____ We should establish asset allocation parameters with the investment manager and then actively participate in and/or supervise the day-to-day selection of investments.

11. How do you feel about giving investment discretion to a third-party investment management firm? Choose one.

_____ Very comfortable   _____ Somewhat uncomfortable

_____ Somewhat comfortable   _____ Very uncomfortable

12. Select the statement that best describes how you currently make investment decisions.

_____ We collect and analyze the facts and make decisions on our own.

_____ Others advise us and we make decisions based on their advice.

_____ Our advisors make the decisions.

13. Please briefly list or describe those aspects of your current investment management process that are working well and those which you believe have problems or could be improved. (Examples include performance, performance reporting, asset allocation, etc.)

Working Well: _____

_____

_____

_____

Concerns—May Need Improvement: _____

_____

_____

_____

_____   _____

This Page Completed By (Name)   Date Completed
Internal Self-Guided Investment Management Assessment   Page 11 of 14

14. Which of the following outside service providers presently provide your organization with investment management assistance?

	Organization	Key Contact	First Service (Date)	Address (City, State)	Phone
Securities Broker/Consultant					
Bank or Trust Company					
Investment Advisor					
CPA					
Attorney					
Insurance Agent or CFP					
Other					
Other					
Other					

This Page Completed By (Name) _____ Date Completed _____

Internal Self-Guided Investment Management Assessment   Page 12 of 14

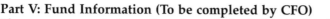

Part V: Fund Information (To be completed by CFO)

Please answer a set of questions for each fund identified in Part II of this questionnaire.

Name of Fund: _____ Type of Fund: _____

1. General Portfolio Objective: (Select one.)

_____ **Capital Preservation**—the preservation of capital with returns exceeding risk-free investments. Accordingly, the risk level should be low with minimal price volatility.

_____ **Income**—modest growth of capital with the generation of income as the primary objective.

_____ **Growth and Income**—primarily oriented toward growth of principal with a minor emphasis on portfolio income. Investments could include equities, debt instruments, and cash or cash equivalents for diversification and risk management.

_____ **Growth**—growth of capital. The portfolio will exhibit increased volatility while expecting to outperform equity indexes over a market cycle.

_____ **Aggressive Growth**—aggressive growth of capital is the primary objective. The portfolio may accept higher volatility associated with aggressive growth while expecting to outperform equity indexes over a market cycle.

2. Investment time horizon most appropriate for this account: (Select one.)

_____ Ten years or more

_____ Five to ten years

_____ Three to five years

_____ Less than three years

3. Target rates of return: 1 year: ___.___% 3 years:___.___% 5 years:___.___%

4. What is the current relative risk tolerance for this fund?

_____ More fluctuation than the market

_____ Approximately the same fluctuation as the market

_____ Less fluctuation than the market

_____ Relative performance measures are inappropriate for this fund

5. What is the maximum loss you could tolerate in this fund over the following time frames?

_____ % per quarter

_____ % per year

_____ % in any two year period

6. Is the fund taxable? _____ yes _____ no

7. If the fund is taxable, give the following:
Income Tax Rate: _____._____% Capital-Gains Tax Rate: _____._____%

8. Other information

Minimum Required Annual Yield (Div. & Interest): $ _____

Anticipated Annual Contributions: $ _____

Anticipated Annual Withdrawals: $ _____

9. Please list the existing assets and attach a current portfolio statement, if available.

Asset Class	Percent Allocated	Dollar Amount
Cash/Cash Equivalents (includes mutual funds)		
Equities (includes mutual funds)		
Bonds (includes mutual funds)		
Real Estate (includes mutual funds, REITs, etc.)		
Private Placements (includes personal business)		
Other Investments (includes mutual funds)		

10. Indicate the current asset allocation percentages and the permitted range if such targets exist. If a category is prohibited, indicate with a "0" maximum percentage. If a category is required, indicate by stating the same percentage for minimum and maximum.

Asset Class	Current	Minimum	Maximum
Cash/Cash Equivalents			
U.S. Stocks			
Foreign Equities			
U.S. Investment Grade Bonds			
Junk Bonds			
Foreign Bonds			
Real Estate (includes mutual funds, REITs, etc.)			
Private Placements (includes personal business)			
Other Investments (includes mutual funds)			

11. Please describe on an attached page the purpose of this fund, any special income or other requirements, any restrictions on investments, and any special reporting requirements.

E-1 Sample Monthly Report

December 31, 1997

Statement of Objectives
Growth of capital.

Current Asset Allocation:

Equity	85%
Fixed Income	0%
Cash Equivalents	15%

Account Summary
The inception date of your account is May 16, 1974.

You initially invested capital of:	$195,211.50
You have withdrawn funds of:	- 726,611.14 net
Your account now has a value of:	$1,027,689.73

Each 100 dollars invested at inception is now worth: $1,601.63

FILE COPY

Fiscal Year: 12

To add to your account, send cash or securities directly to:

Table of Contents

	Section
Portfolio Holdings	I
Transaction Summary	II
Tax Information	III
Performance Summary	IV

If you have questions concerning your statement, please feel free to contact Richard

271

VAN DEVENTER & HOCH

Portfolio Holdings

Security Description	% of Portfolio	Purchase Date	Quantity	Cost per Share	Cost Basis	Market Price Per Share	Market Value	Unrealized Gain/Loss	Annual Income	Annual Yield Cost	Annual Yield Market
Common Stock											
AT&T	2.39	08/19/96	400	37.27	14908	61.31	24525	9617	528	3.5	2.2
Albertsons Inc	2.76	08/01/97	600	36.38	21829	47.25	28350	6521	384	1.8	1.4
Archer-Daniels-Midland	2.60	07/18/97	1230	21.38	26295	21.69	26676	381	246	.9	.9
Bard (CR) Inc	1.83	09/24/93	600	23.07	13842	31.31	18788	4946	432	3.1	2.3
Bell Atlantic Corporation	1.77	07/19/91	200	47.45	9489	91.00	18200	8711	616	6.5	3.4
Bowne & Co Inc	2.73	10/27/95	700	18.81	13167	40.13	28088	14921	252	1.9	.9
Chubb Corporation	2.94	11/28/88	400	13.86	5545	75.63	30250	24706	464	8.4	1.5
Cyprus Amax Minerals Company	1.05	11/29/93	700	21.52	15065	15.38	10763	4302−	560	3.7	5.2
Dayton-Hudson Corporation	1.97	06/27/95	300	23.10	6931	67.50	20250	13319	192	2.8	.9
Dillards Inc-Cl A	1.72	11/22/96	500	30.10	15050	35.25	17625	2575	80	.5	.5
EG&G Inc	2.43	09/26/96	1200	17.35	20820	20.81	24975	4155	672	3.2	2.7
Edwards (A.G.) Inc	4.06	06/30/94	1050	11.54	12117	39.75	41738	29621	546	4.5	1.3
Electronic Data Systems Corp	3.42	09/25/97	800	36.10	28880	43.94	35150	6270	480	1.7	1.4
Federal National Mortgage Assn	4.44	12/14/94	800	18.28	14620	57.06	45650	31030	672	4.6	1.5
First Chicago NBD Bancorp	2.44	01/19/96	300	37.98	11393	83.50	25050	13658	480	4.2	1.9
Genuine Parts Corp	2.31	08/28/97	700	31.23	21858	33.94	23756	1899	672	3.1	2.8
Hartford Financial Svcs Grp	4.10	12/02/94	450	43.38	19519	93.56	42103	22584	720	3.7	1.7
Heinz (H.J.) Company	2.97	04/13/94	600	21.90	13140	50.81	30488	17348	756	5.8	2.5
Louisiana Pacific Corporation	1.85	11/22/95	1000	23.58	23575	19.00	19000	4575−	560	2.4	2.9
Motorola Corporation	2.23	01/16/96	400	48.19	19274	57.19	22875	3601	192	1.0	.8
Norfolk Southern Corporation	2.67	04/28/94	900	21.02	18918	30.50	27450	8532	720	3.8	2.6
Occidental Petroleum Corp	2.85	09/25/97	1000	25.94	25944	29.31	29313	3369	1000	3.9	3.4
Potlatch Corporation	2.09	12/14/95	500	39.94	19968	43.00	21500	1533	870	4.4	4.0
Royal Dutch Petroleum Company	6.33	08/22/88	1200	14.11	16938	54.19	65025	48088	1500	8.9	2.3
Safeco Corporation	2.85	09/28/94	600	26.03	15618	48.75	29250	13632	768	4.9	2.6
Supervalu Inc	3.67	07/29/96	900	27.98	25178	41.88	37688	12510	936	3.7	2.5
Tenneco Inc	1.92	01/28/97	500	42.10	21050	39.50	19750	1300−	600	2.9	3.0
Tribune Company New	4.85	11/07/91	800	18.16	14528	62.25	49800	35272	512	3.5	1.0
Union Pacific Corporation	4.27	08/08/88	700	37.36	26150	62.63	43838	17688	1204	4.6	2.7
Union Pacific Resources Grp	1.62	08/08/88	688	19.99	13752	24.25	16684	2932	138	1.0	.8
Group Totals	85.10				525357		874594	349237	17752	3.4	2.0

VAN DEVENTER & HOCH

Portfolio Holdings

Security Description	% of Portfolio	Purchase Date	Quantity	Cost per Share	Cost Basis	Market Price Per Share	Market Value	Unrealized Gain/Loss	Annual Income	Annual Yield Cost	Annual Yield Market
Cash Equivalents											
Accrued Dividends	.17		1769F	1.00	1770	.00	1770	0	0	.0	.0
Provident Institutional	14.72		0	.00	151326	.00	151326	0	7657	5.1	5.1
Group Totals	14.90				153096		153096	0	7657	5.0	5.0
Total Securities	100.0				678453		1027690	349237	25409	3.7	2.5

VAN DEVENTER & HOCH

Transaction Summary

Transaction Date	Description	Type of Transaction	Quantity	Cash	Capital
11/03/97	Provident Institutional	Money Market Income		465.81	
11/03/97	Expense	Custodian Fee		33.89-	
11/28/97	Provident Institutional	Cash Withdrawal		1309.92-	1309.92-
11/30/97	Provident Institutional reverse entry	Cash Addition		1531.60	1531.60
12/01/97	Archer-Daniels-Midland	Dividend Income		31.50	
12/01/97	Potlatch Corporation	Dividend Income		217.50	
12/02/97	Louisiana Pacific Corporation	Dividend Income		140.00	
12/09/97	Tenneco Inc	Dividend Income		150.00	
12/10/97	Dayton-Hudson Corporation	Dividend Income		72.00	
12/10/97	Electronic Data Systems Corp	Dividend Income		120.00	
12/10/97	Norfolk Southern Corporation	Dividend Income		180.00	
12/11/97	Tribune Company New	Dividend Income		128.00	
12/12/97	Cognizant Corp	Dividend Income		12.00	
12/15/97	Supervalu Inc	Dividend Income		234.00	
12/23/97	Cognizant Corp	Sell	400.00	17409.42	
12/23/97	Dayton-Hudson Corporation	Sell	100.00	6189.79	
12/31/97	Income	Cash Withdrawal		1285.00-	1285.00-
12/31/97		Money Market Auto Transfer		24252.81-	
					1063.32-
		Closing Cash Balance		.00	

VAN DEVENTER & HOCH

Tax Information
Summary of Securities Sold This Tax Year

Description	Quantity	Date of Purchase	Date Sold	Cost Basis	Proceeds	Gain/Loss Short Term	Long Term	Percent
NCR Corporation New	25.000		02/21/97	746.74	869.39		122.65	16.42
Dun & Bradstreet	400.000		04/24/97	8962.62	9859.67		897.05	10.01
Student Loan Marketing	100.000		05/09/97	3522.50	11799.76		8277.26 *234.98	
Reader's Digest Assn	500.000		05/21/97	20780.00	11949.60		8830.40-* 42.49-	
SLM Holding Corp	200.000		07/01/97	7045.00	25854.14		18809.14 *266.99	
BankAmerica Corp Note	25000.000		07/15/97	25282.25	25000.00		282.25-* 1.12-	
First Chicago NBD Bancorp	200.000		08/01/97	7595.00	15266.99		7671.99 *101.01	
Lucent Technologies Inc	129.000		08/11/97	6055.28	10734.05		4678.77 * 77.27	
Calgon Carbon Corporation	1500.000		08/13/97	17870.00	20691.81		2821.81 * 15.79	
Corestates Financial Corp	600.000		10/22/97	15844.80	46250.96		30406.16 *191.90	
Dayton-Hudson Corporation	200.000		11/14/97	4620.67	12992.07		8371.40 *181.17	
Cognizant Corp	400.000		12/23/97	12868.04	17409.42		4541.38 * 35.29	
Dayton-Hudson Corporation	100.000		12/23/97	2310.33	6189.79		3879.46 *167.92	

Net Short Term Gain or Loss		.00
# Net Mid-Term Gain or Loss @ 28%		.00
Net Long Term Gain or Loss @ 28%		1019.70
* Net Long Term Gain or Loss @ 20%		80344.72
Total Gain or Loss - 1997		81364.42

This information is an indication of the data accumulated for your tax year. We believe this information to be accurate, however, please refer to custodian's records for complete details. Our records indicate your Tax I.D. is , and your fiscal year end is December 1997.

VAN DEVENTER & HOCH

Tax Information
Income and Expense Summary Year to Date

Income

Dividends	17,689.92	
Interest	1,500.00	
Money Market Interest	5,658.19	
Total Income		$24,848.11

Expenses

Management Fee	2,727.34	
Miscellaneous Expenses:		
Non-Resident Tax	264.20	
Custodian's Fee	300.07	
Other Custodian Charges	.74−	
Transaction Charges	45.40	
Total Expenses		$3,336.27

This information is an indication of the data accumulated for your tax year. We believe this
information to be accurate, however, please refer to custodian's records for complete details.
Our records indicate your Tax I.D. is , and your fiscal year end is December 1997.

VAN DEVENTER & HOCH

Performance Summary

	Your Account	Selected Indices			
		Cost of Living	Fixed Return	Stock Indices	
Calendar Year	Total Return	Consumer Price Index	Treasury Bills	Standard & Poor's 500	Value Line Geometric
1987	4.78%	4.41%	5.46%	5.26%	−8.32%
1988	13.50%	4.40%	6.38%	16.61%	17.98%
1989	13.10%	4.63%	8.21%	31.67%	13.69%
1990	−4.43%	6.53%	7.63%	−3.16%	−21.33%
1991	22.58%	2.69%	5.41%	30.46%	29.76%
1992	9.83%	3.05%	3.48%	7.66%	10.02%
1993	16.91%	2.75%	2.89%	10.03%	13.59%
1994	.20%	2.70%	4.19%	1.27%	−3.57%
1995	26.90%	2.60%	5.87%	37.57%	22.31%
1996	16.31%	3.30%	5.20%	22.96%	16.00%
1997	28.22%	1.80%	5.36%	33.36%	23.64%

Your **Total Return** includes income and all expenses.
Selected **Stock Indices** include estimated income with no expenses.

Sample Quarterly Report

E-2

Sample Quarterly Report
Performance Summary Sheet
AGGRESSIVE GROWTH MODEL
AS OF Q2 1996

Allocations

Entity Name	Min %	Max %	Assigned %
Van Deventer & Hoch - Eq - Value/Low P/E	0%	40%	35%
Brandes Inv Partners - Intl Eq	0%	40%	35%
Furman Selz Capital Mgt LLC - Sm Cap Domestic Eq	0%	10%	25%
T-Bills	0%	0%	5%

Summary Statistics

Total Quarters	38	# Up Quarters	32	# Down Quarters	6
Highest Quarter		18.28 %	Lowest Quarter		-23.31 %
Highest Year		41.04 %	Lowest Year		-6.34 %
Highest 4 Qtr Period		41.04 %	Lowest 4 Qtr Period		-10.25 %

Performance Statistics

	Annualized Return	Standard Deviation	Value Added	Sharpe's Ratio
Latest Quarter	4.39	.	.	.
Latest 6 Months	8.62	.	.	.
Latest 9 Months	13.85	.	.	.
Latest Year	22.48	.	.	.
Latest 18 Months	22.87	.	.	.
Latest 2 Years	19.04	.	.	.
Latest 3 Years	15.41	3.71	2.39	.
Latest 4 Years	15.72	3.43	2.78	.
Latest 5 Years	17.04	3.39	4.88	.
Latest 10 Years	.	.	.	.
Latest 15 Years	.	.	.	.
Latest 20 Years	.	.	.	.

Quarterly Returns

Year	Qtr 1	Qtr 2	Qtr 3	Qtr 4	Annual
1987	13.03	6.28	13.34	-23.31	4.41
1988	16.27	9.69	0.51	4.91	34.48
1989	8.30	5.91	9.55	2.30	28.54
1990	-2.57	3.11	-12.67	6.75	-6.34
1991	18.28	2.12	8.42	7.69	41.04
1992	3.38	1.44	0.74	6.90	12.94
1993	5.51	2.66	7.94	5.52	23.37
1994	-3.29	-1.52	6.55	-2.34	-0.90
1995	5.12	5.77	7.58	4.82	25.39
1996	4.04	4.39			

Charitable Choices
Aggressive Growth Model
Asset Allocation

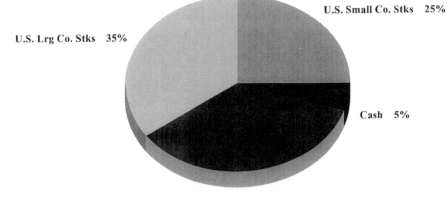

U.S. Small Co. Stks   25%

U.S. Lrg Co. Stks   35%

Cash   5%

Foreign Stocks   35%

Return Comparison
As of Second Quarter 1996

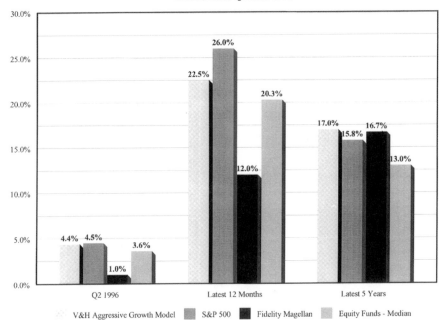

Return vs. Risk Analysis
Third Quarter 1991 to Second Quarter 1996

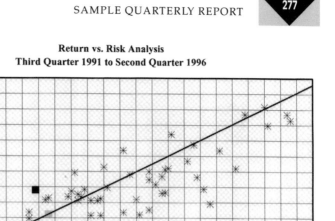

| | T-Bills | U.S. Capital Markets Index | Capital Markets Line | V&H Aggressive Growth Model | CA Growth Mgrs > $100MM |

Relative Performance Measurement
Third Quarter 1993 to Second Quarter 1996

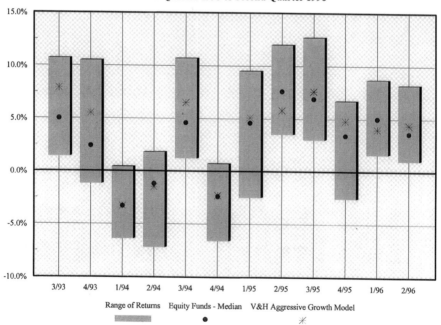

Range of Returns   Equity Funds - Median   V&H Aggressive Growth Model

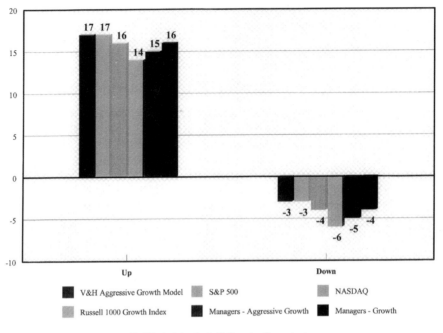

Number of Up & Down Quarters
Third Quarter 1991 to Second Quarter 1996

Legend:
- V&H Aggressive Growth Model
- S&P 500
- NASDAQ
- Russell 1000 Growth Index
- Managers - Aggressive Growth
- Managers - Growth

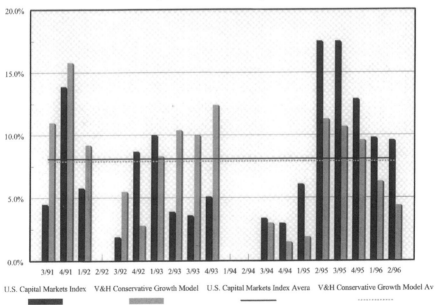

Up Market Analysis (2 Quarter Grouping)
Third Quarter 1991 to Second Quarter 1996

Legend:
- U.S. Capital Markets Index
- V&H Conservative Growth Model
- U.S. Capital Markets Index Avera
- V&H Conservative Growth Model Av

Annualized Returns: Five Year Moving Average
Third Quarter 1991 to Second Quarter 1996

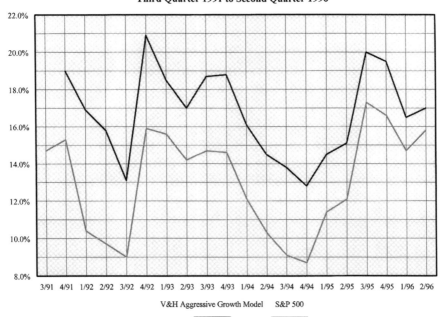

V&H Aggressive Growth Model   S&P 500

F-1 ▼ Sample Endowment Resolution[1]

WHEREAS, American Charitable Organization of Los Angeles, California (ACO) has determined that there will be a long-term, multi-generational need for the services and support it provides to the community; and,

WHEREAS, many of ACO's financial supporters are interested in and capable of making substantial gifts of assets, above and beyond their annual giving; and,

WHEREAS, many of ACO's financial supporters are desirous of having a designated fund to which substantial gifts may be made to enhance the overall, long-term financial strength of the organization and to make it less dependent upon government funding or annual fund raising; and,

WHEREAS, ACO has been advised that it is already the designated beneficiary of a substantial estate, the proceeds from which would be appropriate to establish a long-term endowment fund;

NOW, THEREFORE, BE IT RESOLVED that the Board of Directors hereby establishes the "Endowment and Support Fund of American Charitable Organization of Los Angeles, California." This fund shall be established and operated as follows:

1. The fund shall annually distribute an amount equal to 5 percent of its then current value which shall include contributions to the fund, income earned on such contributions and all gains and losses on such funds, whether realized or unrealized. These distributions shall be made quarterly, by distributing an amount equal to 1.25 percent of the current fair market value of the fund on the first business day of each calendar quarter. To the extent that it may legally do so, ACO shall interpret this policy as satisfying a gift provision which calls for retaining principal and distributing annual "income."

2. The fund may hold either Designated or Undesignated gifts. The quarterly distribution shall be used as directed, to the extent attributable to Designated Gifts, and shall be used as determined by _____ to the extent attributable to Undesignated Gifts.

3. All Designated and Undesignated gifts may be commingled for investment purposes and held in a single portfolio. Such funds shall be invested at the direction of the Chief Financial Officer in accordance with ACO's investment policies, as amended.

---

[1] This resolution is a sample for illustration purposes only and should not be used by any organization unless reviewed and approved by that organization's legal counsel.

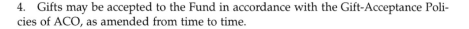

4.   Gifts may be accepted to the Fund in accordance with the Gift-Acceptance Policies of ACO, as amended from time to time.

5.   As all such funds are intended to be perpetual, ACO may not invade principal or loan itself money from the Fund for any reason without a unanimous vote of the Board of Directors. The reason for imposing this requirement is to assure the perpetual existence of the fund while still retaining in the Board the right to invade principal in the event of an occurrence of such magnitude as to threaten the long-term viability of ACO.

  In the event of an invasion of principal, for other than the liquidation of the organization, the amount withdrawn shall be treated as a loan. The Directors shall establish a reasonable schedule for repayment together with interest at the prime rate then charged for commercial loans in the greater Los Angeles area. In the event of a determination to end the work of the Los Angeles Council of the ACO and the subsequent liquidation of its assets, the Board may by unanimous vote utilize the Fund to pay any indebtedness following which the remaining proceeds shall be distributed to such one or more other tax-exempt organizations, of like character, value and aims as those of ACO, as the Board shall determine best able to hold and utilize such funds as an ongoing endowment.

6.   Whenever either soliciting or receiving a gift into the Fund, ACO shall disclose to the actual or potential donor the nature of the fund including:

- The purposes for which the fund is maintained;
- The ability of a donor to direct the use of the proceeds (within the policies established by the Board);
- The fact that the Board of Directors may, in an emergency, invade the principal of the fund over and above the quarterly distribution; and,
- The general nature of the manner in which the funds are invested.

7.   The officers of ACO are hereby authorized and directed to take such actions as may be necessary to carry out the purposes of this resolution.

  IN WITNESS WHEREOF, this Resolution is adopted by the unanimous vote of the Board of Directors on the ____ day of _____, 19___.

By: _____

_____, President

By: _____

_____, Secretary

Sample Endowment Trust Agreement[1]

This Trust Agreement, made and executed this _____ day of _____, 19_____ by and between the American Charitable Organization ("ACO"), _____ (city) _____ (state), and _____ (trust company) _____ (city), _____ (state) as "Trustee."

PURPOSE

WHEREAS the Board of Directors of ACO has approved the creation and establishment of the ACO Trust Fund, hereafter called the fund, for the benefit _____ [*describe area or initiative*];

AND WHEREAS the ACO has authorized and accepted the proposed plan of the fund as hereinafter provided and has approved the form and provisions of this agreement of trust;

AND WHEREAS in order to insure the devotion to such purpose of all contributions made to the fund, it has been determined to place the fund in trust and to delegate certain powers to the Trustee to administer the fund as hereafter set forth;

AND WHEREAS the _____ (Bank or Trust Company) has been selected by the Board of Directors of the ACO to serve as Trustee of said fund and Trustee has signified and by the execution of this trust agreement does hereby signify its willingness to serve as trustee upon the terms and conditions hereafter set forth;

NOW THEREFORE the Board of Directors does hereby sell, assign, transfer, and set over unto the said Trustee all its right, title, and interest in and to such contributions as have been made or may be made to this fund, to be held by said Trustee, but in trust only, for the use, benefit, and behest of the ACO upon the following terms and conditions:

1. DURATION

The trust provisions hereinafter set forth shall be in effect and the trust hereby created shall exist so long as the aforesaid Board of Directors, ACO, or its duly constituted successor, shall continue to operate and exist as a charitable organization as recognized by the IRS under section 501(c)(3) of the Internal Revenue Code.

2. PRINCIPAL FOREVER HELD BY TRUST

Said Trustee shall hold the principal of all money or property given to this fund to invest and reinvest in the exercise of its discretion as trustee, unless the deed or legacy of a particular gift or gifts specifically authorizes or requires its retention and/or use for a specific project.

---

[1] This is a sample endowment trust that creates a permanently restricted fund to be held and administered by a public charity. This form is for illustration purposes only and should not be used by any organization unless reviewed, modified, and approved by that organization's legal counsel.

3. DISTRIBUTIONS FOR CHARITABLE PURPOSES

The fund shall annually distribute an amount equal to 5 percent of its then current value which shall include contributions to the fund, income earned on such contributions and all gains and losses on such funds, whether realized or unrealized. These distributions shall be made quarterly, by distributing an amount equal to 1.25 percent of the current fair market value of the fund as of the last business day of each calendar quarter. The trust shall distribute the amounts so determined not later than the tenth business day of the next succeeding calendar quarter. To the extent that it may legally do so, ACO shall interpret this policy as satisfying a gift provision which calls for retaining principal and distributing annual "income."

The Trustee's sole responsibility with regard to distributions from the fund is to make the distribution to the ACO in accordance with the foregoing provision. The Trustee shall not be responsible for the ultimate distribution and use of the amount of the trust distributions by the ultimate charitable beneficiaries as that responsibility is specifically retained by the ACO as part of its mission. The ACO shall, however, provide the Trustee with evidence of the application of these funds to the stated purposes. The Trustee may, from time to time, with the permission of the ACO accumulate funds for a specific charitable or educational project, provided that any such accrual shall not be unreasonable in amount or duration.

4. POWERS OF TRUSTEE

The Trustee hereunder and its successor is hereby given power and authority subject to the provisions of the Articles and Bylaws of the ACO, to receive, take, hold, use, control, manage, invest, and reinvest the said principal sum, the additions thereto or accumulations thereof, including the proceeds thereof, from time to time, in such bonds, stock, notes, securities, or other property, personal or real, and courses of action, as they shall deem most suitable and they are empowered to vary the trust property, or any part or portion thereof, at pleasure, changing personal to real estate or real estate to personal estate, and to that end to sell any of such property either at public or private sale, with or without notice, and to such person or persons, upon such terms and for such price as to said Trustee may seem expedient and proper, and to that end, to execute, acknowledge, and deliver all necessary deeds, contracts, bills of sale, releases, assignments, or other instruments of writing, either with or without covenant of warranty, necessary or requisite to carry out effectively the purpose, intent, and meaning of this trust, provided, however, that any and all investments or reinvestments shall be in securities and/or property in which, from time to time, it may be lawful to invest trust funds or assets of life insurance companies under the laws of the State of California; except mortgages upon unimproved real estate.

5. SPECIAL POWERS OF TRUSTEE

The Trustee is authorized to retain in the form received and for such time as it deems proper any securities or property forming an original part of the trust fund, or which may hereafter be conveyed to the Trustees to become a part of the fund.

6. INTERRUPTION OF ACO SERVICES

In the event that the Board of Directors of ACO ceases to effectively function as a result of the revocation, suspension, or lapse of its articles of incorporation or otherwise, the Trustee may, in its discretion, continue to distribute funds to or for the benefit of the designated charitable beneficiaries provided that (1) the Trustee is satisfied that such funds will be propertly applied and that (2) the suspension of active Board supervision of ACO is a temporary condition. Whenever either of the foregoing conditions is no longer met, then the Trustee shall accumulate funds for distribution under paragraph 7, below, unless control of ACO is vested in a properly appointed trustee or receiver by a court of competent jurisdiction.

7. TERMINATION OF THE ACO

In the event that the ACO shall cease to exist or function as aforesaid and its activities shall not be revived, then and in that case, the Trustee or its successor hereunder, being in the lawful exercise of its functions herein, is authorized and empowered to use any or all trust funds created, either principal or income thereof, or both, in the cause of furtherance of the work of such one or more charitable or educational organizations as will best satisfy the purposes for which all such funds have been held and maintained. The organizations to which such funds would be distributed must be limited to those described in section 501(c)(3) of the Internal Revenue Code of 1986 (as amended). Upon such application of the property forming the corpus of this trust the same shall cease and determine.

8. BOND AND COMPENSATION OF TRUSTEE

The Trustee and its successor in trust shall serve without the necessity of giving any bond or security for the performance and discharge of its duties and said Trustee may retain such compensation for its services hereunder as may be agreed upon by the ACO, provided, however, that such compensation shall not in the aggregate exceed the amount which said Trustee shall be entitled to receive under the laws of the State of California from time to time in effect.

9. COMPENSATION PAYABLE TO THE ACO FOR ALLOCATION AND ADMINISTRATIVE SERVICES

The Trustee shall pay to ACO an annual fee as compensation for services rendered to or for the benefit of the Trust. Such services include the provision of general and administrative support, the identification of potential charitable beneficiaries of trust distributions and the review of potential charitable beneficiaries to be sure that they are 501(c)(3) organizations that are otherwise qualified recipients of trust gifts or grants. The annual administrative fee shall be ¼ of 1 percent of the net asset value of the trust and shall be payable in quarterly increments of 0.625 percent (6¼ basis points). The fee shall be due and payable by the tenth business day of each calendar quarter and shall be based upon the net asset value of the principal amount then held in the trust as of the last business day of the preceding quarter. Said fee shall be in addition to whatever compensation is payable to the Trustee for its services and to whatever direct expenses are incurred by the trust in carrying out its purposes.

10. METHOD OF CHANGING CORPORATE TRUSTEE

Should unforeseen conditions require that the Trustee resign or be discharged from its duties hereunder, it shall, thirty days in advance of said resignation or discharge becoming effective, submit a written notice of such resignation to the ACO. Such resignation shall take effect upon such date as specified in such notice and thereupon the said Trustee shall be discharged from all further responsibility hereunder upon transferring and delivering the securities, money, and other property then held by it in the fund, to the successor as designated by the ACO. The ACO may, at its discretion, change the Trustee provided it shall submit due notice of said change to the Trustee at least thirty days in advance of said change becoming effective.

11. CAPITAL GAINS/UNDESIRABLE GIFTS

It is hereby declared that the trust property of the fund may be increased from time to time by contributions, donations, or otherwise and in the event the said trust property of the fund shall be added to or increased as aforesaid, the same shall be considered by the Trustee as forming a part of the corpus of this trust and shall be held upon and be subject to the same terms and conditions as herein made applicable to the original fund. Capital gains shall be added to the principal, but the Trustee may determine what shall be considered capital gains and what shall be income, and such determination by the Trustee shall be deemed final. Particular contributions, donations, or legacies offered to the trust fund may be refused either by the Executive Committee or the Trustee, if found by either of them to be inconsistent with the purpose of this trust or impracticable to administer as a part thereof.

12. RECORDS AND REPORTS

The Trustee shall act as depository of the trust funds; shall report to the Executive Committee from time to time as may be required by the Executive Committee, not only as to the status of the funds on deposit, but also with an estimate of net income which will be available from time to time. The Trustee shall also submit to the Executive Committee, within thirty days after the end of each calendar year, an annual statement, and at such other times as may be required by the Executive Committee, shall submit an intermediate statement of the condition of the fund; each such statement shall consist of (a) a complete financial statement of the transactions of the Trustee during the preceding calendar year, if it be an annual statement, or since the last annual statement, if it be an intermediate statement; (b) the amount of income then available for distribution; (c) a list of securities, investments, and cash holdings in the fund; and (d) a general fiduciary report, appropriate to be rendered by such Trustee, including any comments, suggestions, or recommendations which the Trustee may deem appropriate.

13. AGREEMENT

From time to time, if in the judgment of the Executive Committee, any of the provisions of this trust agreement, as it may then exist or be effective, shall be or have become inappropriate or inapplicable to the purposes for which the Executive Committee deems this agreement to have been made, or if in the opinion of the Executive Committee it shall be desirable to rectify any defects and omissions in this agreement or to make any reasonable modifications thereto, which in the judgment of the Executive Committee may be expedient or necessary to give effect to the intent thereof, the Executive Committee shall have the power by an instrument in writing, signed and acknowledged by the officers of the Executive Committee with the approval of the Trustees and the Board of Directors of ACO, to make such modifications, alterations, and supplements, or amendments to the terms and provisions of this agreement as the Executive Committee may deem not inconsistent with the general purposes for which contributions, donations, or otherwise have been made to the fund, and for which this trust agreement shall have been made.

14. SEVERABILITY

To assure further the carrying out of the purposes hereof, each and every one of the provisions of this trust agreement are to be regarded and construed as independent of every other provision. In the event that the final determination of a court of competent jurisdiction shall adjudge that any of the terms, conditions, or provisions of this trust agreement are invalid, such adjudication shall in no way affect the validity of the remaining provisions.

IN WITNESS THEREOF, the ACO and _____ (bank or trust company) have caused these presents to be signed by their respective officers thereunto duly authorized as of this _____ day of _____, 19_____.

American Charitable Organization   **(Bank or Trust Company)**

By _____   By _____
President   President

ATTEST: ATTEST:

_____ (Seal)   _____ (Seal)
Secretary   Secretary

Preamble

It is the policy of the Board of Directors (Board) to treat all assets of the American Charitable Organization (ACO), including funds which are legally unrestricted, as if held by ACO in a fiduciary capacity for the sake of accomplishing its mission and purposes. The following investment objectives and directions are to be judged and understood in light of that overall sense of stewardship. In that regard, the basic investment standards shall be those of a prudent investor as articulated in applicable state laws.

Delegation

The Board has delegated supervisory authority over its financial affairs to the Finance Committee of the Board (Committee). The Committee is responsible for regularly reporting on investments to the Board. In carrying out its responsibilities, the Committee and its agents will act in accordance with these Investment Policies (the Policies) and all applicable laws and regulations. The Board reserves to itself the exclusive right to revise, or grant exceptions to, the Policies.

The Committee is authorized to retain one or more Investment Counselors (Counselors) to assume the investment management of funds and assets owned or administered by the organization. In discharging this authority, the Committee can act in the place and stead of the Board and may receive reports from, pay compensation to, enter into agreements with, and delegate investment authority to such Counselors. When delegating discretionary investment authority to one or more Counselors, the Committee will establish and follow appropriate procedures for selecting such Counselors and for conveying to each the scope of their authority, the organization's expectations, and the requirement of full compliance with these Policies.

Objectives

ACO's primary investment objective is to preserve and protect its assets, by earning a total return for each fund (e.g., Operating Reserves, Charitable Trust Funds, Annuity Reserves, etc.) appropriate to each fund's time horizon, distribution requirements, and risk tolerance.

Asset Mix

To accomplish ACO's investment objectives, the Counselor is authorized to utilize portfolios of equity securities (common stocks and convertible securities), fixed-income securities, and short-term (cash) investments. The actual asset allocations for

---

[1] What follows is a basic and intentionally conservative set of investment policies for a charitable organization. Please note that these policies are only a sample and may not be appropriate for a specific organization without significant modifications and additions. Any investment policies should be reviewed by legal counsel before adoption.

each portfolio shall be set by the Counselor in conjunction with ACO's designated financial officer within the ranges provided in the table below. These ranges can only be modified by the Committee with approval by the Board.

Asset Quality

1. Common stocks—The Counselor may invest in any unrestricted, publicly traded common stock that is listed on a major exchange or a national, over-the-counter market and that is appropriate for the portfolio objectives, asset class, and/or investment style of the fund that is to hold such shares.

2. Convertible preferred stock and convertible bonds—The Counselor may use convertible preferred stocks and bonds as equity investments. The quality rating of convertible preferred stock and convertible bonds must be BBB or better, as rated by Standard & Poor's, or BAA or better, as rated by Moody's®. The common stock into which both may be converted must satisfy the standard of Section 1, above.

3. Fixed-income securities—The quality rating of bonds and notes must be A or better, as rated by Standard & Poor's or Moody's®. The portfolio may consist of only traditional principal and interest obligations (no derivatives) with maturities of seven years or less.

4. Short-term reserves—The quality rating of commercial paper must be A-1, as rated by Standard & Poor's, P-1, as rated by Moody's®, or better. The assets of any money market mutual funds must comply with the quality provisions for fixed-income securities or short-term reserves.

Asset Diversification

The Counselor will maintain reasonable diversification at all times and may not make investments in the equity securities of any one company that exceed 5 percent of the portfolio (at the time of purchase) nor allow the total securities position (debt and equity) in any one company to exceed 10 percent of the portfolio. The Counselor shall also maintain reasonable sector allocations and diversification. In that regard, no more than 25 percent of the entire portfolio may be invested in the securities of any one sector.

Investment Management Limitations

All purchases of securities will be for cash and there will be no margin transactions, short selling, or commodity transactions. In addition, the Counselor may not make direct investments in real estate, loan money (except through the purchase of fixed-income securities as permitted above), or permit the lending, mortgage, pledge, or hypothecation of any assets.

Custody and Securities Brokerage

The Committee will establish such custodial and brokerage relationships as are necessary for the efficient management of the ACO's funds. Whenever the Committee has not designated a brokerage relationship, then the Counselor shall execute transactions wherever it can obtain best price and execution.

Investment Criteria Based on Mission or Social Responsibility

ACO desires to invest in companies whose business conduct is consistent with ACO's goals and beliefs. Therefore, the Counselor will use its best efforts to avoid investing in the securities of any company known to participate in businesses the Board deems to be socially or morally inconsistent with ACO objectives. The Committee will provide the Counselor with a list of mission guidelines.

Reporting Requirements

1. Monthly—The Counselor will provide the Committee with a monthly written statement containing all pertinent transaction details for each separately managed portfolio for the preceding month, including:

- the name and quantity of each security purchased or sold, with the price and transaction date;
- a description of each security including its percentage of the total portfolio, purchase date, quantity, average cost basis, current market value, unrealized gain or loss, and indicated annual income and yield (%) at market; and
- an analysis for the entire portfolio of the current asset allocation by investment category (equities, fixed-income securities, and cash reserves).

2. Periodically—The Counselor shall meet with the Committee semiannually to provide detailed information about (1) asset allocation, (2) investment performance, (3) future investment strategies, and (4) any other matters of interest to the Committee. The Counselor will promptly advise the Committee of any significant changes in its ownership, financial condition, or investment personnel.

3. Annually—The Counselor shall provide an annual summary of all transactions in each fiscal year together with a report of investment performance for the year by portfolio.

Cash Flow Requirements

ACO will be responsible for advising the Counselor in a timely manner of ACO's cash distribution requirements from any managed portfolio or fund. The Counselor is responsible for providing adequate liquidity to meet such distribution requirements.

SAMPLE MAXIMUM PERCENTAGE POLICIES
PER INVESTMENT FUND OR CATEGORY

Investment Fund	*Asset Classes*		
	Equities	**Fixed-Income Securities (U.S. & Corp. bonds)**	**Short-Term Reserves (Cash/1-yr. Notes)**
Operating Reserves	0%	50%	100%
Annuity Reserves	60%	75%	35%
Charitable Trusts	60%	75%	35%
Endowment	80%	50%	20%

G-2 Sample Investment
Policies For Operating
Reserves[1]

Preamble

It is the belief of the Board of Directors (Board) that all funds of American Charitable Organization (ACO) are held by it as a fiduciary either as a matter of law or as a matter of moral obligation. Therefore, even the legally unrestricted funds of ACO are held by the corporation as a steward for the sake of carrying out its mission and purposes. The following investment objectives and directions are to be judged and understood in light of that overall sense of stewardship.

The Board has previously delegated supervisory authority over its financial affairs to the Finance Committee of the Board. In carrying out its responsibilities, the Committee and its agents will be guided by and act in accordance with these Investment Policies (Policies) and all applicable laws and regulations. The Board reserves to itself the exclusive right to revise the Policies.

Operating Reserve Policy

The primary investment objective of ACO is to preserve and protect assets of the organization while earning an appropriate rate of return for each category of assets. To achieve these objectives, ACO's investment account will incorporate three tiers designed to meet the specific safety, liquidity and yield criteria of each category. Those categories are *Operating Cash, Liquid Assets*, and *Investment Assets*, each of which is defined below.

Tier 1—Operating Cash

The purpose of this tier is to assure adequate cash for operations. To achieve this goal, the Committee (acting through its designated agents) will match Tier 1 investment maturities to the organization's cash flow and draw-down requirements. In no event, however, will Tier 1 maturities exceed 180 days.

Tier 2—Liquid Assets

The purpose of this tier is to provide a liquidity reserve above and beyond the cash for operations maintained in Tier 1. When investing liquid assets, the Counselor will emphasize safety, liquidity, and yield, in that order, with staggered maturities to a maximum of (12/24) months.

Tier 3—Investment Assets

This portion of the investment portfolio is designed to maximize yield, consistent with safety of principal. Liquidity is a secondary objective. Maturities should be reasonably laddered out to a maximum of (36/48/60) months.

The Committee shall periodically establish the amounts which shall be maintained in each tier. In doing so, they shall review the prior year's cash-flow requirements and reserve levels as well as the anticipated needs of the organization as presented

---

[1] This is a sample for illustration purposes only and should not be used by any organization unless reviewed and approved by that organization's legal counsel.

EXHIBIT A.

Tier 3—Investment assets	$3,000,000
Tier 2—Liquid assets	$1,000,000
Tier 1—Operating cash—all funds in exess of:	$4,000,000

Targets set by the committee at its meeting on _____, 199___.

to them by the designated financial officer. The initial amounts to be maintained in each tier are set forth in Exhibit A.

The Counselor shall conform the Organization's investments to the targets in Exhibit A as modified from time to time by the Committee. ACO's designated financial officer will be responsible for communicating the cash-flow requirements for Tier 1 to the Counselor in a timely manner and the Counselor may rely and act upon such advice and information.

Asset Quality

Within the three tiers described above, investments shall be made exclusively with the following securities, each of which shall conform to the stated quality requirements.

1. U.S. Treasury and agency securities.
2. Corporate bonds and notes rated A or better by Moody®'s and Standard & Poor's.
3. Commercial Paper rated P-1/A-1 by Moody®'s and Standard & Poor's.
4. Certificates of Deposit and Bankers Acceptances from institutions rated A or better and insured by FDIC in amounts not to exceed $100,000.
5. Repurchase agreements collateralized by U.S. treasury securities.
6. Money market mutual funds, the principal investments of which are instruments described in 1 through 5 above.

All investments shall be diversified in accordance with the requirements of Exhibit B and shall be for cash. There will be no margin transactions, short selling, commodity transactions or use of derivatives. The Counselor will select the broker or brokers to execute all purchases and sales in the best interest of ACO.

Investment Counsel

The Committee of ACO is authorized to retain one or more Investment Counselors (Counselor) to assume the investment management of those funds and assets owned or administered by ACO for itself or for its constituents. In discharging this authority, the Committee shall act in the place and stead of the Board and may receive reports from, pay compensation to, and enter into agreements with such Counselors. The Committee may also grant exceptions to the investment policies provided that such exceptions are promptly communicated in writing to the full board at its next regularly scheduled meeting.

Reporting Requirements

Monthly

The Investment Counselor will provide the Investment Committee of the American Charitable Organization with a monthly written statement that provides all pertinent

EXHIBIT B. American Charitable Organization Investment Policy Guidelines

Investment	Use of Funds	Diversification Guidelines	Maturity Period
U.S. Treasury Securities	Investment assets Liquid assets Operating cash	$500,000 per issue maximum Treasuries and agencies should comprise at least 50% of portfolio	36/48/60 months or less
U.S. Government Agency Securities	Investment assets Liquid assets Operating cash	$500,000 per issue maximum Treasuries and agencies should comprise at least 50% of a portfolio	36/48/60 months or less
U.S. Corporate Debt	Investment assets Liquid assets Operating cash	Minimum A rating * $500,000 per issuer maximum 15% limit on bonds rated A	36 months or less
Commercial Paper	Liquid assets Operating cash	Rated P-1/A-1 * $500,000 per issuer maximum	270 days or less
Certificates of Deposit	Liquid assets Operating cash	Institution rated A or better * $100,000 per issuer maximum FDIC insured	12 months or less
Bankers Acceptances	Liquid assets Operating cash	Institution rated A or better * $500,000 per issuer maximum	270 days or less
Repurchase Agreements	Operating cash	U.S. Treasury collateral only	Overnight only
Money Market Funds	Operating cash		Daily demand

*Ratings are Moody®'s and Standard & Poor's, July 5, 1995

transaction details for each separately managed portfolio for the preceding month, including the following:

1. The name and quantity of each security purchased or sold, with the price and transaction date; and
2. An analysis for each security of its description, percentage of total portfolio, purchase date, quantity, cost basis, current market value, unrealized gain or loss, and indicated annual income and yield (%) at market.

Periodically

The Investment Counselor shall meet as requested by the Investment Committee to provide detailed information about asset allocation, investment performance, future investment strategies, and other matters of interest to the Committee.

Selected Bibliography

The following books and articles are ones that I have found to be either particularly interesting or particularly helpful, in each case for the reasons noted.

RECOMMENDED FOR THE LIBRARY

Andersen, Arthur. *Tax Economics of Charitable Giving.* Washington, DC: Arthur Andersen and Co., May 1995.

A thorough if somewhat dry discussion of the principal tax issues associated with charitable giving. It does a much better job with income tax concerns than with estate and gift tax issues. Updated regularly.

Berry, Wendell. *What Are People For?* San Francisco: Northpoint Press, 1990.

A delightful collection of essays by a farmer, environmentalist, and writer on the importance of people and communities. A valuable counterpoint to our otherwise constant focus on money.

Cary, William L., and Bright, Craig B. *The Law and the Lore of Endowment Funds.* New York: The Ford Foundation, 1969.

Cary, William L., and Bright, Craig B. *The Developing Law of Endowment Funds: The Law and the Lore Revisited.* New York: The Ford Foundation, 1974.

These are the seminal studies whose conclusions and recommendations led to the adoption of the Prudent Investor Rule. While technically dated, the thoughts and observations are still interesting.

Cohen, Zinbarg, and Zeikel. *Investment Analysis and Portfolio Management.* Burr Ridge, IL: Irwin, 1987.

One of the standard textbooks on modern portfolio theory. A good single volume for those who would like to dig deeper.

Downes, John, and Goodman, Jordan Elliot. *Barron's Finance & Investment Handbook* (4th ed.). Hauppage, NY: Barron's Educational Series, Inc., 1995.

An excellent desk reference, available in most bookstores, with a particularly thorough dictionary of investment terms.

Edie, John A., and Smith, Lowell S. "Investing in U.S. Securities is a Violation of Your Fiduciary Duty." *Foundation News.* November 1993.

Edie, John A., and Smith, Lowell S. "Let Go Of Your Old Investment Assumptions." *Foundation News.* January/February 1994.

Really good two-part article that explains why it is no longer appropriate for nonprofit organizations to be invested exclusively in fixed-income. A great piece to give board members who refuse to consider equity investments.

Ellis, Charles D. *Investment Policy: How to Win the Loser's Game.* Burr Ridge, IL: Irwin, 1985.

Dandy little book by a well-known, well-respected institutional consultant on the importance of fundamental policy decisions. I have shamelessly adopted his idea on the importance of getting into the game throughout my own book. Ellis has also edited two collections of articles on investing called *Classics I and II* which are interesting reading for a good cross section of historic Wall Street wisdom.

Graham, Benjamin. *The Intelligent Investor.* New York: Harper and Row, 1973.

Ben Graham, first writing in the 1930s, is considered the father of value investing. Many investment managers respect and pursue his thinking as discussed in this book.

Hopkins, Bruce R. *The Tax Law of Charitable Giving.* New York: John Wiley & Sons, 1993.

A very good book on the taxation of charitable giving. I prefer it to the Arthur Anderson book, cited earlier, because it is more thoroughly annotated and includes case law. Also updated regularly.

Ibbotson, Roger G., and Sinquefield, Rex A. *Stocks, Bonds, Bills and Inflation 1997 Yearbook*. Chicago: Ibbotson Associates, 1997.

When Roger Ibbotson first published this book it was revolutionary in that he painstakingly gathered data on investment performance that had not been readily available previously. While it is no longer the unique publication that it once was, this is still a great source of historical performance information by asset class.

ICFA Continuing Education. "Managing Endowment and Foundation Funds." *Association for Investment Management and Research, Conference Proceedings from March 25–26, 1996*. Charlottesville, VA: AIMR, 1996.

This is an excellent collection of short articles on various aspects of endowment management.

Malkiel, Burton. *A Random Walk Down Wall Street*. New York: W.W. Norton and Company, 1996.

My favorite book on investing. Even if Malkiel were absolutely wrong in his assessment of market efficiency, it would still be a helpful book for the overview it gives of traditional approaches to investing. Fun reading besides.

Neuhaus, Richard John. *Doing Well and Doing Good: The Challenge to the Christian Capitalist*. New York: Doubleday, 1992.

An interesting discussion of an encyclical by Pope John Paul on the role of capitalism in the world. Important reading for anyone who is concerned about the social and moral side of business life.

Restatement of the Law: Trusts—Prudent Investor Rule. St. Paul, MN: American Law Institute Publishers, 1992.

A publication for lawyers, the notes in this discussion of the trust law of investing are the best discussion of the legal history of the Prudent Investor Act that I have found.

Schwed, Fred, Jr. *Where Are the Customers' Yachts?* New York: John Wiley & Sons, 1940.

A humorous look at the everyday life of Wall Street in the 1920s and 1930s. Read for fun.

Scott, David L. *Wall Street Words*. Boston: Houghton Mifflin, 1988.

Not as thorough as the Barron's publication but very easy to use. Good for the nonprofessional.

OTHER INVESTMENT MANAGEMENT ARTICLES AND BOOKS

Aikens, Perrin. "New Restatement of Prudent Investor Rule." *Trusts & Estates*. May 1992.

This book discusses the Third Restatement to the Prudent Investor Rule.

American Association of Fund-Raising Counsel. "Annual Survey of State Laws Regulating Charitable Solicitation." New York: AAFRC, 1996.

This brochure, published annually, lists the requirements and regulating agencies for charitable organizations, solicitors, and fund-raising counsel in each state.

American Association of Fund-Raising Counsel. *Giving USA 1997*. New York: AAFRC Trust for Philanthropy, 1997.

Annual publication of sources and amounts of charitable giving in the United States.

Banz, Rolf. "The Relationship Between Return and Market Value of Common Stocks." *Journal of Financial Economics.* 1981, 3–18.

Basu, Sanjoy. "The Relationship Between Earnings' Yield, Market Value and Return for NYSE Common Stocks." *Journal of Financial Economics.* 1983, 129–156.

Bernstein, Peter L. *Against the Gods: The Remarkable Story of Risk.* New York: John Wiley & Sons, 1996.

Crenshaw, Carol. "Think FASB." *Foundation News and Community.* October 1994.
    Article contains an overview of new Financial Accounting Standards Board statements and their effects on community foundations.

Damato, Karen. "Morningstar Updates Ratings to Reflect Reality." *Wall Street Journal,* October 29, 1996.
    Article points out that mutual fund reporting is becoming style specific. One more example of institutional investment mind-set becoming more widespread.

De Bondt, Werner F.M., and Thaler, Richard. "Does the Stock Market Overreact?" *The Journal of Finance.* July 1985, 793–807.
    Article explores extent to which human behavior can have an effect on stock market prices.

Fabozzi, Frank J. *Bond Markets, Analysis and Strategies.* Englewood Cliffs, NJ: Prentice Hall, 1993.
    Provides a look at bond portfolio strategies and new bond structures.

Fama, Eugene F. "Efficient Capital Markets: A Review of Theory and Empirical Work." *Journal of Finance.* May 1970.
    A summary of research on the random-walk theory by one of its creators. Very technical.

Grant, James. *The Trouble with Prosperity.* New York: Random House, 1996.
    Argues that in order to understand and eventually see the coming downfall of the financially prosperous times of the 1990s one must analyze the cycles the market has gone through in the last 70 years.

Haugen, Robert A. *Modern Investment Theory.* Upper Saddle River, NJ: Prentice Hall, 1997.
    A "textbook-like" book on modern investment theory.

Hoffman, Marc, and Hoffman, Leland, Jr. *Harnessing the Power of the Charitable Remainder Trust.* Charlotte, NC: PhilanthroTec, Inc., 1992.
    A discussion of the many uses of a charitable remainder trust.

Institute of Chartered Financial Analysts. *Improving the Investment Decision Process: Quantitative Assistance for the Practitioner.* Burr Ridge, IL: Dow Jones Irwin, January 19, 1994.
    Essays by various authors on different methods of investment decision making.

Institute of Chartered Financial Analysts. *The Challenges of Investing for Endowment Funds.* Dow Jones Irwin, October 29, 1986.
    Essays by various authors on different aspects of endowment fund investment management.

Keynes, John Maynard. *The General Theory of Employment, Interest, and Money.* New York: Harcourt Brace & Company, 1936.

Loeb, G.M. *The Battle for Investment Survival.* New York: Simon and Schuster, 1957.

Luck, Christopher, and Wood, Kathy. "The CFA Digest." *Association for Investment Management and Research.* Fall 1993, 45–47.
    Interesting synopsis of an article on the cost of screening portfolios for social and moral issues.

Lynch, Peter. *Beating the Street.* New York: Simon and Schuster, 1993.

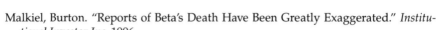

Malkiel, Burton. "Reports of Beta's Death Have Been Greatly Exaggerated." *Institutional Investor Inc.* 1996.
    A short article on the usefulness of Beta.
Makoff, Eileen. "Portfolio Optimization. A Peek Behind the Magician's Curtain." *Morningstar Investor.* August 1995.
    This article cautions about assuming that previous market behavior can be used to determine the best asset allocation to use in a future market, which could have totally different characteristics.
"Market Indexes." *Pensions & Investments,* October 2, 1996.
Markowitz, Harry M. *Portfolio Selection.* Cambridge, MA: Blackwell, 1991.
    The published version of Markowitz's original work on portfolio theory. Very technical.
Massy, William F. *Endowment: Perspectives, Policies, & Management.* Washington, DC: National Association of College and University Business Officers, 1990.
McGough, Robert, and Damato, Karen. "Buying Pressure." *Wall Street Journal,* December 30, 1996.
Modigliani, Franco, and Pogue, Gerald. "An Introduction to Risk and Return." *Financial Analysts Journal.* March/April 1974, 68–80.
Poterba, James M., and Summers, Lawrence H. "Mean Reversion in Stock Prices." *Journal of Financial Economics.* 1988, 27–59.
"Redefining the 'Prudent Investor Rule' for Trustees." *Trusts & Estates.* December 1990.
    This article is an interview with the Reporter of the Prudent Investor Rule for Restatement of Trusts, Edward Halbach. It is primarily concerned with future judicial interpretation of the Prudent Investor Rule.
Ritchie, J. Timothy. "Prudent Investor Rule is Not a Radical Departure." *Trusts & Estates.* January 1991.
Roll, Richard. "Orange Juice and the Weather." *The American Economic Review.* December 1984, 861–880.
Roll, Richard. "R². " *The Journal of Finance.* July 1988, 541–566.
    Outline of different things that cause the prices of stock to change.
Roll, Richard. "What Every CFO Should Know About Scientific Progress in Financial Economics: What Is Known and What Remains to Be Resolved." *Financial Management,* 1994, 23(2), 69–75.
Ross, Stephen. "The Arbitrage Theory of Capital Asset Pricing." *The Journal of Economics.* March 19, 1973, 341–360.
    An evaluation of the Arbitrage Theory of Capital Asset Pricing.
Schmitt, Richard B. "Uncharitable Acts." *Wall Street Journal,* August 27, 1995.
    This is an article primarily about the situation of Richard Barclay and his gift to the University of California at Irvine. He died without having paid the balance of a building fund pledge to the University. The University sued his widow to collect the balance of the pledge.
Schultz, Charles A., J.D. *To Disclose or Not to Disclose.* Camarillo, CA: Crescendo, 1996.
Sharpe, William F. "Asset Allocation, Management Style and Performance Measurement." *Journal of Portfolio Management,* Winter 1992.
Sharpe, William F. "Dynamic Strategies for Asset Allocation." *Financial Analysts Journal,* January–February 1995, 149–160.
Sharpe, William F. "From the Board: The Arithmetic of Active Management." *Financial Analysts Journal,* January–February 1991, 7–9.
Sharpe, William F. "Mutual Fund Performance." *The Journal of Business.* January 1966, 119–138.

This article evaluates mutual fund performance using a) the theory of portfolio selection, b) the theory of the pricing of capital assets under conditions of risk, and c) the general behavior of stock market prices.

Sharpe, William F. "Risk, market sensitivity and diversification." *Financial Analysts Journal*. January/February 1995, 74–79.

Article discusses different types of risk as well as how to calculate market sensitivity and diversification.

Sharpe, William F. and Guy M. Cooper. "Risk-Return Classes for the NYSE Common Stocks 1931–1967." *Financial Analysts Journal*. March/April 1972, 46–81.

Siegel, Jeremy J. *Stocks for the Long Run: A Guide to Selecting Markets for Long-Term Growth*. Burr Ridge, IL: Irwin, 1994.

Tregoe, Benjamin B., Zimmerman, John W., Smith, Ronald A., and Tobia, Peter M. *Vision in Action: Putting a Winning Strategy To Work*. New York: Simon and Schuster, 1989.

Watkins, Charles M. "Tax Sheltered Annuities: A Ticking Time Bomb?" *Christian Management Report*. August 1995.

This article is about the increasing governmental supervision of nonprofit retirement plans.

Welch, Lyman W. "How the Prudent Investor Rule May Affect Trustees." *Trusts & Estates*. December 1991.

This article states the basic principle of the Prudent Investor Rule, explains how it differentiates itself from prior legislation, and discusses the revision as it was adopted in Illinois.

Williams, Arthure, III. *Managing Your Investment Manager*. Burr Ridge, IL: Business One Irwin, 1980.

Williamson, J. Peter. *Funds for The Future: College Endowment Management for the 1990s*. Westport, CT: The Common Fund Press, 1993.

Willis, Robert T., Jr., CPA. "Prudent Investor Rule Gives Trustees New Guidelines." *Estate Planning*. November 1992.

NEW ERA ARTICLES

Andringa, Robert. "If It Sounds Too Good To Be True. . . ." *Advancing Philanthropy*. National Society of Fund Raising Executives, 1996.

Blum, Debra. "Shepherding Christian Charities." *The Chronicle of Philanthropy*, December 12, 1996.

Bulkeley, William. "Nonprofits Sue. . . ." *Wall Street Journal*, May 9, 1996.

Carton, Barbara. "Unlikely Hero." *Wall Street Journal*, May 19, 1995.

Dobrin, Peter. "London Charity Linked. . . ." *Philadelphia Inquirer*, June 1, 1995.

Downs, Jere, and Kaufman, Marc. "Two Helped Hundreds." *Philadelphia Inquirer*, June 1, 1995.

Downs, Jere, Sataline, Suzanne, and Kaufman, Marc. "State Probes." *Philadelphia Inquirer*, June 2, 1995.

Gorenstein, Nathan. "Rockefeller Gave Bennett Millions. . . ." *Philadelphia Inquirer*, June 1, 1995.

Greene, Stephen G., and Williams, Grant. "A Plan for New Era's Recovery." *The Chronicle of Philanthropy*, July 11, 1996.

Power, William. "Philadelphia Wonders How It Got Fooled." *Wall Street Journal*, July 18, 1995.

Putka, Gary. "Pennsylvania Seeks to Freeze. . . ." *Wall Street Journal*, May 17, 1995.

Rebello, Joseph, and Johnson, Constance. "New Era Told to Liquidate. . . ." *Wall Street Journal*, May 22, 1995.

Rottenberg, Dan. "Some Refused To Enter." *Philadelphia Inquirer*, June 7, 1995.

Rubin, Daniel, and Ditzen, L. Stuart. "Charity's Collapse. . . ." *Philadelphia Inquirer*, June 1, 1995.

Rubin, Daniel, Lounsberry, Emilie, and Roche, Walter F. "Bennetts Purchase. . . ." *Philadelphia Inquirer*, June 7, 1995.

Rubin, Daniel, and Slobodzian, Joseph A. "Bennetts Get Less." *Philadelphia Inquirer*, June 14, 1995.

Rubin, Daniel, and Slobodzian, Joseph A. "New Era Creditors." *Philadelphia Inquirer*, June 26, 1995.

Stecklow, Steve. "Bennett in Videotaped Talks. . . ." *Wall Street Journal*, November 1, 1995.

Stecklow, Steve. "Crumbling Pyramid." *Wall Street Journal*, May 16, 1995.

Stecklow, Steve. "False Front." *Wall Street Journal*, May 19, 1995.

Stecklow, Steve. "Feeding the Frenzy: A New Era Consultant Lured Rich Donors Over Pancakes, Prayers." *Wall Street Journal*, June 2, 1995.

Stecklow, Steve. "Incredible Offer." *Wall Street Journal*, May 15, 1995.

Stecklow, Steve. "IRS Is Studying. . . ." *Wall Street Journal*, May 24, 1995.

Stecklow, Steve. "New Era Trustee Files. . . ." *Wall Street Journal*, June 26, 1996.

Stecklow, Steve. "New Era Trustees. . . ." *Wall Street Journal*, December 15, 1995.

Stecklow, Steve. "New Era's Bennett Made $15,000 Loan. . . ." *Wall Street Journal*, June 15, 1995.

Stecklow, Steve. "New Era's Head. . . ." *Wall Street Journal*, September 30, 1996.

Stecklow, Steve. "Payback Time." *Wall Street Journal*, January 24, 1996.

Index

Absolute return goals, *see* Performance standards
Accounting, 9, 103–108, 154, 155–156, 157–159
Accounting-based financial statement, 155, 157–159
Advisors, 113–115, 230. *See also* Consultants
American Charitable Organization (ACO), xiv, 3, 11, 35, 79, 83, 92, 121, 122, 154, 173, 205, 227
American Law Institute, 30
Annuities:
 annuity trust, 195
 charitable-gift annuity, 197–198
 gift annuity, 32, 193, 198, 202–204
Applicable Federal Rate (AFR), 194–195
Assessment:
 of development, 98–102
 of funds, 117–121
 of investment accounting, 103–108
 of investment advisors, 113–115
 of investment management, 7–8, 95–98
 of investment philosophy, 108, 111–113
Asset allocation, 8, 36, 41, 42, 52–58, 63–69, 127, 160
Asset classes, 65–67
Assets:
 capital reserves, 92, 93
 operating reserves, 92
 permanent funds, 92, 94–95
 planned-gift assets, 92, 94
 retirement funds, 92, 93–94
Association of Independent Certified Public Accountants (AICPA), 156
Attorneys, 230
Audit, *see* Assessment

Bank of America, 55n9
Beneficiary, 13, 14, 15
Bennett, John G., Jr., 221–222
Bequest, 193–194
Beta, 47–49
Black, Fisher, 48
Board of directors, 84–85. *See also* Conflicts of Interest
Broker, *see* Consultants *and* Securities Brokerage *and* Stockbrokers

California Securities Statute, 32
Capital asset pricing model (CAPM), 36, 48–51
Capital gains, 4, 42

Capital Markets Research, 169
Capital reserves, *see* Assets
Capitalization, (cap), 129. *See also* Market segment
Cash management, 52–55, 134
Certificate of Deposit (CD), 93
Charitable lead trust, *see* Trusts
Charitable organizations, xi, 3, 5, 9, 15, 32–33, 34, 95, 175, 219, 232
Charitable remainder trust (CRT), *see* Trusts
Charitable-gift annuity, *see* Annuities
Common Fund, 65–67, 161–162
Common law, 12, 16–17, 18
Compliance, *see* Investment policies
Conflicts of interest, 220–221
Constriction, *see* Laws and legal developments
Consultants:
 broker-consultants, 138–139
 equity managers, 129–133
 fixed-income managers, 134–136
 "general contractors," 128, 137
 institutional consultants, 137–138
 investment advisors, 123, 128, 129–136
 "pure" investing firms, 138
Cotrustees, *see* Trustee
CPAs (certified public accountants), 230
Credit quality, 134
Custody, 124, 140–145

Dean Witter, 138
Delegation of investment responsibilities:
 hiring help, 8–9, 28, 123
 legal aspects of, 19, 22, 27–30
 diligence in, 29, 147–149
Development (fund raising):
 assessment, 96, 98–102
 goals, 233
 investment policies, 10
Due diligence, *see* Delegation of investment responsibilities
Discounted present value, 179
Diversification, 26, 34, 42, 48, 51–52
Donors, 174, 211, 212, 213–217
Dow, 39
Duration, 44, 136. *See also* Maturities

EAFE index (Europe and the Far East), 129
Efficient frontier, 36
Ellis, Charles, 39
Endowments, 20–22, 95, 183–186, 190–191, 280–286

Equity managers, *see* Consultants
Evangelical Council for Financial Account-
    ability, 222n11
Expenses:
    external expenses, 231
    internal expenses, 231
    or investment, 222–223
    soft expenses, 231–232

Fama, Eugene, 36
Fannie Maes (Federal National Mortgage As-
    sociation), 181
FASBs (FASB standards), 156, 157
Fiduciary, 12, 13, 16
Fiduciary duty,13, 14, 15, 212–214
Finance committee, *see* Investment com-
    mittee
Financial Accounting Standards Board
    (FASB), 156
501(c)3, 9, 32
Fixed-income investments:
    collaterized mortgage obligation (CMO),
        181–182
    custody choices for, 143
    inflation effect on, 20, 27
    junk bonds, 182–183
    longer-term, 177–181
    short-term, 175–177
    total return of, 42–43
Fixed-income managers, *see* Consultants
Ford Foundation Studies, 20–22, 173
Foundation for a New Era in Philanthropy,
    see New Era for Philanthropy Fund
Fund raising, *see* Development (fund
    raising)

GAAP (generally accepted accounting prin-
    ciples), 156
"General contractors," *see* Consultants
Gift annuity, *see* Annuities
Gift-acceptance policy, 218–219, 250–256
Ginnie Maes (Government National Mort-
    gage Association), 181
Growth *see* Portfolio style

Harvard College v. Amory, 16
Hindsight, *see* Standard of care
Hiring help:
    administering trusts, 216–218
    advisors, 233–234
    delegation of investment management,
        8–9, 28, 123
Hustlers, *see* Scams

Ibbotson Associates, 169
Income, 4
Income spending policy, *see* Spending Pol-
    icies
Indexing, 40
Index fund, 39–40. *See also* Mutual funds
Inflation, 20, 45. *See also* Standard of care
"Inflation plus" standard, *see* Performance
    standards
Internal Revenue Service (IRS), 156, 201, 219
Investing, 4–5
Investment accounting, 103–108
Investment advisors, *see* Consultants
Investment Advisors Act of 1940, 128n5, 141
Investment assessment, *see* Assessment
Investment committee, xii, 87–90, 229–230
Investment goals, *see* Investment phi-
    losophy
Investment grade, 182
Investment laws, *see* Laws and legal develop-
    ments
Investment management, xiii, 8–9, 74–75,
    123, 124–128, 134
Investment management assessment, *see* As-
    sessment
Investment management performance stan-
    dards, *see* Performance standards
Investment philosophy, 15, 108–111, 207–209
Investment policies:
    compliance, 234–235
    diversification, 51–52
    goals in, 95, 111–113, 117, 232–233
    implementing, xii, 86, 227–228
    participation, 6–7
    reasons for, 3, 4–6, 10, 224–225
    sample policies, 224–225, 287–292
Investment regulations, *see* Restrictions
Investment reporting, *see* Performance re-
    porting

Junk bonds, 134, 182–183

Laws and legal developments:
    common law, 12, 16–17, 18
    constriction, 17–18
    Harvard College v. Amory, 16
    Investment Advisors Act of 1940, 128n5,
        141
    investment laws, 6, 11, 12, 16, 30, 33
    legal list statutes, 18–19
    Philanthropy Protection Act (PPA), 5–6,
        32
    Prudent Investor Rule, 6, 12, 16, 22–23,
        30–31, 33, 203, 207, 208

Prudent Man Rule, 6, 12, 16–20, 203
Restatement of the Law of Trusts, 30–31
securities laws, 12, 31–33
Securities Act of 1933, 31–32
Taxpayer Relief Act of 1997, 195n7
trust laws, 13, 15, 19, 27
Uniform Management of Institutional
    Funds Act (UMIFA), 22–30, 33,
    242–245
Uniform Prudent Investor Act (UPIA), 6,
    23–30, 33, 217, 246–249
Lewis, C.S., xi
Liabilities, 5–6, 19, 28–30, 212
Lintner, John, 48
Liquidity, 160
Lynch, Peter, 76

Macaulay, Frederick, 136
Malkiel, Burton, 41, 133n7
Manageable funds, 231
Management style, 129–131
Market efficiency, 35, 36, 37–41
Market segment, 129, 134
Market timing, 131
Markets, 129, 134
Marking to market, 155, 156–157
Markowitz, Harry, 35, 36, 47, 48
Maturities, 134–136. *See also* Duration
Merrill Lynch, 138
Mobius, 169
Modern portfolio theory, *see* Portfolio theory
Money market funds, 54, 141–143
Moody's {{registerserif}}, 182
Morgan Stanley EAFE index, *see* EAFE
    index
Mutual funds, 8, 19, 32, 39

NASDAQ (National Association of Securi-
    ties Dealers Automated Quotations sys-
    tem), 51
NAV (net asset value), 55n9, 141–142
Nelson, 169
Net worth, 185
New Concepts in Philanthropy Fund, *see*
    New Era for Philanthropy Fund
New Era for Philanthropy Fund, 223–226
New York Stock Exchange, 40, 51, 128
Nondelegable duties, *see* Trusts
Nonprofit organizations, *see* Charitable or-
    ganizations

Operating reserves, *see* Assets
Organizational structure, 6–7, 86, 97–98

Paine Webber, 138
Participation, *see* Investment policies
Performance reporting, 9, 157, 163–170,
    271–279
Performance standards:
    absolute return goals, 160–161
    absolute standards, 159–161
    "inflation plus" standard, 154–155, 160,
        161
    relative standards, 161–163
Permanent funds, *see* Assets
Permitted investments, *see* Standard of care,
Philanthropy Protection Act (PPA), 5–6, 32
Planned gifts:
    as assets, 92, 94
    gift-acceptance policy, 218–219, 250–256
    liabilities of, 6
    restrictions on, 8, 201, 203–204, 219
    trusts and annuities, 193–197
Policy, *see* Investment policy
Pooled gifts, 197–199
Pooled-income funds, 31, 32, 193, 199
Portfolio style, 131–132
Portfolio theory:
    asset allocation, 52–58
    diversification, 48–52
    historic patterns, 74–76
    lowering risks, 58–62, 65
    origins of, 6, 35–36
    rebalancing, 68–69
Prudent Investor Rule, 6, 12, 16, 22–25, 30–
    31, 33, 203, 207, 208
Prudent Man Rule, 6, 12, 16–20, 203
Prudential, 138
Pure consulting firms, *see* Consultants
Purity, *see* Restrictions

Quantifiability, *see* Risks

Random walk theory, 36–39
Reaching for yield, 188–190
Remainder trusts, *see* Trusts
Request for Proposal (RFP), 147, 149,
    233–234
Research, financial, 133, 136
Resources, 7
Restatement of the Law of Trusts (also
    called the Restatement or Restatement
    Third of Trusts), 30–31
Restrictions:
    for gift annuities, 203–204
    IRS regulations on planned gifts, 201, 219
    investment regulations, 8, 12
    socially responsible investing, 8, 207–209

Retirement funds, *see* Assets
Return on investment, 4–5
Risk:
  assessment of, 113
  definition of, 45
  kinds of, 45, 74
  measurement of, 46–48
  tolerance for, 8
  vs. return, 41
  vs. reward, 36, 45–46
Risks, kinds of:
  complexity, 74, 76
  credit, 182
  fixed-income, 177–181
  inflation , 45
  innovation , 74, 76–77
  isolation, 74, 78–79
  liquidity, 45
  market, 45, 62
  quantifiability, 74, 77–78
  specific, 45, 62–63
Rockefeller, Lawrence, 222

Scams:
  hustlers, 223–224
  scam proofing, 222–223
Sector, 51, 189
Sector rotation, 131
Securities, 31
Securities Act of 1933, 31–32
Securities and Exchange Commission (SEC), 123, 128n5, 156
Securities brokerage, 128, 145–146
Securities laws, *see* Laws and legal developments
Self-guided internal investment management assessment, 7, 95, 97–121, 230, 257–270
Service providers, 9, 28, 123, 146, 147
Sharpe, William, 36, 48
Simon, William, 222
Smith Barney, 138
Socially responsible investing, *see* Restrictions
Spending policies, 186–190
S&P 500 (Standard & Poor's 500 Stock Index), 5, 48, 49, 51–52, 159
Standard deviation, 46, 46n6, 48, 57, 60
Standard of care:
  defined in UMIFA and UPIA, 23–27
  hindsight, 25, 27
  inflation, 26–27

permitted investments, 23–24, 27
  total return, 25–26, 27
Stock market, 5
Stockbrokers, 128, 138

Taxpayer Relief Act of 1997, 195n7
Time frame, 7–8, 42, 69–72
Time horizon, 72–73
Total return, 41, 42–44. *See also* Standard of care
Trust, willlingness to, *see* Vulnerabilities
Trustee:
  cotrustees, 217
  definition of, 13
  institutional trustees, 215
  reasons against serving, 211–215
  reasons for serving, 210–211
Trusts:
  nondelegable duties, 19
  trust laws, 13, 15, 27
  trust relationships, 13
Trusts, kinds of:
  charitable lead trust, 193, 196–197
  charitable remainder trust (CRT), 8, 14, 193, 194–195, 201
  constituency trust, 15
  express trust, 14, 16
  flip trust, 174, 195n8
  implied trust, 14–15
  net income trust, 174–175, 201
  public trust 15
  remainder trust, 196, 201–202.
  unitrust, 195

Uniform Management of Institutional Funds Act (UMIFA), 22–30, 33, 242–245
Uniform Prudent Investor Act, (UPIA) 6, 23–30, 33, 217, 246–249
U.S. government securities, 20, 175
Unitrust, *see* Trusts

Value, *see* Portfolio style
Vanguard S&P 500 Index Fund, 77
Variance, 46–48. *See also* Standard deviation
Volatility, 49, 60, 72, 74, 75
Vulnerabilities, 5–6, 206, 219

Wrap fee or program, 138–139, 139n9

Yield, 42, 43, 44, 188
Yield curve, 175–177, 178